MW01229427

The unfinished Capitol dome provides a backdrop for the first inauguration of Abraham Lincoln on March 4, 1861. The exterior of the dome was completed in time for Lincoln's second inauguration four years later.

THE AMERICAN WAR

A HISTORY OF THE CIVIL WAR ERA

Third Edition

Gary W. Gallagher

Joan Waugh

Published by Flip Learning

Request for permission to reproduce selections from this book should be mailed to:
Flip Learning, 288 Nimitz Ave, State College, PA 16801.

FlipLearning.com

Third Flip Learning paperback edition May 2023

ISBN-13 979-8-9858492-7-1

For information about special discounts for bulk purchases,
please contact Flip Learning Sales at sales@fliplearning.com.

Printed in the United States of America

5   7   9   10   8   6   4

For our undergraduate students at Penn State,
The University of Virginia, and UCLA.

ACKNOWLEDGMENTS

THIS BOOK GREW out of extended discussions about the readings we assign in our undergraduate courses on the era of the Civil War. The conversations included many friends in the field, whose scholarship has shaped our understanding of the origins, conduct, and consequences of the war. In a typically generous allocation of their time, Bill Blair, Steve Cushman, Matt Gallman, and Carrie Janney read all of the manuscript. Hal Jespersen proved to be the ideal cartographer, displaying good humor and great efficiency in preparing the maps. At Flip Learning, Christian Spielvogel provided constant support of the type authors crave but too seldom receive. Jennifer Backer and Kate Hunter helped immeasurably during the editing process. All of these people made the project a delightful experience.

DIGITAL FEATURES

The interactive version of *The American War* includes the following features:

- ▷ Filmed debates between the authors on topics such as the "inevitability" of secession, war, and Confederate defeat.
- ▷ 40+ interview-style videos embedded within the textbook, including a dozen that feature Gary Gallagher on location at several battlefield sites.
- ▷ 100+ hyperlinks to important online resources.
- ▷ PowerPoint slide presentations available as an instructor resource at the end of each chapter.
- ▷ Auto-graded quizzes at the end of each chapter.
- ▷ Embedded discussion questions so that students can engage one another directly within the textbook.

VitalSource Digital
ISBN: 979-8-9858492-9-5

Paperback/Digital Bundle
ISBN: 979-8-9858492-6-4

NEW TO THIS EDITION

To keep up with current scholarship on the Civil War and Reconstruction periods, new or revised material has been incorporated throughout *The American War* on the following topics:

▷ **Chapter 3**: Guerrilla Warfare

▷ **Chapter 8**: The Struggle for Women's Voting Rights

▷ **Chapter 9**: Did the War End in the Spring of 1865?

▷ **Chapter 11**: Was Reconstruction a Lost Moment?

▷ **Chapter 12**: Acknowledging the War's Dark Side

▷ **Further Reading**: More than two dozen additional titles that combine accessibility and sound scholarship, including thirteen in a new section devoted to photographs and art.

DIGITAL VIDEO LIST

CHAPTER 1

- ▷ A Perception of Two Worlds
- ▷ Free Labor Ideology
- ▷ Free Labor & Northern White Unity
- ▷ Slavery on the Eve of Civil War
- ▷ Slavery's Expansion
- ▷ Slavery & Southern Society
- ▷ Hidden Complexities of Slavery
- ▷ Author Discussion #1 - Was Secession and War Inevitable in the 1850s?
- ▷ Fire-Eaters & Abolitionists
- ▷ Kansas-Nebraska Act
- ▷ Rise of the Republican Party
- ▷ John Brown's Raid
- ▷ Response to John Brown
- ▷ Cinematic - Lincoln at Cooper Union
- ▷ Republican Threat to the South
- ▷ Southern Reactions to Lincoln
- ▷ South Carolina Secedes
- ▷ No Room for Compromise
- ▷ Lincoln Argues for War
- ▷ Lincoln Miscalculates Unionist Support in the South
- ▷ Reactions to Fort Sumner

CONTENTS

INTRODUCTION

THE AMERICAN WAR tells the story of the compelling conflict that marked one of the great defining moments in U.S. history. Long-simmering sectional tensions reached a critical stage in 1860-61 when eleven slaveholding states seceded and formed the Confederate States of America. Political disagreement gave way to war in April 1861, as Confederates insisted on their right to leave the Union and the loyal states refused to allow them to go. Nothing in the nation's history had prepared Americans for the scale of military fury and social disruption that ensued. Four years of fighting claimed more than a million military casualties (of whom as many as 750,000 may have perished), directly affected the lives of hundreds of thousands of civilians, and freed four million enslaved African Americans. The social and economic system based on chattel slavery that the seceding states had sought to protect lay in ruins. The durability of the Union had been confirmed, as had the supremacy of the national government over the individual states. In the longer term, preservation of the Union made possible the American economic and political colossus that figured so prominently in twentieth- and twenty-first-century history.

The issues at stake in this era—sovereignty and freedom—reached from the highest levels of the constitutional and political arena into the lives of ordinary people, North and South, black and white, soldiers and civilians, men and women. *The American War* provides readers interested in the Civil War and Reconstruction with an understanding of the dramatic political and military events and personalities, as well as an appreciation of the sheer tragedy of the war. This fascinating story is set within a chronological framework that analyzes the larger social and economic processes that transformed the nineteenth-century United States. Those who read *The American War* will be well prepared to debate and discuss three major questions that have captured the attention of generations of Americans since the end of the conflict: What were the causes of the Civil War? Why did the Union prevail over the Confederacy? Was Reconstruction a success or failure? They will also understand how Americans who experienced the conflict interpreted and remembered it.

The American War reflects the wide diversity of historical scholarship about the period. No student of this complex era can be considered well educated without a solid introduction to the coming of the war, the rise of the Republican Party, the presidency of Abraham Lincoln, the establishment of the Confederate States of America, the military ebb and flow of the conflict, and the turmoil of Reconstruction. In short, constitutional, political, military, diplomatic, and economic issues are addressed in the chapters, with a good mixture of people, places, laws, events, battles, and well-known social movements. Similarly, readers must be aware of the cultural, social, racial, and gender issues that have cast new light on traditional assumptions. The life of the common soldier, changing women's roles in society, the revolutionary nature of enrolling black soldiers to fight for the Union, the breakdown of slavery, and the complexities of bringing the reality of emancipation to bear upon an embittered white southern population are all important aspects of the era that are well covered in *The American War*.

Above all, we hope this overview of the most tumultuous period in our history conveys a sense of how profoundly it touched the lives of millions of Americans. We hope as well that readers will understand, even more than 150 years after the first guns fired at Fort Sumter, that it remains impossible to grasp the larger sweep of U.S. history without coming to terms with the American War.

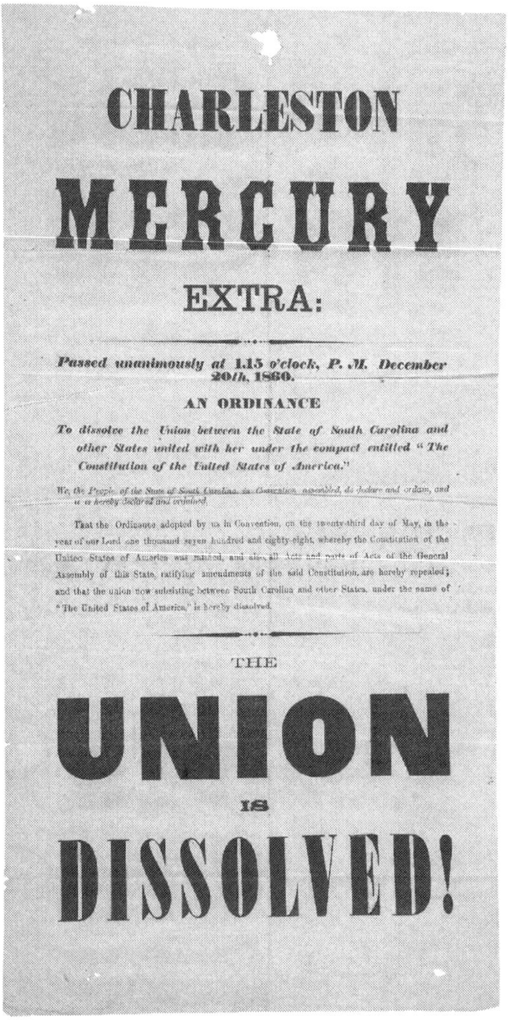

CHARLESTON

MERCURY

EXTRA:

Passed unanimously at 1.15 o'clock, P. M. December 20th, 1860.

AN ORDINANCE

To dissolve the Union between the State of South Carolina and other States united with her under the compact entitled " The Constitution of the United States of America."

We, the People of the State of South Carolina, in Convention assembled, do declare and ordain, and it is hereby declared and ordained,

That the Ordinance adopted by us in Convention, on the twenty-third day of May, in the year of our Lord one thousand seven hundred and eighty-eight, whereby the Constitution of the United States of America was ratified, and also, all Acts and parts of Acts of the General Assembly of this State, ratifying amendments of the said Constitution, are hereby repealed; and that the union now subsisting between South Carolina and other States, under the name of "The United States of America," is hereby dissolved.

THE

UNION

IS

DISSOLVED!

Plate 1. Broadside announcing South Carolina's secession from the United States. Printed in Charleston on December 20, 1860, this document became an iconic symbol of the break-up of the Union.

CHAPTER 1

EXPANSION, NATION, AND PERCEPTION:
THE ROAD TO SECESSION AND WAR

SECTIONAL TENSIONS ALWAYS formed part of the American political landscape. Delegates to the Philadelphia convention in the summer of 1787 agreed to a series of compromises relating to the institution of slavery, without which passage and ratification of the Constitution would have been impossible. During the decades leading up to the secession crisis of 1860-61, disagreements between slaveholding and free states occasionally mushroomed into major political crises. Yet it is crucial to remember that Americans did not know they were living in the "antebellum" period. That term, taken from Latin for "before the war" and now applied to the years 1820-60, came into use only after the nation emerged intact from four years of appalling slaughter. Most citizens of the prewar era spent relatively little time thinking about geographical differences and had no sense that violence would soon engulf the republic. Then as now, concerns about home and family, about work and business, and about local politics usually predominated.

Powerful ties connected citizens across sectional lines, while other factors served to divide residents of the North from those in the South. Political and cultural ligaments included a common language, a Protestant Christianity that claimed millions of adherents, and a shared history that celebrated the revolutionary generation's successful rebellion against Great Britain. At the same time, northern and southern states indisputably developed in divergent ways that can be traced to the institution of slavery. Historians have disagreed about whether the North and South had become quite separate civilizations by the late 1850s. Were they a true nation? Or two geographical regions sharing common federal boundaries but divided across a political and ideological frontier delineated by slavery?

Often overlooked in this scholarly debate is the fact that substantial numbers of white northerners and southerners *believed* there were troubling divisions. In any era and circumstance, perception usually trumps reality in dictating behaviors because people act according to what they perceive to be the truth—however that perception might differ from reality. By the eve of the Civil War, northerners saw in the South a society fundamentally—and many would have said perniciously—shaped by the presence of slavery. For their part, white southerners thought northerners an antagonistic and meddling people determined to undermine the South's slavery-based social system. It mattered little whether a real chasm split the nation's populace. The *New York Daily Tribune* put it well in the spring of 1856: "The truth is, that though we are but one nation we are two peoples. We are a people of equality, and a people of inequality. We are a people of Freedom and a people of Slavery. . . . These two peoples are united by a bond of political union, but whenever a collision comes which brings out the peculiar characteristics of the two, they are seen to be as unlike as almost any two civilized nations on the face of the globe." That same year, a young

North Carolina cadet at West Point offered the southern viewpoint. "Our manners, feelings & education is as if we were different Nations," he wrote, predicting eventual division along regional lines. "Indeed, everything indicates plainly a separation."

I. SECTIONS AND PERCEPTIONS

An observer seeking major themes in American life between 1820 and 1860 could craft a narrative largely devoid of sectional issues. These years witnessed a revolution in communications and transportation that dramatically shrank time and space. The electrical telegraph, famously demonstrated with Samuel F. B. Morse's message from Washington to Baltimore in May 1844, opened breathtaking possibilities. By 1861, Western Union's transcontinental lines connected to the Eastern seaboard and California, and in 1858 the first transatlantic cable linked Europe and North America (it soon failed and not until 1866 would a reliable cable be laid). Railroads expanded exponentially during the last two decades before the war, from just fewer than 3,000 miles of track in 1840 to more than 30,000 in 1860. The telegraph and trains allowed information, goods, and people to move much faster, increasing the pace of life and commerce in ways that left people somewhat flabbergasted. (Telegraphy and railroads would play major roles in the military story of the Civil War.) Population growth also maintained a dizzying pace, averaging more than 33 percent a decade between 1820, when Americans numbered just more than 9,500,000, and 1860, when the total approached 31,500,000. Of the later figure, more than four million were foreign-born and approximately 10 percent Catholic—major increases as percentages of the whole population from earlier decades and largely a result of German and Irish immigration.

The observer similarly could focus on headlines dealing with significant events unconnected to sectional disputes. Toward the end of the prewar period, for example, the Panic of 1857 and the Colorado gold rush of 1858-59 garnered massive attention throughout the nation. Part of a wider world economic crisis, the panic hit the North harder than the South and caused considerable dislocation in the railroad industry, agricultural markets, and the banking sector for more than a year. The discovery of precious metals in Colorado, which inspired the cry "Pike's Peak or Bust," lured more than 100,000 immigrants to the Rocky Mountain region. (By way of comparison, 75,000-90,000 gold-seekers flooded into California during the gold fever of 1848-49.)

Despite such important themes and events, a narrative ignoring sectional stresses would be grossly misleading. Any perceptive observer would notice trends in development that help illuminate why the nation confronted a profound sectional crisis in 1860. The North's population grew far more rapidly, allowing the nonslaveholding states to gain an increasingly lopsided majority in the national House of Representatives and win control of the Senate when California entered the Union in 1850. Admission of Minnesota in 1858 and Oregon a year later added to the free state advantage. Most of the nation's new immigrants settled in the North, many in rapidly growing cities that made the region far more urban than the slaveholding South (one-quarter of northerners lived in towns and cities by 1860, one-tenth of southerners). Of the twenty-five most populous cities in 1860, nineteen were in free states. The North also possessed most of the nation's industrial, commercial, and financial strength. Yet a substantial agricultural sector employed roughly 40 percent of the region's workers in 1860. Yeoman farmers with relatively small holdings dominated northern agriculture.

Religion helped shape northern economic and social life. A vibrant form of Yankee Protestantism trumpeted the virtues of hard work and thrift, while warning against abuse of alcohol or excess of any type. This religious strain helped create an environment conducive to capitalist expansion and the development of an American industrial and commercial giant. The same Protestant ethic prompted many northerners to embrace reform movements that sought to curb drinking, enhance public education, improve conditions in prisons and asylums for the mentally ill, and, most important in terms of sectional relations, end the institution of slavery. Significant elements of the northern populace resisted the models of reform, purposeful labor, and material acquisition—including many Democrats, urban Catholics, and residents of the lower sections of the midwestern states who looked south across the Ohio River for many of their economic, familial, and social ties. But the North's political and economic leadership tended to subscribe to the Yankee Protestant ethic, thereby setting a standard for the entire section.

By the mid-1850s, the free labor ideology had taken firm root across much of the North. It taught that labor and capital need not be at odds. Every man in the United States (only white men could vote in most places, and women occupied a distinctly disadvantaged legal position), proclaimed Whigs and later Republicans who espoused the free labor ideology, possessed almost limitless potential. Poorer men could use their own labor to acquire capital, ascend from the ranks of workers to become property owners, and create a comfortable and rewarding life for themselves and their families. Harsh inequalities of wealth among northerners suggested that this ideal remained far from assured, but political leaders such as Abraham Lincoln, himself a remarkable example of how a poor man could rise, painted a picture of glorious capitalist development. "The prudent, penniless beginner in the world, labors for wages awhile," stated Lincoln in 1859, "saves a surplus with which to buy tools or land, for himself; then labors on his own account another while, and at length hires another new beginner to help him." This was "*free* labor—the just and generous, and prosperous system, which opens the way for all—gives hope to all, and energy, and progress, and improvement of condition to all."

Many northerners believed the social and economic structures in the South mocked the democratic promise bequeathed to the nation by the founding generation. They claimed slaveholding oligarchs controlled the region and circumscribed potential for economic improvement. For these critics, the South harbored a lazy, cruel, poorly educated, violent people stained by the taint of slavery and opposed to the ideas that would allow the United States to fulfill its capitalist destiny. Because slavery closed opportunities to small farmers and degraded white working-class southerners by forcing them to compete with enslaved African Americans, the free labor ideology could not flourish below the Mason-Dixon Line. That failure, argued free labor advocates, in turn compromised the future of the entire nation. As Senator Henry Wilson of Massachusetts put it, the institution of slavery created "a commanding power, ever sensitive, jealous, proscriptive, dominating, and aggressive, which was recognized and fitly characterized as the Slave Power."

The slaveholding South presented many striking contrasts to the North. After 1800, when Virginia had been the most populous and important state in the nation, the region consistently lost ground in terms of comparative population. Its networks of roads, railroads, and canals lagged far behind those of the North. Roughly 80 percent of its population labored in agriculture—double the percentage in the free states—and the overwhelming bulk of southern wealth was invested in slaves and land. Large slaveholders dominated the region politically and socially, producing cash crops of cotton, sugar, tobacco, and rice that made them the single richest group of people in the nation. Southern cotton fed northern and European textile mills, as well as contributing enormously to the nation's favorable balance of trade. Cities were fewer and smaller than in the North, white southerners on average less well educated, and southern religion, though predominantly Protestant as in the North, more concerned with personal salvation than with reforming or improving society. Abolitionism found barren ground in the South, and by the 1850s most white southerners had adopted a stance affirming slavery as a "positive good" for both masters and those held in bondage.

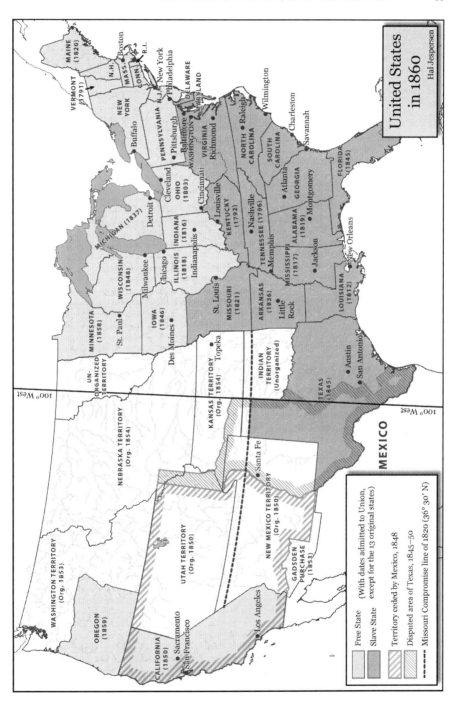

United States in 1860

Hal Jespersen

Free State (With dates admitted to Union,
Slave State except for the 13 original states)

Territory ceded by Mexico, 1848

Disputed area of Texas, 1845–50

Missouri Compromise line of 1820 (36° 30' N)

Slavery served not only as a form of labor control but also as the key to the South's social order. Only about one-third of white southern families owned slaves, and most of those held fewer than five. Just 12 percent of the slaveholders owned twelve or more slaves, the dividing line often given between a plantation and a farm. But all white southerners had a stake in the system of slavery because, as white people, they belonged to the region's controlling class. No matter how wretched their condition, they were superior, in their minds and according to the social and legal structure of southern society, to the millions of enslaved black people. White southerners, regardless of economic status, were made equal by the fact of black slavery. For this reason, and because of genuine fear of what would happen should large numbers of black people be freed in the South, white southerners saw slavery as a necessary and generally beneficent institution and reacted very defensively to criticism from the North.

During the antebellum years, many white southerners held a set of negative stereotypes about the North. They considered northerners a cold, grasping people who cared little about family and subordinated everything to the pursuit of money and material goods. They also believed northerners too quick to judge others, insistent on forcing their reforming beliefs on all Americans, and, most ominously, intent on interfering with a southern society dependent on slavery to exert social and economic control over black people.

II. TERRITORIAL EXPANSION AND ESCALATING TENSIONS

The sectional crisis reached a molten intensity in connection with expansion into the federal territories. Aware of its growing inferiority in population, the South thought it necessary to maintain parity in the U.S. Senate, where each state had two representatives regardless of population. The North, equally cognizant of its edge in population, insisted that it should wield greater influence in government. White southerners also asserted that their "peculiar institution," as slavery was called, must be able to expand into the new areas lest their economy stagnate. Beginning in the late 1840s, large numbers of northerners supported a free soil movement that sought to prevent slavery's introduction into the territories. Many of those calling for free soil in the West, it should be noted, were as prejudiced against black people as any southern slaveholder. The population of the free states in 1860 was 98.8 percent white, and most residents thought in terms of federal territories reserved for free white men and their families.

A number of mileposts marked the road of sectional friction. In 1820, the Missouri Compromise restricted slavery in the Louisiana Purchase country to land below 36 degrees, 30 minutes north latitude. Missouri entered the Union as a slave state and Maine as a free state, thereby preserving the balance of power in the Senate and setting a precedent for admitting free and slave states in pairs that would hold for the next thirty years. Alarmed by heated congressional debates over Missouri, the aged Thomas Jefferson likened the issue to a "firebell in the night" and "considered it at once as the knell of the Union." In 1831, Nat Turner's bloody slave uprising in Southside Virginia and the founding of William Lloyd Garrison's abolitionist newspaper *The Liberator* spawned concern among white southerners. The admission of Texas as a slave state in 1845 and the war with Mexico in 1846-48 brought vast new western lands into the Union. The North staked out its position in 1846 with the Wilmot Proviso, which called for excluding slavery from any territory taken from Mexico. The proviso, which passed the House of Representatives but failed in the Senate, served warning to the South that a good part of the North meant to bar slavery from all new territories.

Crisis followed crisis rapidly after 1848, a year in which the Free Soil Party mounted a ticket for the presidency headed by former Democratic president Martin Van Buren. The Compromise of 1850, in addition to ending the South's parity in the Senate with the admission of California as a free state, forced a tougher fugitive slave law on the North. Two years later, Harriet Beecher Stowe's novel *Uncle Tom's Cabin* was published and reached a huge audience in the North and in England, winning untold converts to the anti-slavery cause. The Kansas-Nebraska Act of 1854 sought to apply the doctrine of "popular sovereignty," which allowed the people of a territory, rather than the federal government, to decide whether they would accept slavery. Many northerners argued that this violated the Missouri Compromise by reopening to slavery parts of the Louisiana Purchase territory. Virtual civil war erupted in Kansas, as slaveholders and free staters fought to gain control of the area. In 1856, Charles Sumner of Massachusetts was brutally beaten on the floor of the Senate by Representative Preston Brooks of South Carolina after giving a no-holds-barred speech opposing the spread of slavery into Kansas. Brooks's action, together with the white South's overwhelmingly positive reaction to his assault on Sumner, seemed to confirm stereotypes of slaveholders as quick to resort to violence when anyone challenged them.

The Supreme Court's Dred Scott decision in 1857, supported strongly by Democratic president James Buchanan, seemingly guaranteed a slaveholder's right to take chattels anywhere in the territories and possibly anywhere in the free states. Outraged northerners denounced the decision, written by Chief Justice Roger B. Taney of Maryland, as proof that a "slave power conspiracy" in government gave the South clout far out of proportion to its population.

In fact, the South had wielded disproportionate influence in national government for many decades. Between George Washington's assuming the presidency in 1788 and the election of 1860, slaveholders or pro-southern northern Democrats held the presidency for sixty years. The Supreme Court also often seemed to favor the slaveholding states, and because of the three-fifths compromise of the Constitution—which counted enslaved African Americans as three-fifths of a person for purposes of representation and taxation—each white voter's ballot in a slaveholding state counted for more than one cast by a voter in a free state. When white southerners claimed to be a mistreated minority in national politics, many northern citizens countered that it was the majority in the North that had been denied the full influence their numbers deserved.

In the 1840s and 1850s, crucial national institutions failed to cope with increasing sectional tensions. Several Protestant denominations, including the Baptists and Methodists, split into northern and southern branches over the issue of slavery. The Whig Party broke apart in the early 1850s, its southern and northern wings hopelessly at odds. Meanwhile, the Democratic Party became in effect a southern-dominated sectional party that elected "doughfaces"—the derisive term for "northern men of southern principles" such as Franklin Pierce and James Buchanan—to the presidency. In the minds of many in the free states, the Democratic Party served as a mere tool of slaveholding oligarchs. The Republican Party, a purely sectional organization with no appeal in the South, first ran a presidential candidate in 1856, its platform calling for a total ban on slavery in the territories. White southerners quickly associated Republicans with abolitionists—though the two were by no means synonymous.

Perceptions on each side reached a point by the late 1850s where many northerners or southerners showed little inclination to view the other section sympathetically or even realistically. Each side expected the worst from the other. The white South imagined the North as a land of abolitionists and Republicans intent on killing the institution that served as the foundation of southern economics and society. The North deprecated a South of aggressive slaveholders who used the national courts and doughface allies in the presidency and Congress to frustrate the nation's progress toward greatness as a free labor, capitalist state. In October 1859, John Brown's raid on Harpers Ferry sent shock waves through both sections. Slaveholders denounced Brown as a terrorist who sought to foment servile insurrection among millions of slaves. Opinion in the North fell along a wide spectrum, though enough people supported Brown to inspire tremendous fear in the South. Ralph Waldo Emerson, the famed essayist and lecturer, typified the latter group. Speaking in Boston a month after the failed raid, he remarked of the soon-to-be-executed Brown: "He believes in the Union of the States, and he conceives that the only obstruction to the Union is Slavery, and for that reason, as a patriot, he works for its abolition."

III. THE ELECTION OF 1860 AND SECESSION OF THE LOWER SOUTH

The presidential election of 1860 unfolded amid escalating sectional animosity and laid bare the profoundly disruptive influence of slavery-related issues. Unable to agree on a policy in the territories, the Democratic Party split into northern and southern wings, which chose as their respective standard-bearers Stephen A. Douglas of Illinois, who supported the idea of popular sovereignty, and John C. Breckinridge of Kentucky, who called for the right to take slaves into all territories. The Republicans nominated Abraham Lincoln on a platform that emphasized the need to bar slaves from all the territories, and a fourth party, the Constitutional Unionists, selected an aging Tennessee Whig named John Bell, who said nothing about the territories and called for subordination of all interests to the goal of preserving the Union. Although Lincoln and the Republicans did not appear on the ballot in ten slaveholding states, it soon became clear that the populous free states would give them victory. A dispirited South plunged into gloomy anticipation of a Republican occupying the presidency, while many across the North happily envisioned an end to the pro-southern Democratic stranglehold on the office.

Slaveholders had reason to fear Lincoln and his party. The Republican candidate's "House Divided" speech of June 1858 seemed to spell doom for the long-term prospects of the South's ruling class. "A house divided against itself cannot stand," Lincoln had affirmed, adding: "I believe this government cannot endure, permanently half slave and half free. I do not expect the Union to be dissolved—I do not expect the house to fall—but I do expect it will cease to be divided. It will become all one thing or all the other." For their part, most white southerners would have endorsed the ideas in Alexander H. Stephens's famous "Cornerstone Speech" delivered soon after Lincoln's inauguration in March 1861. The foundations of a southern nation, said the Georgian, would rest "upon the great truth that the negro is not equal to the white man; that slavery, subordination to the superior race, is his natural and moral condition." This "great physical, philosophical, and moral truth," together with a desire to protect vast wealth and the power it conveyed, lay at the heart of southern determination to protect the peculiar institution.

Numbers highlight the contentious nature of the election and its possible financial implications for the South. Lincoln received 180 electoral votes to a combined 123 for his three opponents but polled almost a million fewer popular votes. If the other candidates had consolidated their electoral totals, Lincoln still would have won. Confronted with a bleak prospect of becoming an ever-smaller minority within the nation, residents of the fifteen slaveholding states discussed how the incoming administration's positions on slavery-related issues might threaten their economic and social stability. The 1860 census revealed that slaveholders controlled more wealth than any other segment of American society. On a per capita basis, South Carolina and Mississippi—where slaveholders composed the highest percentage of white citizens—stood first and second in wealth. The value of property in enslaved people exceeded $3 billion—a sum far greater than the combined total of the nation's manufacturing establishments and railroads.

Several months after Lincoln's election, Jefferson Davis summarized the thinking of many slaveholders in the wake of the election. The Republicans' intention to exclude slavery from the territories, observed Davis, would have the effect of rendering "property in slaves so insecure as to be comparatively worthless, and thereby annihilating in effect property worth thousands of millions of dollars." Beyond the economic dimension, many slaveholders and nonslaveholders believed Republicans might pursue policies that would weaken white social supremacy in the South. Perhaps most obviously, a Republican president could appoint justices to the Supreme Court who would not follow Chief Justice Taney's pro-southern example.

People in all of the slaveholding states grappled with the question of how to react to Lincoln's election. Public opinion fell into three broad categories. Immediate secessionists favored individual action by separate states, while cooperationists, who also supported secession, preferred joint action by all or at least most of the South. Unconditional Unionists rejected the idea of secession altogether, insisting that slavery and all other southern interests could be protected most effectively under the Constitution. In the end, seven states concluded that Lincoln's triumph justified taking the drastic step of leaving the Union. The breakdown was geographical. Between December 20, 1860, and February 1, 1861, all of the Lower South seceded. South Carolina led the way, voting to depart from the United States on December 20, followed by Mississippi (January 9), Florida (January 10), Alabama (January 11), Georgia (January 19), Louisiana (January 26), and Texas (February 1). Just 32 percent of the South's white population lived in the Lower South, but these seven states were home to 47 percent of the enslaved population and had the highest rates of slaveholding among white households. In two of the seven, South Carolina and Mississippi, slaves composed a majority of the population.

The fact that eight slaveholding states chose not to secede inspired hope for compromise among friends of the Union in the free states and south of the Potomac and Ohio rivers. The states that rejected

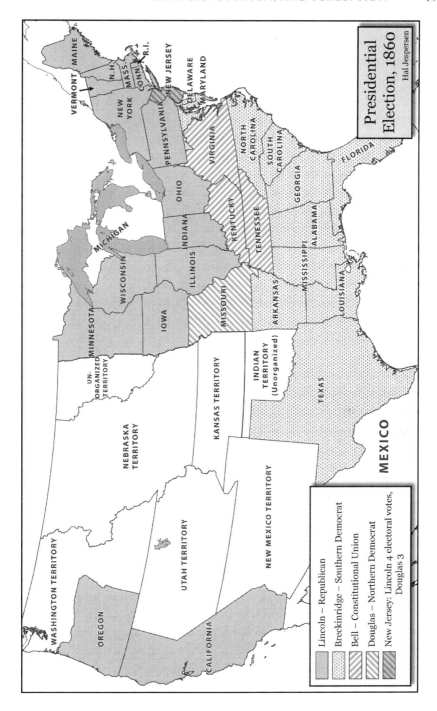

Presidential Election, 1860

Hal Jespersen

Lincoln – Republican

Breckinridge – Southern Democrat

Bell – Constitutional Union

Douglas – Northern Democrat

New Jersey: Lincoln 4 electoral votes, Douglas 3

secession in the months after the election, typically labeled the Upper South and the Border States, far outstripped the Deep South in white population, manufacturing capacity, and other important ways. The Upper South—Virginia, North Carolina, Tennessee, and Arkansas—claimed more than 35 percent of the South's white people, while the Border States—Missouri, Kentucky, Maryland, and Delaware—counted 33 percent. More than 52 percent of all enslaved people also resided in these eight states. Although they refused to embrace secession for themselves, most citizens in the Upper South and Border States argued that the Lower South had the right to secede and opposed any federal action to compel reunification of the United States.

IV. THE ROAD TO FORT SUMTER

While events in the South played out, northerners debated the constitutionality of secession. Unfortunately for anyone who sought an easy answer, the Constitution did not address the subject of secession directly. This left room for heated disagreement. Republicans generally castigated pro-secessionists as enemies of the Union who menaced the accomplishments of the founding generation, but many northern Democrats deplored the idea of forced reunion. A British observer who met with a group of prominent New York Democrats in March 1861 recorded his impressions of the clashing opinions. Republicans considered secession to be nothing but "treason," he noted, and accused the South of contemplating it long before the crisis of 1860-61. Among Democrats, in contrast, sentiment ran powerfully against deploying any kind of force to compel wayward states to rejoin the Union. "The feeling ag[ains]t the use of coercive means," recorded the Englishman, "is very strong & general."

The seven seceding states monitored debates elsewhere but moved forward to establish a new slaveholding republic. Representatives from all but Texas met in Montgomery, Alabama, in early February 1861

(Texas sent delegates later) and within five weeks formed the Confederate States of America, with its capital in Montgomery and a provisional government headed by Jefferson Davis and Alexander H. Stephens as president and vice president. The Confederate constitution, adopted on March 11, closely resembled that of the United States in many respects but unequivocally protected slavery and affirmed the rights of states.

President Buchanan and other politicians in Washington groped for a solution that would restore the Union during the ten weeks following South Carolina's secession. The president, who fit comfortably within the doughface element of the Democratic Party, claimed to believe secession illegitimate but blamed Republicans for the crisis, took no steps to enforce federal law in the seceded states, and suggested a constitutional amendment protecting slavery in the territories to placate the South. Other proposed compromises also placed the burden of concessions on the North and the Republicans, including the most famous one, named for venerable Senator John J. Crittenden of Kentucky. Among other things, Crittenden called for opening to slavery all territories south of the old Missouri Compromise line of 36 30—something the Republicans could not accept without breaking faith with all who had cast ballots for Lincoln.

This tense period offered up a little-known attempt at compromise by means of a thirteenth amendment to the Constitution. Championed by a group of Upper South Unionists and northern leaders who hoped to arrest and reverse the secessionist frenzy, it forbade any future amendment that would empower Congress to abolish or interfere with slavery in states where it already existed. The Corwin Amendment, so called because Republican congressman Thomas Corwin of Ohio introduced it in the House of Representatives, received the necessary two-thirds majority in both chambers of Congress, and on March 2, 1861, outgoing president James Buchanan signed it as a symbolic gesture of support (the president has no legal role in amending the Constitution). This action reflected the fact that in the early spring of 1861 a majority of white people in the free states, including Abraham Lincoln, were constitutional conservatives who believed the republic's founding document prevented Congress from abolishing slavery in the southern states. During his first weeks in office, Lincoln sent letters to each state governor conveying the proposed amendment and calling attention to Buchanan's endorsement. By the end of May, Kentucky, Ohio, and Rhode Island had ratified the amendment, and Maryland and Illinois later followed suit. But the outbreak of violence soon doomed this effort to find a peaceable solution to the sectional crisis.

Abraham Lincoln took office on March 4, 1861, and made several crucial points in his inaugural address. He insisted that the Union was perpetual and promised to "hold, occupy, and possess" all federal property that had not already passed into Confederate hands, signaling a sharp change from Buchanan's policy. He laid blame for the crisis directly on secessionists: "In *your* hands, my dissatisfied fellow countrymen, and not in *mine*, is the momentous issue of civil war. The government will not assail *you*. You can have no conflict, without being yourselves the aggressors." Lincoln understood the powerful pull of the concept of Union to millions of Americans, and he closed on a lyrical note. "We are not enemies, but friends," he insisted: "We must not be enemies. . . . The mystic chords of memory, stretching from every battle-field, and patriot grave, to every living heart and hearthstone, all over this broad land, will yet swell the chorus of the Union, when again touched, as surely they will be, by the better angels of our nature."

Shortly after Lincoln's inauguration, events reached a violent climax at Fort Sumter, a federal installation in Charleston harbor. Lincoln claimed Sumter as U.S. property, while Confederates countered that it lay on South Carolina soil and thus belonged to their new nation. The fort's garrison needed to be supplied, and Lincoln, pressed by northern opinion not to abandon Sumter, decided to send an unarmed vessel with provisions. He alerted South Carolina's governor and hoped the slaveholding states that remained in the Union would be sympathetic. Jefferson Davis's government, under similar pressure from their citizenry to seize the fort, wished to avoid firing the first shot. In the end, the Confederates asked Major Robert Anderson, the fort's commander, to surrender his garrison before the relief ship arrived. Anderson refused, and on April 12 the Confederates commenced a bombardment. Thirty-six hours later, the fort capitulated. On April 15, Lincoln issued a call for 75,000 ninety-day volunteers to suppress the rebellion. "I appeal to all loyal citizens to favor, facilitate and aid this effort," wrote the president, "to maintain the honor, the integrity, and the existence of our National Union, and the perpetuity of popular government; and to redress wrongs already long enough endured." All who opposed this assertion of federal authority should "disperse, and retire peaceably to their respective abodes within twenty days from this date."

The firing on Fort Sumter and Lincoln's call for volunteers marked the final scenes in a long-running drama of sectional tensions that stretched back many decades. No one at the time knew exactly what lay ahead, but people in the United States and the Confederacy understood they had reached a momentous point. "Never was known such excitement as was caused by Mr Lincoln's proclamation," a woman in eastern North Carolina wrote in her diary. "The whole South flew to arms." Far to the northwest in Indiana, another diarist recorded his reaction to the news. "[T]he surrender of Ft. Sumter confirmed," he began, " . . . North & South Both preparing for war—one the South flushed with victory at the surrender & the other ready to resist the injury & disgrace of flag & country." The stage had been set for the most transformative event in U.S. history.

Plate 2. "Scott's Great Snake." This cartoon map, published in 1861, illustrates what became widely known as Winfield Scott's Anaconda Plan to defeat the Confederacy by sealing its coasts and taking control of the Mississippi River.

CHAPTER 2

TWO REPUBLICS GIRD FOR WAR

THE MONTHS FOLLOWING Abraham Lincoln's call for 75,000 volunteers witnessed an explosion of activity and heated rhetoric as two nations prepared to fight. The eight slaveholding states still in the Union made final decisions regarding secession that greatly affected the size and scope of the ensuing conflict. Military and political leaders on both sides oversaw mobilization of manpower and material resources and formulated strategic plans. Across the United States and the Confederacy, citizens expressed fervent support for their governments and causes. Innocent of the vast carnage that would engulf their societies, many people seemed to welcome war as a release after years of pent-up sectional wrangling. "Slaveholding begets and fosters the war spirit," cheered a newspaper editor in Richmond, Virginia, adding, "Let us all make up our minds for a long and bloody war . . . . if need be until the

North gets sick of it. . . . War will do us no harm and much good." In New York City, a Republican lawyer struck a similarly strident pose. "So Civil War is inaugurated at last," he observed in his diary in the wake of Sumter's fall. "God defend the Right. The Northern backbone is much stiffened already."

I. THE UPPER SOUTH AND THE BORDER STATES TAKE SIDES

The four states of the Upper South considered Lincoln's call for military action against the Confederacy unacceptable. Unwilling to coerce other slaveholding states, Virginia, Arkansas, North Carolina, and Tennessee left the Union between mid-April and early June, bringing the number of Confederate states to eleven. These actions virtually guaranteed a longer and much bloodier conflict because they greatly increased the Confederacy's war-making capacity. Virginia, Tennessee, and North Carolina ranked first, second, and third in white population—and thus in potential military recruits—among the seceding states, and the Upper South contained more than half of the fledgling nation's industrial capacity. Virginia was especially important. With it, the Confederacy gained the extensive industrial and commercial strength of Richmond, powerful ties to Revolutionary leaders including George Washington (the Great Seal of the Confederacy would feature Washington), and the services of Robert E. Lee, who would tower over all other southern military figures. Partly in acknowledgment of Virginia's supremacy, the Confederacy transferred its capital from Montgomery to Richmond in May. Abraham Lincoln grasped the implications of Virginia's choice, acidly commenting in a message to Congress on July 4 that the Old Dominion's leaders and citizenry had "allowed this giant insurrection to make a nest within its borders."

The Border States took longer to make their decisions. Only Delaware, the smallest and least populous, demonstrated firm loyalty to the

United States. Missouri, Kentucky, and Maryland engaged in heated and often violent internal struggles, with secessionists mounting sustained efforts to align with the Confederacy. Maryland posed a special problem for the Lincoln administration—should it secede, Washington, D.C., would lie inside Rebel territory. Lincoln approved extraordinary—and constitutionally questionable—actions to keep Maryland in the Union. As for Kentucky and Missouri, their status remained uncertain until Unionists triumphed in the autumn of 1861. During the course of the war, bitter guerrilla fighting plagued Missouri and Kentucky, and rump versions of their governments sought admission to the Confederacy. Confederates willingly added stars to their national flag for the two states, though few serious observers actually believed the charade. The Border States contributed approximately 240,000 soldiers to the Union effort (nearly 42,000 of them black men) and at least 75,000 to the Confederacy. More important, by holding onto the Border States the Lincoln government controlled the Ohio River and access to its major tributaries as well as manufacturing and agricultural resources greater than those in the Upper South. In 1863, West Virginia became, in effect, a fifth Border State when Unionists from the mountainous western regions orchestrated the departure of fifty counties from Confederate Virginia. Thirty-two thousand West Virginians donned blue uniforms (196 of them black), while 15,000 joined Confederate military units.

Although disappointed that four slaveholding states rejected secession, the Confederacy's white citizenry embarked on their quest for nationhood imbued with feelings of southern community. Formed during the antebellum decades, their identity as members of a slaveholding society transcended state boundaries and promoted a seamless transition to a new Confederate loyalty. As the war began, a woman in Richmond expressed determination that reflected a merging of her southern loyalty and new Confederate identity. "We must all work for our country," she stated, " . . . . very weak in resources, but strong in stout hearts, zeal for the cause, and enthusiastic devotion to our beloved South; and while men are making a free-will offering of their life's blood on the altar of their country, women must not be idle."

Confederates believed their nation carried forward the work of the Revolutionary generation. They trumpeted the right to self-determination enshrined in the Declaration of Independence, accusing Republicans and the North of breaking faith with the Founders. In the Confederate interpretation, sovereign states had come together to establish the nation under a Constitution that protected slavery and included a fugitive slave clause. Secession represented a legal reassertion of that sovereignty to block Republican efforts to destroy slaveholders' property rights and by extension the southern social system predicated on white supremacy. Edward Porter Alexander, a young Georgian who resigned from the U.S. Army to join the Confederacy, summed up a common perception regarding the magnitude of the Republican threat: "I believe the interests of humanity, civilization, and self-preservation call on the South to secede, and I'll go my arm, leg, or death on it." For white southerners such as Alexander, "civilization" and "self-preservation" carried very specific meanings relating to a society whose legal and political structures guaranteed white control over millions of enslaved black people and their labor.

Loyal citizens of the United States also aligned themselves with the Founders. They pointed out that the preamble to the Constitution begins with "We the People," thereby countering the idea that sovereign states had forged the nation. One of the hardest things to grasp is why huge numbers of northern men would risk their lives in a conflict that never posed a direct threat to their families, farms, homes, and towns. The answer lies in a very widespread devotion to the meaning of the Union. Those who venerated the Union claimed that petulant slaveholding oligarchs, unhappy with the results of a presidential election untainted by corruption at the polls, had dismantled the constitutional edifice built on the Revolutionary generation's sacrifices. A

Union unique in its guarantees to "the people" of a voice in their own governance and economic opportunity could be vindicated only if citizen-soldiers stepped forward. Beyond the borders of the United States, the future of democracy in a western world ruled by aristocrats and monarchists similarly depended on a war to save the Union.

A Union rally attracted a vast crowd in New York City on April 20. Thousands of people sang "The Star-Spangled Banner" and roared their support when Major Robert Anderson, Fort Sumter's Kentucky-born commander, made an appearance. A witness remarked that the "Union mass-meeting was an event. Few assemblages have equaled it in numbers and unanimity." A Connecticut soldier offered an individual tribute to the meaning of Union, explaining his refusal to accept secession in language echoed in countless other letters and diaries: "[If] traitors be allowed to overthrow and break asunder ties most sacred—costing our forefathers long years of blood and toil, all the hope and confidence of the world in the capacity of men for self government will be lost."

II. WHICH SIDE SHOULD WIN?

With the Border States secured, the United States comprised twenty-three states to the Confederacy's eleven and possessed undeniable advantages of manpower and economic capacity (admission of West Virginia and Nevada during the war brought the U.S. total to twenty-five). This has led to a widespread—and thoroughly wrong-headed—belief that Union victory was inevitable. Confederates battled against impossible odds, goes a common interpretation. No backward-looking, agricultural, slaveholding society could compete against a modernizing capitalist adversary built on free labor. In reality, the chances for Confederate success much exceeded those of the colonies against mighty Great Britain during the Revolution—something well understood by people on both sides. As one highly placed Confederate put it in the autumn of 1861, history offered no instance of "a people as numerous as we are inhabiting a country so extensive as ours being subjected if true to themselves."

An examination of relative strengths and weaknesses underscores why each side could have won. Numbers favored the United States. According to the 1860 census, the loyal states contained 22,260,836 people, of whom 21,472,897 were white (96.5 percent; if the Border States are left out, the percentage rises to 98.8) and 787,939 black (432,650 of them enslaved). The Confederate population included 5,447,220 white residents and 3,521,110 enslaved and 132,760 free black people—a total of 9,101,090. The loyal white population, from which more than 90 percent of Union soldiers would be drawn, thus outnumbered the Confederate white population by nearly 4-1. Enslaved labor allowed the Confederacy to mobilize a much higher percentage of its military-age white males (at least 85 percent compared to about 50 percent for the United States), and Border States, as already mentioned, sent another 75,000 men into southern armies. But approximately 100,000 black men and 105,000 white Unionists from the Confederacy fought in blue uniforms. Overall, the United States drew on a much deeper pool of manpower, placing approximately 2,200,000 men into the army compared to 800,000-900,000 for the Confederacy.

The United States held an even more impressive edge regarding a broad range of commodities required to wage war. Factories in the loyal states accounted for virtually all of the firearms, shoes and boots, woolens, and locomotives produced in the nation. The vast majority of deposits resided in northern banks, railroad mileage in the North more than doubled that in the Confederacy, and iron production in free states outstripped that in the South by 15-1. The Confederacy would create substantial war industries during its four-year history but never came close to matching the industrial muscle of the United States.

Professional military forces constituted a third Union advantage—

though one less substantial than the others already mentioned. The U.S. Army, fewer than 15,000 strong, was scattered across the American landscape in small units, and most of the fewer than fifty naval vessels in commission patrolled waters far from the United States. Moreover, most of the navy's ships were designed for ocean-going service rather than the coastal and riverine action that would dominate operations against the Confederacy. By the end of the war, the United States would have more than seven hundred warships in service, but few people could have imagined that in April 1861.

The balance sheet also included significant Confederate advantages. Most obviously, conditions for victory favored the Confederacy. It need only convince the loyal citizenry that subduing the rebellion would cost too much human and material treasure. A tie was thus as good as a win and required no projection of southern military power into the United States, no occupation of U.S. territory. The American Revolution presented a powerful example of how a weaker combatant could prevail by exhausting a stronger one's will to persevere. In this struggle between two democratic republics, civilian populations would be the key—something Abraham Lincoln, Jefferson Davis, Robert E. Lee, Ulysses S. Grant, and other perceptive political and military leaders realized. When one side's civilians reached their breaking point, whatever the real condition of the armies in the field, the war would end. This meant that the Confederacy, which lacked the resources to defeat the United States in an absolute sense, could win its independence.

Geography also favored the Confederacy. Spread over more than 750,000 square miles, intercut with imposing mountain ranges, and served by a substandard network of all-weather roads and railroads, it posed massive logistical obstacles to invading Federal forces. Although less compelling than the spectacle of armies locked in combat at places such as Gettysburg and Shiloh, the task of feeding and clothing huge numbers of soldiers, as well as the thousands of horses and mules that

labored alongside them, would be essential to success. It is instructive
to think of the challenge Union planners confronted in this way: every
time the Army of the Potomac—the largest and most important of the
Union forces—stopped for the night, it became the second largest city
in the Confederacy, topped in size only by New Orleans. British armies
during the Revolution had faced a comparable logistical challenge, and
more than once the sheer size of the American hinterlands had proved
a powerful ally to the colonists. Moreover, a 3,500-mile coastline and
open border with Mexico rendered an effective Union naval blockade virtually impossible, which meant the Confederacy would be able
to import at least some of the weapons, clothing, and other things
its armies would require. On the negative side, major rivers such as
the Mississippi, the Tennessee, the Cumberland, and the James ran in
the wrong direction from the Confederate perspective, offering Union
forces avenues of advance rather than posing easily defended barriers.

Fighting for home ground also gave Confederates an edge. Soldiers
defending hearth and family typically display greater resolve than those
seeking to conquer and occupy an opponent's territory. A Georgia soldier deployed to Virginia in May 1861 spoke to the importance of
place: "Oh, who could breath[e] this air, who trod this soil . . . and not
be ready to fight . . . . I cannot help thinking that some of the most
sanguinary battles of modern times are destined to be fought upon this
soil. Great God! Nerve us for the conflict!" Confederates often likened
Federal military forces to Hessians, the mercenaries Great Britain had
used during the Revolution, or to Vandals, the Germanic people who
sacked Rome and spread terror through parts of the empire. Both epi-
thets captured the sense of struggle for home against a brutal outsider.

Neither the United States nor the Confederacy possessed a clear
advantage in talented commanders. The persistent myth that superi-
or Confederate generalship succumbed in the end to overwhelming
Union manpower and resources collapses under scrutiny. The Civil War
would be the first in American history largely directed by graduates of

West Point. During the war with Mexico, West Pointers had acquitted themselves very well in subordinate roles—some of the brightest, such as Lee, George B. McClellan, and P. G. T. Beauregard, served on General Winfield Scott's staff. The junior officers from the mid-1840s advanced to the top echelons of responsibility during the Civil War, heading armies and holding key advisory positions to both Lincoln and Davis. These men had taken the same classes from the same professors at West Point, learned the same lessons under Scott and Zachary Taylor in Mexico, and shared a military heritage stretching back to Washington and the citizen-soldiers of the Continental Army. Inevitably, some applied their knowledge more effectively than others, and each side had its share of successes and failures. In the end, the United States would find more officers capable of directing armies effectively, something no one could have predicted at the war's outset. But on the whole the quality of generals proved very similar.

One variable could throw off any reckoning of the Confederacy's likelihood of success. As with so many other factors, this one had a connection to the Revolutionary War. Everyone knew colonial victory would have been impossible without the intervention of France after the battle of Saratoga in 1778. French regulars and naval strength under the Comte de Rochambeau and the Comte de Grasse set up victory at Yorktown in 1781, and French pressure applied to British interests elsewhere in the world mightily assisted the American Rebels. The possibility of foreign intervention, particularly by Great Britain or France, was much on the minds of the Lincoln and Davis administrations throughout the war. Many Confederates initially believed British dependence on southern cotton to feed its voracious textile industry would prove decisive, while some abolitionists doubted that either France or Great Britain, which had abolished slavery in their colonies in the 1830s and 1840s, would align with the Confederacy. The question of foreign intervention in the North American conflict would remain a lively one through the first eighteen months of the war and still had relevance as late as the autumn of 1863.

In summary, the United States possessed considerable advantages, but the Confederacy by no means faced a hopeless struggle. Other nations had won against longer odds, and no one should fall prey to what might be called the Appomattox syndrome. That flawed way of looking at the conflict begins with knowledge of U.S. victory, assumes that was the only possible outcome, and works backward to locate evidence of why the Confederacy failed. This can lead to a linear understanding of Union victory built on a model of constantly eroding Confederate morale ground down by internal tensions and inexorable Federal power sternly applied. Stronger popular will in the United States did win out, but only after Confederate military successes and political strife in northern states brought moments of despair that almost settled the issue in favor of the Rebels.

III. PRESIDENTS, GENERALS, AND STRATEGIC PLANNING IN 1861

Information from the battlefronts dominated newspaper coverage throughout the war, shaping national morale as well as perceptions about political and social questions. The secession of Virginia and transfer of the Confederate capital to Richmond focused early military planning on the upper reaches of the Confederacy. As the two sides wrestled with how best to prepare for and conduct their initial campaigns, the hundred-mile strip of land between Washington and Richmond assumed primacy as the likely cockpit of the war. In terms of overarching goals, the Confederacy sought to counteract whatever moves the United States initiated, hoping to defend its borders and establish independence. Lincoln and his advisors confronted the far more daunting task of marshaling and projecting military power to compel the wayward states to return to the Union.

The rival presidents brought strikingly different credentials and personalities to their role as commander in chief. Lincoln's military service consisted of a few weeks as captain of Illinois militia during the Black Hawk War of 1832. He had never witnessed combat. Limited in national political experience to a single congressional term in the mid-1840s, he never held a substantive administrative post before assuming the presidency. Davis, in contrast, graduated from West Point in 1828, commanded a Mississippi regiment at the battle of Buena Vista during the war with Mexico, served as an innovative secretary of war during the administration of Franklin Pierce in the 1850s, and twice chaired the Senate's Committee on Military Affairs. A good listener and quick learner who initially leaned on Winfield Scott, Lincoln could put his ego aside in dealing with difficult generals such as George B. McClellan. In time, he gained confidence in his own opinions and pressed commanders to apply superior Union resources relentlessly. Davis proved more prickly in dealing with subordinates, engaged in some protracted and counterproductive feuds, sometimes sought to function as commander in chief and general in chief simultaneously, and occasionally supported loyal officers despite poor performances on the battlefield. Overall, both men dealt with profoundly difficult challenges and acquitted themselves well.

General in Chief Scott took the lead in devising a strategic blueprint to defeat the Confederacy. A hero of the War of 1812 and the war with Mexico, he had been the most important American general for many years and, though in his mid-seventies, could apply vast experience and a first-rate intellect to the issue at hand. In the spring of 1861, he proposed a strategy reminiscent of that used against Mexico. The United States had blockaded Mexico's gulf coast, sought to isolate its northern provinces, and eventually mounted a major invasion against the Mexican capital. Scott similarly envisioned a naval blockade of the Confederacy and a combined army-navy strike down the Mississippi River to split the southern republic into two pieces. Should the Rebels continue to resist after the loss of key ports and control of the Mississippi, the United States might have to "[c]onquer the seceding States by invading armies." These proposed operations, dubbed the "Anaconda Plan" because they sought to squeeze the life from the Confederacy, would take several months to organize and, cautioned the aging general, might stretch over two or three years and require 300,000 men to execute. Although he retired in the autumn of 1861, Scott had sketched a scenario very similar to what actually took place during the war.

Well aware of political pressures on Lincoln to strike an immediate blow, Scott and other veteran officers counseled against precipitate action. They knew it took time to train raw troops and collect supplies—military realities lost on many newspaper editors and members of Congress. In the first innocent spring and summer of the war, however, exuberance and impatience prevailed. President Lincoln succumbed to the notion that a quick victory might crush the rebellion and avoid protracted bloodshed, supporting a campaign aimed at a Rebel force positioned some thirty miles west of Washington. In response to officers who claimed recent recruits were unready to fight, the president responded, "You are green, it is true; but they are green, also; you are all green alike." This way of thinking set in motion what would become known as the campaign of First Bull Run or Manassas.

IV. THE CAMPAIGN OF FIRST BULL RUN

The largest army ever fielded by the United States, 35,000 strong and commanded by General Irvin McDowell, camped just across the Potomac River from Washington in early July. A second Union general, Robert Patterson, guarded the lower Shenandoah Valley near Harpers Ferry with 18,000 men. Two Confederate forces confronted their Union opponents. P. G. T. Beauregard, the "Hero of Sumter," occupied Manassas Junction with 20,000 men, while General Joseph E. Johnston was near Winchester with another 12,000 troops. The Confederates enjoyed what military officers called interior lines. This meant that Johnston, by making use of the Manassas Gap Railroad, could reinforce Beauregard more quickly than Patterson could move to join McDowell.

McDowell marched toward Beauregard's army on July 16. He expected Patterson to pin Johnston down in the valley, thereby denying the Rebels a chance to combine their forces. Making very slow progress, the Union army reached Centreville before noon on July 18. By that time, Beauregard, well informed about McDowell's plodding advance, had placed his units in a defensive position covering key fords and bridges across a stream called Bull Run. Preliminary skirmishing that afternoon yielded a Confederate success and prompted McDowell to pull back and consider his options. Unknown to him, Patterson had bungled his mission in the valley, and Johnston had begun to shift his small army to the railroad that would take them on to Manassas Junction.

McDowell failed to engage the Rebels again until the morning of July 21. Three days had elapsed since initial contact, affording time for most of Johnston's troops to join their comrades posted along Bull Run. Yet the initial stage of the battle favored McDowell. More than 10,000 Federals crossed Bull Run and in sharp fighting pushed the Rebel left flank back to a high plateau called Henry Hill. Confederates from the morning's fighting rallied on that site as other regiments came to their support. At a critical juncture, a South Carolina officer sought to inspire some troops who had been scattered in earlier action. Pointing toward Virginia units led by General Thomas J. Jackson, Barnard E. Bee shouted: "Yonder stands Jackson like a stone wall; let's go to his assistance!" Thus did Jackson, forever after known as "Stonewall," receive the most famous nickname of the war. More than two hours of sustained combat on Henry Hill swung against the Federals as Confederate reinforcements applied increasing pressure. Shortly after four o'clock, a number of Union units, including those led by future army commander William Tecumseh Sherman, withdrew toward a ford and bridge across Bull Run.

Raising the Rebel Yell for one of the first times in the war, Confederates built momentum and forced their enemy into full retreat. Civilians who had come from Washington to witness a Union victory found themselves swept up in a mass of soldiers, pieces of artillery, supply wagons, and carriages. Congressman Alfred Ely of New York, captured during the chaotic aftermath of the battle and treated roughly by a hot-tempered Confederate colonel, found himself en route to imprisonment in Richmond. The Confederates, nearly as disorganized in victory as their beaten foe, failed to mount a pursuit that could prevent McDowell's demoralized army from reaching the safety of Washington.

First Bull Run gave citizens in both the Confederacy and the United States a small taste of the horrors to come over the next four years. Casualties exceeded those of any previous battle in American history. Approximately 18,000 men on each side participated in the fighting, which resulted in nearly 3,000 Federals and 2,000 Confederates being killed, wounded, or taken prisoner. Morale soared across the Confederacy, while the loyal citizenry of the United States braced for a longer and harder war.

For the rest of the summer, volunteers swelled the ranks of both armies. Three-quarters of a million men entered U.S. service, challenging the government's ability to clothe, feed, and arm them. More than 200,000 Confederates were in uniform by the end of the first week of August, and congressional legislation authorized another 400,000 enlistments. Where and how these soldiers would go into action prompted intense speculation and concern. John Beauchamp Jones, a clerk in the Confederate War Department whose voluminous diary contains invaluable information and gossip, complained on August 24: "We are resting on our oars after the victory at Manassas, while the enemy is drilling and equipping 500,000 or 600,000 men. . . . We are losing precious time." Another diarist, Benjamin Brown French, provided an equally valuable perspective from the U.S. capital. Writing five days af-ter Jones, he also expressed frustration. "The war does not seem to lead to much fighting about here now," he complained, "but there must be some soon; things cannot remain as they now are long. Two armies, *looking each other in the face*, must fight soon!" Neither diarist could know that several months of military stasis lay ahead—or that a round of operations in the spring of 1862 would shake both the United States and the Confederacy to their foundations.

Plate 3. Both sides accused the other of committing military atrocities through-out the war. This sketch from *Harper's Weekly* is titled "The Rebels Bayonetting Our Wounded on the Battle-Field, at Bull Run."

Plate 4. Dead Confederate soldiers near the Dunker Church at Antietam. This image, together with others made on the battlefield by photographer Alexander Gardner, provided viewers with graphic evidence of the war's carnage.

CHAPTER 3

WAR IN EARNEST:
SHIFTING MILITARY TIDES IN 1862

AN EXPANDING WAR'S hard realities engulfed the United States and the Confederacy in 1862. Following a generally quiescent autumn of 1861, military operations entered a far more active and bloody phase during the first six months of the new year. Shiloh and the Seven Days, battles on a scale utterly unprecedented in American history, rocked the respective home fronts between early April and the first week of July, and the remainder of 1862 witnessed large-scale campaigning across a huge landscape. Union and Confederate politicians struggled to satisfy the conflict's voracious appetite for manpower and money, adopting policies that would have been unthinkable in a peacetime environment. In his first annual message to Congress on December 3, 1861, President Lincoln expressed hope that efforts to suppress the rebellion would not "degenerate into a violent and remorseless revolutionary struggle." Yet both sides learned, as 1862 progressed, the age-old lesson that major wars unleash powerful social and political forces that rage beyond expected boundaries.

I. THREE THEATERS OF WAR

The military story of the war played out in three principal geographical theaters. The Eastern Theater embraced most of Virginia, parts of western Maryland, and the lower tier of counties in central Pennsylvania. This arena experienced by far the most concentrated combat. More men became casualties within twenty miles of Fredericksburg, Virginia, than in any other Confederate state, and overall nearly 450,000 of the war's 1.1 million casualties occurred in the Eastern Theater. Several factors conspired to focus attention on the East. It contained the two national capitals, which were separated by just a hundred miles, and boasted the conflict's two most famous armies—the Army of the Potomac and the Army of Northern Virginia. It was the theater closest to most large northern cities and thus to newspapers that reached a huge audience, and British and French observers habitually gauged the progress of the war by what transpired in Virginia. Finally, Robert E. Lee's emergence in late 1862 as the preeminent Rebel general gave additional weight to events in the East. It was a measure of the predominance of the Eastern Theater in the minds of people in the United States and the Confederacy that Appomattox, where Lee surrendered to Ulysses S. Grant in April 1865, marked the effective end of the war.

The Western Theater sprawled across many states and offered a portable feast of military action as U.S. armies penetrated ever deeper into the Confederacy. Early in the conflict, it stretched from the Ohio River on the north to the Gulf of Mexico on the south, with eastern and western limits defined by the Appalachian Mountains and the Mississippi River. By the end of the conflict, western armies had fought through Georgia and into the Carolinas, setting up a final scene

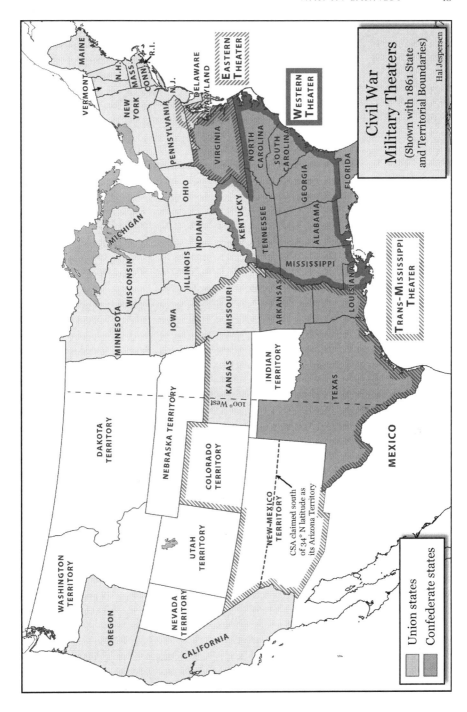

Civil War
Military Theaters
(Shown with 1861 State
and Territorial Boundaries)

Hal Jespersen

EASTERN THEATER

WESTERN THEATER

TRANS-MISSISSIPPI THEATER

MAINE

VERMONT

N.H.

MASS.

CONN.

R.I.

NEW YORK

PENNSYLVANIA

N.J.

DELAWARE

MARYLAND

VIRGINIA

NORTH CAROLINA

SOUTH CAROLINA

GEORGIA

FLORIDA

OHIO

MICHIGAN

INDIANA

ILLINOIS

KENTUCKY

TENNESSEE

ALABAMA

MISSISSIPPI

WISCONSIN

MINNESOTA

IOWA

MISSOURI

ARKANSAS

LOUISIANA

INDIAN TERRITORY

KANSAS

TEXAS

100° West

DAKOTA TERRITORY

NEBRASKA TERRITORY

COLORADO TERRITORY

NEW-MEXICO TERRITORY

CSA claimed south
of 34° N latitude as
its Arizona Territory

MEXICO

WASHINGTON TERRITORY

UTAH TERRITORY

NEVADA TERRITORY

OREGON

CALIFORNIA

Union states
Confederate states

at Durham Station, near Raleigh, where General William Tecumseh Sherman presided over the capitulation of the last significant Confederate field army. The Army of Tennessee, initially called the Army of the Mississippi, carried the burden of southern defense in the West, while on the Union side three armies named after prominent rivers, the Armies of the Tennessee, the Cumberland, and the Ohio, projected U.S. power into the rebellious states. The Western Theater contained crucial logistical resources, as well as New Orleans, the Confederacy's largest city and most important port, Nashville, Memphis, Atlanta, and other vital centers of commerce and communication.

The third and largest theater was the descriptively named Trans-Mississippi, which extended north to south between the borders with Canada and the republic of Mexico and east to west from the Mississippi River to the Pacific Ocean. Although accorded some attention in strategic planning by both sides, operations west of the Mississippi never rivaled in scale or importance those in either the Eastern or Western Theater. The most consequential military and political events in the Trans-Mississippi occurred in Arkansas, Missouri, Texas, western Louisiana, and Indian Territory (present-day Oklahoma). U.S. armies gained early control in portions of this region, especially those closest to the Mississippi, while other places, most notably Texas, experienced almost no Union incursions. The long border between Texas and Mexico allowed movement of goods into the Confederacy, and French intervention in Mexico added a diplomatic dimension to affairs in the Trans-Mississippi. On May 12-13, 1865, near Brownsville, Texas, a heavy skirmish at Palmito Ranch marked the final significant clash of the war. The part of the Trans-Mississippi west of the 100th Meridian, which embraced everything from western Kansas, Nebraska, and the Dakotas to the Pacific Coast and from the Texas panhandle across modern-day New Mexico and Arizona to California, remained peripheral to the Civil War. It witnessed very little military action between the United States and the Confederacy—none that had any appreciable effect on the conflict's outcome, though a small Rebel force moved up the Rio Grande from El Paso in 1861-62 and reached the vicinity of Santa Fe, New Mexico Territory, before retreating back to Texas in the late spring.

II. CAMPAIGNS IN THE WESTERN THEATER THROUGH JUNE

The military spotlight shined first in 1862 on the Western Theater, where a spectacular series of Union victories seemingly portended an early end to the conflict. General Albert Sidney Johnston presided over the Confederate defense, seeking to block four main avenues of advance along the Mississippi, Tennessee, and Cumberland rivers and a railroad that connected Louisville, Kentucky, and Nashville, Tennessee. From west to east, Confederate forces at Columbus, Kentucky (on the Mississippi), Fort Henry (on the Tennessee), Fort Donelson (on the Cumberland), and Bowling Green, Kentucky (on the railroad) awaited Union offensives. General Henry W. Halleck, the senior Union officer in the theater, targeted the two forts as Johnston's weak point, hoping that their capture would force abandonment of the entire southern line and allow Union forces to occupy Nashville.

Halleck selected Ulysses S. Grant to lead the offensive, a choice that introduced the person who, next to Lincoln, would contribute most to defeating the Confederacy. The thirty-nine-year-old Grant had experienced a good deal of failure before the war but quickly demonstrated unusual gifts as a field commander. Assisted by a naval flotilla, his small army seized Fort Henry on February 6 and Fort Donelson ten days later. Approximately 15,000 Confederates laid down their arms at Fort Donelson after Grant offered terms requiring their "unconditional and immediate surrender"—earning the victorious general the nickname "Unconditional Surrender" Grant. While Grant smashed the center of Johnston's line, a second Union army moved south along the railroad toward Nashville, occupying the city on February 25. The loss of Nashville cost the Confederacy a strategic hub of transportation and communications and significant site of war production. Johnston's defensive line had crumbled, and by the first week of April Grant had proceeded up the Tennessee River to Pittsburg Landing, a few miles north of the Tennessee-Mississippi border. A diarist in Richmond termed the loss of Nashville a "calamity" but mustered a degree of resolve: "We must run the career of disasters allotted us, and await the turning of the tide."

The Davis administration sought to counter defeats in the West by concentrating more than 40,000 men under Johnston at Corinth, Mississippi, for a counterblow against Grant. On April 6, Johnston's soldiers struck Grant's slightly larger army near a country Methodist church called Shiloh. During two days of combat, the Federals absorbed heavy blows and gave up a good deal of ground but, reinforced by 18,000 men, eventually drove the Confederates from the field and back into northern Mississippi. The battle of Shiloh established a ghastly standard of slaughter that made First Bull Run seem little more than a skirmish. Casualties approached 11,000 for the Confederates and more than 13,000 for Grant, a total that exceeded the number of Americans who had fallen in battle during the Revolutionary War, the War of 1812, and the war with Mexico combined. Albert Sidney Johnston was mortally wounded on the battle's first day, prompting Jefferson Davis to remark, "[O]ur loss is irreparable."

Over the course of the next two months, more disheartening news greeted Confederates. On April 25, a small fleet under David G. Farragut, who later would become the first admiral in the U.S. Navy, seized the riverfront at New Orleans. Four days later the Stars and Stripes flew over City Hall and the Custom House. Never again would Confederates command the economic gateway to the Mississippi River Valley. Although more than a year would pass before Union forces gained final control over the full length of the river, in practical terms the Mississip-

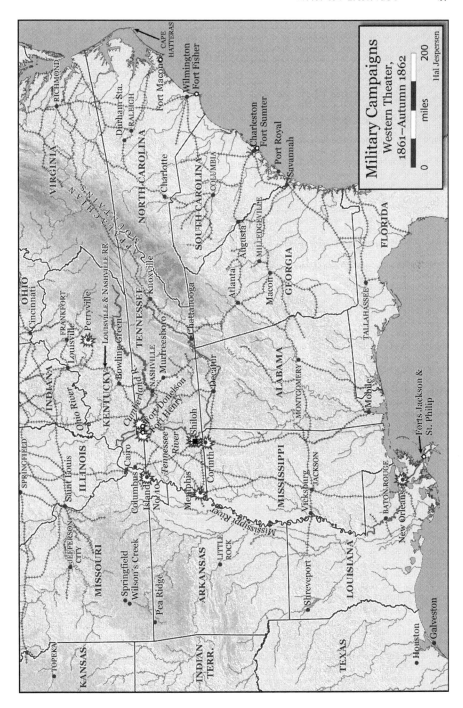

Military Campaigns
Western Theater,
1861–Autumn 1862

Hal Jespersen

0   miles   200

pi ceased to be a Confederate waterway just more than a year after the guns at Sumter had signaled the outbreak of violence. By the second week of June, Memphis also had fallen and a Union army of 100,000 occupied Corinth.

U.S. forces in the Western Theater had cleared Rebels from Kentucky and much of Middle and West Tennessee, taken control of the upper and lower Mississippi River, and stood positioned to plunge deeper into the Confederate hinterlands. Winfield Scott's strategic vision was being implemented, and leaders destined to play major roles in Union victory—Grant and his friend William Tecumseh Sherman, who also fought at Shiloh, Halleck, Farragut, and others—had begun their rise to prominence.

III. CAMPAIGNS IN THE EASTERN THEATER THROUGH THE SEVEN DAYS

The Eastern Theater presented a more complex picture of mixed Union and Confederate success. In November 1861, thirty-four-year-old George Brinton McClellan replaced Winfield Scott as general in chief of U.S. armies. McClellan also took the field at the head of the Army of the Potomac, which he had organized and christened in the dark weeks following First Bull Run. Intelligent, charismatic, and well informed about military theory and practice, McClellan considered himself the ablest officer in the nation and expressed impatience with Winfield Scott and contempt for President Lincoln. "I went to the White House shortly after tea where I found '*the original gorilla,*' about as intelligent as ever," he wrote to his wife regarding Lincoln shortly after succeeding Scott: "What a specimen to be at the head of our affairs now!" McClellan instilled a culture of aversion to risk within the high command of the Army of the Potomac, devoutly hoped to keep the war within limits, opposed forced emancipation, and made little effort to hide his opposition to much of the Republican Party's agenda.

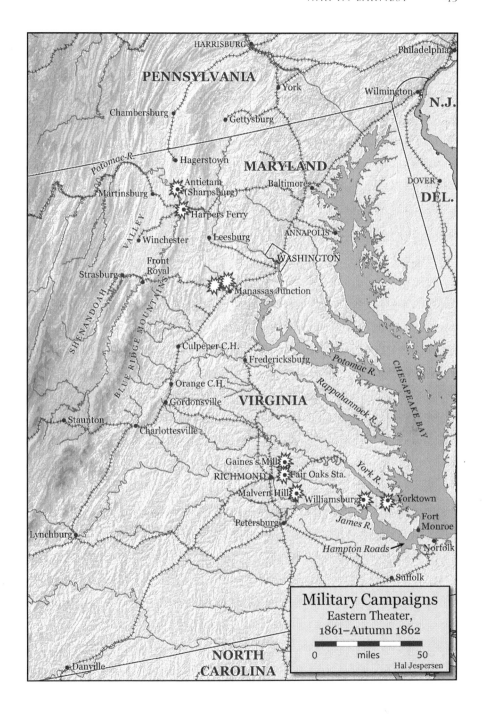

Military Campaigns
Eastern Theater,
1861–Autumn 1862

0   miles   50

Hal Jespersen

Throughout the autumn and winter of 1861-62, McClellan declined to advance against Confederates near Manassas Junction and proved reluctant to advise Lincoln of his plans. Lincoln grew weary of this behavior, and some prominent Republicans accused McClellan of harboring secret sympathy for the Rebels. The exasperated president removed McClellan as general in chief in early March, naming Halleck to replace him in July. Still at the helm of the Army of the Potomac, McClellan finally launched a campaign against Richmond in March. He confronted Joseph E. Johnston's army between the York and James rivers below Richmond, taking Yorktown and Williamsburg en route to reaching the outskirts of the Confederate capital by the end of May. On May 31, Johnston was wounded at the battle of Seven Pines or Fair Oaks, and Robert E. Lee assumed charge of the Confederate army opposing McClellan. The serendipity of combat thus ushered into field command the man who, more than any other, would sustain the Confederate people's hopes for independence over the ensuing three years. In the moment, many Rebels feared that Lee, who had begun the war with a large reputation but subsequently fallen in public estimation, would prove too timid to save their capital. Seldom has any citizenry so badly miscalculated in assessing a general. As one officer later observed, Lee proved to be "decidedly the most audacious commander who has lived since Napoleon."

Between June 1 and July 1, Lee took the initiative, throwing McClellan on the defensive and battering him in what became known as the Seven Days battles. Reinforced by Stonewall Jackson's forces, fresh from success in the Shenandoah Valley, the Confederates at Richmond numbered approximately 90,000 against McClellan's 100,000. In five separate clashes, including Gaines's Mill on June 27 and Malvern Hill on July 1, attacking Confederates suffered more than 20,000 casualties while inflicting 16,000—a butcher's bill that far surpassed even Shiloh's. A woman in Richmond described an endless number of wounded soldiers clogging the city. "We lived in one immense hospital," she observed, "and breathed the vapors of the charnel house." McClellan had abandoned all offensive thoughts as soon as Lee mounted his first assaults, conceding the initiative to an opponent who knew what to do with it. After Malvern Hill, McClellan retreated a few miles down the James River, a movement that angered some subordinates who knew the Army of the Potomac had held a strong position. General Philip Kearny, a fiery veteran who had lost an arm in the war with Mexico, observed bitterly that McClellan's order to withdraw "can only be prompted by cowardice or treason."

The Seven Days marked a grand turning point in the war. Few campaigns, including Gettysburg and Vicksburg, had equally far-reaching consequences. As McClellan approached Richmond, southern civilian morale had been very low because of Union successes in the Western Theater. Had their capital fallen, it is difficult to imagine what would have sustained Confederates going forward. The war might well have ended in the summer of 1862 with George B. McClellan as the great national hero and slavery largely intact. McClellan's constrained approach to war would have proved equal to the task of restoring the Union. Instead, Confederate expectations soared at the news of Richmond's deliverance, and Robert E. Lee began his ascent to an unrivaled position of national trust. McClellan's retreat hit especially hard across the loyal states because hopes had been so high based on news from the Western Theater.

Observers in London and Paris decided the Confederacy was winning the war—a measure of the degree to which McClellan's failure in the Eastern Theater overshadowed the abundance of good news for the Union in the Western Theater. Lincoln understood this phenomenon, complaining to a French diplomat in August: "[I]t seems unreasonable that a series of successes, extending through half-a-year, and clearing more than a hundred thousand square miles of country, should help us so little, while a single half-defeat should hurt us so much."

IV. GUERRILLA WARFARE

By the time of the Seven Days battles, unconventional warfare posed problems for both the United States and the Confederacy. In late July 1862, German-born scholar Francis Lieber informed General Henry W. Halleck that he was studying "the very important question" of depredations perpetrated by irregular forces in Missouri. Halleck agreed that something needed to be done, which helped inspire Lieber to codify the rules of war in a document signed by President Lincoln and issued as General Order No. 100 in April 1863. "Gen Halleck called upon me, after my correspondence with him, to write a pamphlet on guerrillas," explained Lieber, "which I did. . . . I wrote to Halleck that he ought to issue a Code on the Law of Nations so far as it relates to the armies in the field." The Confederacy addressed the challenge of controlling its guerrilla units with the Partisan Ranger Act of April 1862, only to repeal it less than two years later when irregular forces proved resistant to any type of discipline.

Over the course of the war, a few thousand guerrillas contributed to chaotic social conditions in a number of places, most obviously in parts of Missouri and areas radiating out from the spine of the Appalachian Mountains. Civilians suffered amid an escalating drama of brutality, reprisals, and freebooting lawlessness. Perhaps the most notorious incident occurred at Lawrence, Kansas, on August 21, 1863, when Confederate guerrillas under William Clarke Quantrill burned much of the town and murdered more than 150 male civilians

Such reprehensible activities did not play a major role in shaping the military outcome of the Civil War. First to last, conventional armies composed of citizen-soldiers waged operations that dictated swings of national morale, determined control over the most important waterways and logistical areas of the Confederacy, and, ultimately, decided the fate of slavery. The overwhelming majority of soldiers fought in regular units commanded by duly appointed officers. The actions of outliers such as Quantrill and "Bloody Bill" Anderson, as well as the headline-grabbing exploits of John Singleton Mosby in Virginia, scarcely influenced any campaign in a meaningful way.

Some historians believe the Confederacy should have pursued a wide-scale guerrilla resistance. They argue that southern manpower within this context would have lasted almost indefinitely and that the northern public lacked the commitment to suppress dedicated guerrillas. If subjected to the realities confronting the Confederacy, however, a guerrilla-based "war of liberation" seems an anachronistic pipe dream. It is inconceivable that Confederates would have shunned prominent West Pointers such as Robert E. Lee, Joseph E. Johnston, and P. G. T. Beauregard in favor of unknown men who would command small bands of partisans. Guerrilla war also would have been inappropriate for the kind of nation Confederates hoped to establish. They envisioned taking their place among recognized western states, a goal that demanded creation of formal governmental institutions—including a national army and navy. In his inaugural address, Jefferson Davis spoke to his fellow citizens of "the position which we have assumed among the nations of the earth." Great Britain and France would not have been favorably impressed by a fledgling Confederacy that relied on guerrilla units rather than on a formal army.

The threat of social chaos in a slave-based society also stood as a major obstacle to a Confederate policy of guerrilla war. The approach of Union forces understandably provoked alarm among Confederates about the consequences for their enslaved laborers. Late-antebellum fears of insurrection and reactions to Union invaders strongly suggest that Confederates would have opposed a guerrilla strategy that accelerated the process of bringing enslaved people into contact with Federal armies. It strains credulity to believe Jefferson Davis's government would select a strategy calculated to undermine economic and social control over millions of black people. In a careful reckoning of factors that led to defeat, Robert Garlick Hill Kean, who headed the Confederate Bureau of War, spoke to this point, pronouncing "Slavery an inherent weakness when deeply invaded, from [African Americans'] desertion to the enemy and joining their army as recruits."

V. CONFLICTS WITH NATIVE AMERICANS

During the summer of 1862, Dakota Sioux warriors cut a violent swath through much of Minnesota. The uprising grew out of the federal government's failure to deliver promised supplies, left more than 500 white civilians dead, and created panic across the state. Fighting in Minnesota raises the question of how best to treat conflicts with Native Americans between 1861 and 1865, most of which occurred in the trans-100th Meridian West. It is most fruitful to interpret struggles that pitted Indians against the U.S. Army and territorial military units as chapters not of the Civil War but of a much longer historical narrative. They fit within a framework that connects innumerable incidents from the Tidewater and Pequot wars of the seventeenth century to Wounded Knee in 1890. Three of the most written about examples involved the uprising in Minnesota, the forced resettlement of Navajos in Arizona and New Mexico in 1863-64, and the slaughter of approximately 150 Cheyenne and Arapaho people, including many women and children, at Sand Creek, Colorado Territory, in 1864. These kinds of incidents would have taken place, at some point and in some fashion, in the absence of the four-year bloodletting triggered by sectional wrangling.

Continuities among Indian wars across time abound. During the summer of 1863 in Cañon de Chelly, Colonel Christopher "Kit" Carson's command destroyed corn on which Navajos, in Carson's words, "were depending entirely for subsistence" during the upcoming winter. Carson's actions mirrored attempts to deny Native Americans sustenance and shelter that went back to "feed fights" in the colonial era or, nearer the Civil War, to Colonel William J. Worth's tactics during the Second Seminole War in 1841-42. The relocation of the Dakota Sioux in Minnesota and, more famously, the "Long Walk" of 8,000-9,000 Navajos from Arizona to the Bosque Redondo near Fort Sumner, New Mexico, recalled the "removal" of the "Five Civilized Tribes," so called in the nineteenth century, from the Old Southwest to what is now Oklahoma. Wartime friction with Indians also inspired debates about methods that had arisen in earlier eras. One side, usually dominated by white voices from frontier areas, called for unrestrained war against Indians. In this vein, Colonel John M. Chivington, who led Colorado and New Mexico units at Sand Creek, claimed "that to kill them is the only way we will ever have peace and quiet in Colorado." Others decried such brutality, as when Congressman Thaddeus Stevens of Pennsylvania remarked in May 1864 "that, in nine cases out of ten, Indian wars have been produced by the provocations of the whites."

Most people at the time certainly considered clashes with Native Americans to be separate from the war between the armies of the United States and the Confederacy. John G. Nicolay, sent by Abraham Lincoln to report on the violence in Minnesota in 1862, wrote: "Compared with the great storm of rebellion which has darkened and overspread our whole national sky, the Indian war on our northwestern frontier has been a little cloud 'no bigger than a man's hand.'" An Iowan deployed to Dakota Territory in 1862 affirmed that such duty "is not the height of our ambition. We are anxious to take an active part in this struggle for national existence, and distinguish ourselves . . . in maintaining our country's rights and restoring peace and harmony to its now torn and distracted States." In the summer of 1865, an officer in a Union cavalry regiment put the case very succinctly. Hearing a rumor that his unit might be sent to deal with Native American raiding, he told his father he had no desire, in the wake of victory over the Rebels, "to chase Indians." "After the work of the past four and a half years," he wrote in explicitly distinguishing between the sectional and Indian conflicts, "it would seem boys play."

VI. TURNING TOWARD AN ALL-ENCOMPASSING WAR

The Seven Days persuaded many in the United States that a harsher type of war would be necessary to subdue the Confederacy. Lincoln moved closer to abolitionists and Radical Republicans who had demanded seizure of slaves and other property belonging to Rebels. Affected by the outcome of the Seven Days, Lincoln informed his cabinet on July 22 that he intended to issue a proclamation of emancipation that would deny black labor to the southern war effort. Congress, meanwhile, had put the finishing touches on the Second Confiscation Act, a measure passed on July 17 and designed in part to free all slaves held by Rebels. Radical Republican Charles Sumner explicitly tied passage of this act to Union military failure in the Richmond campaign. "[T]he Bill of Confiscation & Liberation, which was at last passed, under pressure from our reverses at Richmond," wrote Sumner in early August, "is a practical act of Emancipation." Had McClellan been the victor in July 1862, he certainly could have pressed his case for a softer policy toward Confederates more effectively. The consequences for millions of enslaved African Americans might have been momentous.

By the end of July, people in the United States and the Confederacy knew that enormous sacrifice and loss likely would be necessary to win the war—and that the national governments would expand their authority to meet demands for men, money, and material resources. The national debt for the United States stood at approximately $62 million in 1860. By the end of 1862, it had soared to nearly $310 million, and by 1865 it would approach $2.5 billion (the latter two figures do not include Confederate national debt). The United States took unprecedented steps regarding taxation during the first year of the war. On August 5, 1861, Congress passed the first federal income tax in the nation's history, imposing a 3 percent levy on all incomes over $800 a year (most working men earned less than that). The much more comprehensive Internal Revenue Act of 1862, signed by President Lincoln on July 1, included excise taxes on liquor, tobacco, and other products, inheritance taxes, and a graduated income tax of 3 percent on incomes of $600-$10,000 and 5 percent on those above

$10,000. Congressman Thaddeus Stevens of Pennsylvania, a Radical Republican who chaired the Ways and Means Committee, remarked that "the rich and the thrifty will be obliged to contribute largely from the abundance of their means" but "no burdens have been imposed on the industrious laborer and mechanic." These and other taxes funded approximately 21 percent of the war effort.

Before passage of the Internal Revenue Act, the government also had begun issuing bonds and printing paper treasury notes to offset spiraling war-related costs. Bonds eventually accounted for 66 percent of federal revenues and paper money for 13 percent. The Legal Tender Act of February 25, 1862, authorized the Treasury Department to issue $150 million in notes—commonly called "greenbacks"—that would be redeemable for all debts public and private except custom duties and interest on government bonds. Treasury notes long had been a feature of American finance but never before denominated legal tender. Opponents of the Legal Tender Act, who included a large majority of the Democrats in Congress, pointed to the worthless paper money of the Revolutionary War and insisted people never would accept greenbacks as a worthy substitute for silver or gold. They were proved wrong. By the end of the war, nearly $450 million in greenbacks had been placed in circulation.

A looming shortage of manpower also threatened the Lincoln government in the wake of the Seven Days. Volunteering had dropped off dramatically, and summer and fall operations would require full ranks in all the armies. Union leaders took a two-pronged approach. On July 1, Lincoln sent a call to the loyal governors for 300,000 volunteers to serve for three years, with quotas assigned to each state according to its population. The president hoped fresh recruits would "bring this unnecessary and injurious civil war to a speedy and satisfactory conclusion." Governors offered bounties to would-be volunteers, but Congress also raised the specter of federal compulsion on July 17 with the Militia Act, which authorized the president to call state militia into national service for a period of nine months. This act allowed, but did not require, the enrollment of black men for duty in noncombatant and combat roles. On August 4, the War Department further burdened the states with a demand for 300,000 nine-month militia—bringing the total call since early July to 600,000. If the states did not produce the requisite number of militia, the War Department would take over the process of enrollment—in effect, instituting a federal draft. The national government never had compelled citizens to serve, so this represented a major break with tradition that many considered a profound abridgment of individual rights and liberties.

In the end, the states supplied enough men to satisfy Lincoln and the War Department. Secretary of War Edwin M. Stanton had stipulated that any three-year volunteer above the target of 300,000 would equal four nine-month volunteers, and 421,000 three-year recruits and 88,000 nine-month militiamen entered the Union ranks. To meet the militia quotas, however, some states resorted to drafts, which spurred violent protests. Democrats took the lead in opposition, with Irish and German Catholics among the most vociferous. The crisis passed without direct federal conscription, though the fear in many quarters of vastly increased central power lingered.

The Confederacy more than matched the United States in expanding the role of national government. This phenomenon, ironic for a republic allegedly devoted to state rights, stemmed in large part from the need to mobilize a high proportion of human and material resources to counter Union military operations. The most drastic expression of growing central power came on April 16, 1862, with passage of the first national military draft in American history. The impending loss to the Confederate army of scores of thousands of men who had volunteered for twelve months' service in the spring and early summer of 1861 led to this legislation. Robert E. Lee, who supported a central government capable of doing whatever necessary to win the war, put the case this way: "The great object of the Confederate States is to bring the war to a successful issue. Every consideration should yield to that; for without it we can hope to enjoy nothing we possess, and nothing that we do possess will be worth enjoying without it." The legislation not only made all white males between eighteen and thirty-five liable for three years' service, but it also extended by two years the obligation of those already in the army who had volunteered in good faith for one year. Two subsequent revisions of the legislation, passed in September 1862 and February 1864, changed the age limits, which finally were set at seventeen to fifty, and kept all soldiers in uniform for the duration.

The conscription act triggered protests across the Confederacy but in the long term served its supporters' purpose. Many inside and outside the army considered it a violation of individual liberties by a dangerously intrusive government in Richmond. Until rescinded in December 1863, a provision of the initial act allowed a draftee to hire a substitute to take his place—which provoked charges that the conflict would become "a rich man's war but a poor man's fight." State rights advocates also weighed in with vigor, none more pointedly than Governor Joseph E. Brown of Georgia, who described the act as a "bold and dangerous usurpation by Congress of the reserved rights of the States." Yet despite ongoing unhappiness with conscription that manifested itself in violence, desertion, and opposition to the war, most Confederates accepted the need for legislation that placed the largest number of men into uniform. Without conscription, it is difficult to see how the Confederacy could have sustained itself beyond the summer of 1862.

Like the United States, the Confederacy also relied on taxes, loans, and paper money to fund the war. Congress passed a modest property tax in August 1861 but waited until April 1863 to enact a broad array of taxes that included a graduated rate on incomes rising from 1 percent on those of $1,000-$1,500 to 15 percent on those greater than $10,000. A "tax-in-kind" also took 10 percent of crops such as corn, wheat, and sweet potatoes from farmers, who were allowed to set aside prescribed amounts of food for their families before the levy was applied. Overall, taxes yielded just 5 percent of the estimated $2.1 billion it cost to wage the Confederate war. Government loans provided another 35 percent, and, ominously, paper notes accounted for the remaining 60 percent. The Confederate government authorized more than $500 million in paper money by the end of 1862, and the amount escalated as the conflict continued. A combination of plentiful paper money, shortages of goods produced by the Union naval blockade, and disruptions to the transportation network by military campaigning created perfect conditions for rampant inflation, which by 1865 approached 9,000 percent in parts of the Confederacy. The United States, by contrast, raised more than $4 billion to run the war and coped with inflation of roughly 80 percent.

One last aspect of Confederate supply deserves mention—though it did not take full effect until the spring of 1863. On March 26 of that year, Congress passed an impressment law that allowed officials of the War Department to purchase animals, food, and fuel at prices set by the government. The law also stipulated that slaves could be impressed to work on fortifications and other war-related projects. This legislation gave formal sanction to actions that had occurred since the beginning of the war and represented another controversial expansion of central power that stirred up hot debate. Farmers complained that prices were set below true market value, and slaveholders accused the government of disrupting normal agricultural production and mistreating impressed slaves. The Davis administration persisted in the policy, which transferred hundreds of millions of dollars of goods and labor from the private sector to help sustain the war effort.

VI. CONFEDERATE COUNTEROFFENSIVES IN THE EAST AND WEST

Military campaigning through the summer and autumn of 1862 featured dramatic shifts in momentum. The Confederacy, after veering toward the precipice of national defeat in early June, mounted offensives that carried the war into the United States in both the Eastern and Western theaters. The changing Union attitude toward waging the conflict showed clearly in Virginia, where General John Pope, posted to the East after achieving success along the Mississippi River, headed a new Army of Virginia. Pope vowed to confiscate Rebel property, execute guerrillas and arrest anyone who assisted them, and expel from Union lines any Confederate civilian who refused to take the oath of allegiance to the United States. Although Pope did not implement all of his threats, Confederates fully understood that the war was taking a harder turn. Jefferson Davis labeled Pope's orders "infamous" and instructed Robert E. Lee to inform the Federals that Confederates would not "consider any officers hereafter captured from Genl. Pope's Army as prisoners of war." They would, instead, be treated as criminals unprotected by the formal rules governing military operations.

Between the end of July and mid-September, Lee reoriented the war in the East from the outskirts of Richmond to the Potomac frontier. Once certain McClellan was being withdrawn from the vicinity of Richmond, he concentrated against Pope, who was maneuvering in north-central Virginia. On August 28-30, the armies collided on the old battlefield of First Bull Run. In what became known as the battle of Second Bull Run or Manassas, heavy Union assaults pushed Stonewall Jackson's troops to the limit before a massive counterattack by James Longstreet's Confederates crushed Pope's left flank and set in motion another ignominious Union retreat. More than 9,000 Rebels and 16,000 Yankees fell in the battle, and Pope was removed from command shortly thereafter. Lee decided to pursue his advantage by taking the war across the Potomac into Maryland and Pennsylvania, hoping to improve his logistical situation, give Virginia a respite from the presence of the armies, recruit Marylanders for the Army of Northern Virginia, and complicate Republican chances for success in the upcoming fall elections. Faced with a deepening crisis, Lincoln turned to

Plate 5. Alexander Gardner's photograph, taken in early October 1862, documented a tense meeting between George B. McClellan and Abraham Lincoln on the Antietam battlefield. McClellan's failure to pursue the defeated Confederate army after the battle helped convince the president to remove him from command.

McClellan to reinspire Pope's beaten troops and blunt Lee's invasion.

Lee crossed the Potomac during the first week of September with an army worn out from many weeks of campaigning and fighting, plagued by logistical problems, and weakened by straggling and desertion. Fewer than 40,000 men shouldered muskets on September 17, when they met the Army of the Potomac's 85,000 along Antietam Creek in western Maryland. In the bloodiest single day in American history, nearly 12,500 Federals and 10,500 Confederates fell in combat that pressed Lee's army to the edge of disaster. Only the timely arrival of a small number of reinforcements and McClellan's decision not to commit thousands of fresh reserves allowed Lee's exhausted men to hold on. "[F]or me to give an idea of the fierceness of the conflict, the roar of musketry, and the thunder of artillery," wrote a South Carolinian shortly after the battle, "is as utterly impossible as to describe a thousand storms in the region of Hades." Lee's army stood defiantly on the field on September 18 before retreating across the Potomac that night. A tactical stand-off on September 17, Antietam became a strategic Union triumph when Lee withdrew.

McClellan's failure to pursue the Rebels deeply disappointed Abraham Lincoln, who considered Antietam a great lost opportunity to inflict a more grievous wound on Lee's army. Yet he thought it enough of a success to issue his preliminary proclamation of emancipation on September 22—something he had held off doing since July in anticipation of a military victory. Political leaders in London and Paris, who had interpreted the Seven Days and Second Bull Run as harbingers of Confederate independence, backed away from some type of intervention after receiving news of Lee's retreat. Lee returned to the Confederate side of the Potomac, where he maintained a menacing position, and McClellan refused to advance against him. Citizens in the United States breathed a sigh of relief, while Confederates tended to view the entire military drama from the Seven Days through Antietam, which included Stonewall Jackson's capture of more than 12,000 Union soldiers at Harpers Ferry on September 15, as, in the words of one editor, a "remarkable campaign . . . extending from the banks of the James river to those of the Potomac" that "impressed the world with wonder and admiration."

Far to the west, other Confederates marched north toward Kentucky in August and September. They hoped to gather supplies, recruit in Kentucky, and clear Middle Tennessee of Federal forces. General Braxton Bragg's Army of the Mississippi, numbering some 35,000, and General Edmund Kirby Smith's optimistically named Army of Kentucky, 10,000 strong, entered the Bluegrass State, capturing thousands of Union soldiers and drawing General Don Carlos Buell's 50,000-man Army of the Ohio out of Tennessee. Buell reached Louisville, where he showed little inclination to confront the invaders. As with Marylanders when Lee's army appeared, Kentuckians did not flock to the Confederate banner—"The people here have too many fat cattle and are too well off to fight," groused Bragg—though many seemed to cheer the Rebels on. In early October, Bragg attended the inauguration of a Confederate governor of Kentucky in Frankfort (whose legitimacy depended entirely on the presence of Confederate military forces).

The campaign reached a climax on October 8 in the battle of Perryville. Amid stifling heat and a punishing drought, portions of Buell's and Bragg's armies blundered into one another on October 7, setting the stage for the main fighting the next day. A seesaw contest yielded 4,200 Union and 3,400 Confederate casualties and closed with a slight tactical advantage to the Rebels. But two days later the Confederates began to withdraw from Kentucky, and November found Bragg's army, which was renamed the Army of Tennessee, near Murfreesboro, some thirty miles southwest of Nashville.

The autumn of 1862 closed with northern elections and changes in the Union high command. Republicans suffered a significant setback in the House of Representatives—Democrats picked up twenty-eight seats but remained a minority—and lost the governorships of New York and New Jersey. The Senate remained firmly Republican. During the election, Democrats pronounced the war a bloody failure and railed against higher federal taxes, the prospect of adding emancipation to the Union's war aims, a prospective draft, and what they saw as Lincoln's violations of civil liberties. *Harper's Weekly* ascribed Democratic successes to "a general dissatisfaction with the results of the war." The high optimism of late spring 1862 had given way to weariness with a conflict that consumed men and money at alarming rates. "No nation in the world," suggested *Harper's*, " . . . ever placed itself, its sons, its means, its liberties, and its life so wholly and unreservedly in the hands of its Government as we did a year ago. The people of the North asked each other—what has Mr. Lincoln done with what we gave him? And voted accordingly."

Lincoln recognized the need to bring fresh leadership to the Union high command, replacing McClellan and Buell with Major Generals

Ambrose E. Burnside and William S. Rosecrans. Although winter campaigns were logistically difficult, he would encourage aggressive moves
against the Rebels before the end of the year. Confederates paid attention to such news, as when a South Carolina woman observed in
her diary, "McClellan has been superseded by Burnside, because he
would not advance & all Yankeedom is in an uproar about it." Many
in the Confederacy connected Lincoln's action to abolitionists' unhappiness with "Little Mac," which they took as evidence of deep political
divisions in the United States. The specter of emancipation, believed
untold Confederates, would stiffen Rebel resolve never to capitulate to
the Yankees. In this vein, one Richmonder asserted that Lincoln's preliminary proclamation would "intensify the war, and add largely to our
numbers in the field." In both the United States and the Confederacy,
people detected the onset of the kind of "remorseless revolutionary
struggle" Lincoln had hoped to avoid in the innocent early phase of the
war.

Plate 6. Soldiers from the 3rd Georgia Infantry. Typical of men who volunteered in huge numbers on both sides early in the war, these three served with the Confederate army in Virginia. One was discharged before seeing combat, the other two were killed at the battle of Malvern Hill on July 1, 1862.

CHAPTER 4

A WAR OF CITIZEN-SOLDIERS

A MAJORITY OF the more than three million men who made up the armies of the Civil War were volunteers. Fifty percent of the pool of eligible men, approximately 2.2 million, served for the United States, while the Confederacy mustered at least 850,000, roughly 85 percent of its military-age white men. These amateur soldiers fought for a variety of reasons and reflected their respective societies in terms of education, economic position, and religious beliefs. Northern or southern, the common soldiers who made up the volunteer armies of the Civil War knew that previous wars had called upon white male citizens to drop their ordinary occupations and spring into action to serve their nation. In fact, the term "citizen-soldier" was deeply rooted in the nation's history. Young men understood that the privilege of citizenship in a democracy required taking up arms and defending community and country against dangerous enemies or domestic threats. When the war was over, citizen-soldiers would return to their normal lives, knowing they had fulfilled their duty and with the expectation of rewards from a grateful country. This had been the case in the Revolutionary War, the War of 1812, and the Mexican-American War of 1846-48.

I. MOTIVATION AND CHARACTERISTICS OF SOLDIERS

From the beginnings of their country, Americans did not trust professional armies, relying instead on local and state militias composed of citizen-soldiers or, as was the case with the war against Mexico, swearing volunteers organized by state directly into federal service. The professional army was tiny and viewed with suspicion. In fact, politicians regularly threatened to close the United States Military Academy at West Point, believing it propagated a class of officers, loyal to a military organization rather than to the whole nation, that could pose a threat to democratic institutions. The notion of the citizen-soldier, on the other hand, evoked popular will and representative government. In line with this tradition, the United States and the Confederacy raised the majority of their men calling upon the ideal of the citizen-soldier.

The typical citizen or common soldier of the Civil War enlisted early, in 1861 or 1862, and stayed to the end, if he lived. Union volunteers typically served out their term of enlistment—whether nine months, two years, or three years. In contrast, Confederate soldiers tended to serve for the duration of the conflict because their Congress passed legislation keeping them in the ranks. Most on both sides were young, between the ages of eighteen and twenty-four. They were most likely to have been born in a rural area and to be a farmer or the son of a farmer, but many were skilled laborers, fishermen, lumberjacks, businessmen, clerks, and college students. The majority who volunteered were white, Protestant, and literate. Civil War soldiers were the best educated in the history of warfare, and their letters home attested to their ability to express themselves. Federals and Confederates alike left a treasure trove of letters, diaries, journals, and memoirs affording subsequent generations of historians the opportunity to reconstruct their daily lives and personal perspectives in great detail.

Common soldiers were not only literate but also interested in politics and ideas and understood why they were fighting. The earliest volunteers tended to be the most enthusiastic and eloquent in expressing idealism. This statement from a private written early in the war illuminates northern patriotism: "When we reflect that we are standing on the outer verge of all that is left of the American Union, and nothing but darkness and rebellion is beyond . . . we feel a thrill of pride that we are permitted to bear a part in maintaining our beloved Government." Other letters from Union soldiers showed that many linked the struggle of 1861-65 to that of 1776-83. "Our Fathers made this country, we, their children are to save it . . . ," wrote an Ohio lieutenant: "Without Union & peace our freedom is worthless." Another Ohioan explained that to "admit the right of the seceding states to break up the Union at pleasure" likely would result in "military license, anarchy, and despotism." These men expressed the sentiment, so well articulated by Abraham Lincoln, that preserving the Union was the preeminent goal of the war.

Although Union remained the primary goal for northern soldiers, a sizable number, after 1863, endorsed emancipation. "I have no heart in this war if the slaves cannot be free," declared a young Wisconsin private in 1863. An Illinois volunteer placed slavery at the core of the sectional disturbance but betrayed little sympathy for black people: "If the Negro was thought of at all, it was only as the firebrand that had caused the conflagration—the accursed that had created enmity . . . between the two sections, and excited the fratricidal strife." In truth, most U.S. soldiers supported the destruction of slavery as the best means to restore their country and punish slaveholders responsible for the conflict, while resisting or opposing advancement for former slaves beyond freedom.

Southern soldiers fought to protect their land from northern invasion, for Confederate independence from what they perceived as Union tyranny, and for state rights. A Georgian explained that "The wicked fanaticism of the North by its unjust and unconstitutional aggression with vile taunts and hypocritical sneers compelled us to sever the bands that once bound us together," while another declared: "We are fighting for the Constitution that our forefathers made and not as old Abe would have it." Although a large number of slaveholders fought for the Confederacy, higher than their percentage of the white population, the majority of its soldiers owned no slaves. Why, then, did they fight so hard and so long for their country's independence? The answer is that most southerners, in and out of the military, believed they had a stake in preserving an economic, political, and social system that privileged all white people, not just the elite class. A volunteer bitterly referred to the Union forces as an "abolitionist army," and a weary veteran of the Army of Northern Virginia declared of the black units in Petersburg: "Our boys went mad when they found they had to fight Negroes." This type of anti-emancipationist sentiment, so prevalent late in the war, strengthened Confederate resolve to save their white republic. Whether Union or Confederate, all soldiers claimed ideological inheritance from the American Revolution, and all would agree, one way or another, with President Lincoln when he said that slavery "was somehow the cause of the war."

The average Union or Confederate soldier had little money or property but nursed great ambitions for both. He was probably not married, although a significant number already had tied the knot. He eagerly accepted the monthly pay (initially $11 per month for Confederate and $13 for Union soldiers), the bonuses, and even the land that would come to him as part of his service—and rightly so, for these rewards were a part of the rich tradition of the American citizen-soldier. (By the second year of the war, the southern soldier had little expectations of such rewards.) He loved the excitement, the martial music, the parades, and the hoopla that accompanied the earliest calls for men. Often his motives for enlisting were mixed: peer pressure, social expectations, dreams of military glory, regular pay and bounties, patriotism, and hatred of the enemy all played a part in the final decision.

Overall, American men shared romantic ideas about being a soldier. The concept of courage was considered most important to the psychological makeup of a warrior. Courage has two definitions. One is "action taken without fear," the one most men aspired to in the ideal. The other definition is "action taken even with fear." Men were supposed to be brave in battle and by doing so would achieve their manhood, discharge their duty, and honor their God and their country. One northern soldier defined this type of practical courage: "The Man who does not dread to die or to be mutilated is a lunatic. The man who, dreading these things, still faces them for the sake of duty and honor is a hero." Courage was often tied to a love of country, the feeling commonly called patriotism. The excitement of the early days of the war is reflected in this letter from a northerner: "The air is full of calls for men who are patriotic to enlist. I really inwardly feel that I want to go do my part as a man." A soldier from Iowa added, "The majority of our Citizens are full of patriotism and express their willingness to stand by the Old Stars and stripes and protect it from dishonor." A Confederate counterpart echoed the sentiment: "What is life worth under a government that cannot be enjoyed?"

Most of all, the citizen-soldier of the Civil War reflected the deeply held values of individualism, family, community, church, and country in Victorian America. It is important to understand that this was not, for the most part, a war fought by the poor for the rich. The families of Civil War soldiers represented the very heart of the United States and the Confederacy as they were constituted in 1861.

There were many men, however, who fell outside the broad depiction of the typical or common citizen-soldier. The 175,000 Germans,

150,000 Irish, 50,000 British, 50,000 Canadians, and smaller numbers of Italians, Scandinavians, and Hispanics who served the Union differed significantly from the majority of native-born white volunteers. Roughly half a million foreign-born soldiers served in the Union army (25 percent of the whole number), while within the Confederate ranks the number and percentage were much smaller. More than 180,000 black men mustered into the U.S. Army after the Emancipation Proclamation was issued on January 1, 1863. While slaves played an indispensable role in sustaining Confederate armies by performing a variety of noncombatant tasks, they did not serve as soldiers. A few Native American units were raised—mostly for the Rebel cause, but some fought in the Union army as well. Draftees, bounty jumpers (men who accepted a monetary bonus to enlist and then deserted), and the criminal element that were a part of the armies also departed dramatically from the norm.

For the Civil War's typical young warriors, shared ideas and feelings created a powerful bond between volunteers in camp, on the march, and fighting on the battlefields and those who stayed home. Hamlets, towns, and cities followed their "boys" throughout the war. Countless soldiers' newsy letters were printed in hometown newspapers for all to read and discuss. Strong local and state loyalties sometimes superseded national ones, especially in the early days. Both federal governments relied heavily on the common people, the middling classes, to support the war effort through men, supplies, and money. This was not a modern war with a well-oiled propaganda machine. Both initial enthusiasm and later dissent for the war came from a grassroots perspective.

In one sense, the young men who served in the war never left home. They joined local outfits, first a company and later a regiment, which were made up of other youths whom they knew well. Coming from one geographical area brought communal feeling and ensured a measure of stability in the ranks. It was common for brothers, cousins, and even fathers and sons to enlist together. In the beginning, soldiers' mothers, wives, sisters, and sweethearts provided homemade uniforms, food, and supplies and sewed the regimental flags. In many instances, the enlisted men elected the company and regimental officers. The officers themselves, as untrained and innocent in the ways of war as the raw recruits, were only slightly older and better off than the men they led. When the war became hard and casualties exacted a terrible toll, the community suffered the losses together. Replacements sometimes came from the same locality. Recruiting became much more difficult everywhere as losses rose dramatically through the four years of struggle.

II. THE SOLDIER'S LIFE

At first, young volunteers in the North and South acted as if they were on their way to a huge party, imbibing alcohol, singing songs, generally having a good time, and resisting unwanted orders from superiors. They soon found out about the more unpleasant realities of military life. Recruits began their training in a company, which with an enrollment of one hundred men was the smallest cohesive unit in the war. (Later in the war, after combat and disease had taken their toll, companies averaged fewer than fifty men.) Companies were formed locally in towns, small cities, and counties. Each company was led by a captain, usually elected by the soldiers in a popularity contest. Two lieutenants, five sergeants, and eight corporals completed the unit's leadership.

The recruit's first excitement came when he and his comrades took a crowded train ride to a distant camp in his state. Many were thrilled by this trip because few ever had traveled very far from home. Here the young volunteers experienced the first inkling of the dreadful boredom of the military camp where they would spend much of their time. Almost always, camp was smoky, dirty, and filled with equally confused men wondering when the war would start in earnest for them. On arrival, the recruits would be put up in huts or tents to await a process of entering Union or Confederate service. It was at this time that the limitations of camp life became evident. A soldier in the 93rd Illinois Infantry summed up his frustrations when he wrote his parents from camp in 1862: "They keep us very strict here, it is the most like a prison of any place I ever saw. . . . It comes rather hard at first to be deprived of liberty." A Rebel from Louisiana echoed the Yank's complaint when he commented from a camp in Alabama that "A soldier is not his own man. He has given up all claim on himself."

A couple of days would pass, and then recruits would be asked to sign enlistment papers, if they had not already done so. A superficial medical examination would declare the soldier fit for service. Only the grossest and most obvious physical or psychological deformity or defect would send a man home, at least in the first year and a half. Before a recruit was officially in the army, one more important step remained. The whole company had to be sworn into Union or Confederate service. This process was called "mustering in," and once completed the unit officially entered national service to be grouped with nine other companies to form a regiment. Once mustered, anyone who left camp without permission would be declared absent without leave and subject to punishment. Records from both armies reveal that approximately 15 percent of Confederate and 12 percent of Union forces eventually were lost to desertion.

Strict military discipline hit the citizen-soldier hard. After the initial excitement wore off, the untested farm boys, city clerks, students, and mechanics had to learn to be soldiers. At first, the typical volunteer had a difficult time accepting the steady discipline, the six hours or more of daily drilling, and the mastery of skills such as the nine steps required to fire a muzzle-loading rifle.

Camp life for an infantry soldier included more than frequent drill. Homesick men eagerly awaited mail from family and friends, tending to write many more letters than they received. Their letters often complained about terrible food, described the weather or the countryside, and related funny stories about comrades. Even more common were the countless letters expressing warm affection and longing for the comforts of home and loved ones. Many an hour was spent reading the Bible, various religious tracts, newspapers, classic literature, or, more commonly, the cheap "dime novels" that flooded the camps. Soldiers frequently organized athletic contests including baseball, football, foot-racing, and wrestling or engaged in fierce snowball fights during the long winter encampments. Plays, concerts, and singing around the fire—"Home Sweet Home" was a particular favorite—were all part of relieving the dreary routine of camp for soldiers.

Debates were popular among the men in the Army of the Potomac. In November 1863 one topic of choice was "Do the signs of the times indicate the downfall of our Republic?" Surely President Lincoln had this type of activity in mind when he described Union troops as "thinking bayonets." Men enjoyed playing checkers, chess, and poker, but soldiers also engaged in activities not mentioned in letters to pious parents or worried spouses. Visiting houses of prostitution often brought venereal disease, with cures often proving worse than the infection. "Besetting sins" also included gambling, drinking, vicious practical jokes, and swearing, all of which proved rampant among young men on both sides. One self-identified Christian soldier expressed frustration at being exposed to all the "profanity, filthy talk and vulgar songs" of military life.

Court-martial records reveal the contempt citizen-soldiers often held for their commanding officers. A northern soldier called one superior "a damned son of a bitch, a damned tyrant, a damned puppy, a damned rascal," while a Confederate described a colonel as "an ignoramus fit for nothing higher than the cultivation of corn." Still another Rebel private declared all officers "not fit to tote guts to a bear." The bottom line was that officers—whether volunteers or West Point trained—had to earn and keep the common soldier's respect.

Military records show that alcohol consumption caused the worst

Plate 7. "Christmas Eve, 1862." Artist Thomas Nast showed strong ties between the military and home fronts in this illustration. It features a Union soldier looking at photographs of his loved ones and a woman praying for his safety while their children sleep.

misbehavior among soldiers and afflicted all ranks. Men drank to relieve boredom, because they were lonely, to give them courage, or just for fun. The favored drink smuggled into camps was whiskey, sometimes referred to as "rot gut." A soldier from Indiana described his whiskey as a combination of "bark juice, tar-water, turpentine, brown sugar, lamp-oil and alcohol." Such liquor had nicknames like "Old Red Eye," "Rifle Knock-Knee," and "Help Me to Sleep, Mother."

Punishment for out-of-control drinking and other infractions promoted discipline that would make for battle-ready combat troops. Unfortunately, punishments could be meted out unfairly. It was up to the commanding officer to set the tone. Most of the penalties were based on humiliation. The most common ones made offenders march through camp with signs denoting their crime—such as "thief" or "coward."

Other punishments forced transgressors to wear a barrel shirt, drag a ball and chain, or suffer the very painful "bucking and gagging." A soldier described a comrade's bucking and gagging in a letter home: "A . . . piece of wood was placed in his mouth and a string tied behind his ears kept it in position," then "the man was seated on the ground with his knees drawn up to his body. A piece of wood is run through his legs, and placing his arms under the stick on each side of his knees, his hands are then tied in front, and he is as secure as a trapped rat." That soldier remained in the position, enduring excruciating pain, for several hours. Long jail terms, branding, and dishonorable discharges could be expected for serious breaches such as desertion or repeated insubordination. Approximately five hundred Civil War soldiers, most of them convicted of desertion, were executed by firing squad or hanging.

Volunteers found solace in many places, but a majority embraced religion. Signing up for service in the army often strengthened the volunteer's desire to join his Christian beliefs with faith in his country's cause. Trust in God played a large part in sustaining morale and providing a community of like-minded comrades while simultaneously diminishing the fear of dying. Officers tended to encourage their men's religious conversion because it bolstered discipline and fostered a fighting spirit. Chaplains, ministers, priests, and even some rabbis for the approximately ten thousand Jewish soldiers flourished, and field services were usually well attended. In addition to comfort, religion gave the volunteer a sense of control over his fate, something to cherish within the uncertainty of wartime.

Letters from men on both sides demonstrate that religious faith was more prevalent than in modern times. Some soldiers believed God personally watched over them, while others prayed for a good death, a sentiment often echoed by their parents. Revivals swept through Confederate camps in 1862 and 1863, driven by the desolation of defeat and the ever-present fear of death. Diaries and journals reveal especially strong expressions of religious faith just before a battle. One North

Carolinian vividly described a Christian comrade exhorting the deity on behalf of his company as the first shots were fired. The man removed his hat, glanced upward toward heaven, and cried, "Lord, if you ain't with us, don't be agin us. Just step aside and watch the damndest fight you are ever likely to see!"

Those in the newly mustered regiments of 1861 and 1862 could expect within a few weeks to receive a uniform and equipment to replace, or to supplement, what they had brought from home. The most important items, besides a musket and bayonet, were a haversack (a type of shoulder bag), a cup, a plate, utensils, a canteen, a blanket, and a tent. Men definitely would not want to be without trousers, shirt, socks, hat, coat, and shoes, although the Confederate gray uniform (sometimes more of a butternut color after 1862) was not as well made as the Union's dark blue frock coats and light blue trousers. Many soldiers started out with other possessions, including luxury items such as extra blankets, pillows, and clothes, but they soon discarded them as too cumbersome to carry easily. Enlisted men matured quickly, and the experienced soldier knew to throw away all but absolute necessities.

Longing for loved ones and home and aggravation with poor food and long hours of training coexisted with the process by which men forged loyalties to their regiments. Four or more of those regiments made up a brigade, two or more brigades a division, and two or more divisions a corps—each unit of organization, along with the officers who commanded them, becoming part of the soldier's martial world and identity. As they continued drilling and got used to their equipment, adjusted to their officers, and read newspapers that predicted imminent battles, the young men contemplated the unpredictable, unknowable, and scary nature of the war.

III. CAMPAIGNING, COMBAT, AND COMRADESHIP

When his unit was finally called into action, the volunteer spent little time on serious reflection while on the march toward an unknowable destination. One Confederate veteran remembered some enjoyable marching times when he and his comrades engaged in singing, joking, and various pranks, concluding: "Troops on the march were generally so cheerful and gay that an outsider . . . would hardly imagine how they suffered." And suffer they did, as soldiers learned through experience how to march twenty miles a day—an average steady pace for veterans—through heat and cold, rain and snow, and mud and dust on all manner of roads.

Mostly, they were constantly hungry and always on the lookout to forage good food to supplement their sparse army diet. Union soldiers munched on hardtack, beans, and salt pork while Confederates consumed cornbread, potatoes, bacon, pork, and peas. "Rotten, mean, mouldy bread, and parched beans for coffee," one Indiana soldier complained, "are a common occurrence." There was no shortage of available foodstuffs for either side during the Civil War, but inefficient supply systems, corruption, and incompetence often stopped delivery to the front. Even usually well-fed U.S. soldiers suffered from the lack of fresh fruit, vegetables, and meat. All volunteers regularly endured long periods of time without sufficient food or water and despite their weakened condition had to learn to march, fight, or build fortifications at a moment's notice.

Food might be a problem while campaigning, but a first battle posed the men's biggest test. That test was universally called "seeing the elephant" by nineteenth-century men who appropriated the phrase from their boyhood excitement at the first sign of the circus. Many writers have described the early Civil War military clashes as fights between two armed mobs. This was courage tested, and many failed at first. The noise, the smoke, the fear of death were indescribable, and thousands ran from the battlefield. Who could blame them? They were not professional soldiers but volunteers who expected the war to be an adventure that would be over in a few months. A Confederate who fought at First Bull Run later described his feelings after that clash: "Surely, surely, there will never be another battle . . . I believe too, no soldier in the ranks ever wanted to go into a second battle." Courage for these men boiled down to being able to follow orders and stay in line. "Oh how I wish I was a dwarf, just now, instead of a six-footer," moaned a Mississippian who faced his initial combat experience at the bloody battle of Shiloh. The best officers respected these amateur soldiers and understood that most of the scared ones would come back to the camps chastened and ready to do better next time.

The average soldier became seasoned soon enough at places called Bull Run, Shiloh, Antietam, Stones River, Fredericksburg, Chancellorsville, Vicksburg, and Gettysburg. The majority of enlisted men and officers learned their jobs well, and some found they actually enjoyed soldiering. Keeping up the fighting spirit, or morale, was vital—and that often came from winning battles, despite the great costs. Some men coped well with the horrors of the battlefield, but others experienced intense psychological trauma, the equivalent of what modern experts call "combat stress" or "shell shock." The chaos of the battlefield inverted all rules of the normal world, leading soldiers at times to fear that they had lost their humanity. They had seen friends and perhaps a family member or two die horribly in battle. Death became an unwelcome but familiar presence, leaving behind devastated and decimated families.

Two examples will illustrate the wrenching experience. Mississippi-born brothers Jud and Cary Smith both died of wounds received at the battle of Malvern Hill, as did their father, who also served as a Confederate soldier. Far to the north, parents and a surviving sister suffered an inconsolable loss as two brothers from Boston, Charles and James Lowell, were killed fighting in different Virginia battles. The lyrics of George Root's popular and haunting song "The Vacant Chair" offered a sad metaphor for domestic loss: "We shall meet but we shall miss him. / There will be one vacant chair." Duty to country was tested sorely by years of increasingly brutal warfare that laid waste to a whole generation of men. A sad veteran of a depleted regiment wrote in 1864, "How many forms had vanished! How many voices had been hushed!"

Disease turned out to be even deadlier than bullets, and two soldiers died for each man killed or mortally wounded in battle. Urban dwellers escaped the worst of childhood diseases, but most rural men and boys had never experienced measles and mumps, or scarlet fever and whooping cough. Especially in the early part of the war, vulnerable young men were crowded in camps with tens of thousands in close quarters as the viruses raged through the ranks. Immune to medical ministrations, measles killed many volunteers. Unsanitary conditions added to soldiers' miseries, as malnutrition and contaminated water caused or complicated illness, and poorly dug latrines made the rivers, creeks, and ponds from which they drank even more dangerous than usual.

Unfortunately for sick or wounded men, doctors often did more harm than good. If the citizen-soldier sustained an injury to a vital organ, death was all but certain. If he survived his initial wounding, his fate could be worse than death. Conditions in field hospitals on both sides were appalling and only somewhat better in the large medical facilities in Washington, D.C., Nashville, Tennessee, and Richmond, Virginia. Although conditions improved as the war progressed, soldiers rightly dreaded hospitals and the overworked and unprepared doctors who staffed them. Medical knowledge was primitive by modern standards. The most common painkiller was laudanum (an opiate), and almost all operations were performed with the patient under some kind of sedative, usually ether or chloroform. For these wounded warriors, the only operation that could be performed with good results was bullet extraction. It was a simple proposition. If the bullet or lead fragment hit a bone in an arm or leg, amputation almost always resulted. The greatest danger to the patient came after the operation when gangrene and other infections caused high death rates.

Many who lost an arm or leg survived the surgery, escaping gangrene but dying later when pneumonia besieged their weakened bodies. The medical ignorance of the era made even minor infections deadly when soldiers' wounds were treated with dirty instruments or touched by the unwashed hands of doctors who then spread rather than halted infections. Internal surgery was nonexistent, and surgeons left those men who suffered stomach wounds pretty much on their own to survive or die. They had no choice. Field doctors fixed their attention on the soldiers who could be immediately saved by amputation or another medical procedure. The postwar landscape attested to the bittersweet success of the surgeon's skill as many thousands of empty-sleeved or legless veterans were a common sight in towns and cities across the country.

As the war ground on, thousands of volunteers confronted the trials associated with capture and imprisonment by the opposing army. By 1865, approximately 410,000 men had fallen into enemy hands. Overall, 215,000 Rebels and 195,000 Yankees endured imprisonment, with 56,000 dying in confinement, representing about 9 percent of the fallen in the war. Earlier American conflicts failed to offer guidance on what to do with the huge numbers of troops captured in the Civil War. Early in the war, the United States and the Confederacy signed a cartel that sought to avoid accumulating prisoners. The agreement called for the exchange of captured men and, if one side took more than the other, the paroling of the remainder. A paroled soldier pledged not to take up arms again until exchanged for a man captured by the other side. This system initially worked well, but as the battles got bigger and bloodier, the logistics of making provisions for prisoners stretched the limits of both sides.

After 1863, the system of exchange broke down—partly over the Confederacy's official refusal to treat captured black soldiers as prisoners of war. Prisoners were lodged in roughly 150 facilities that ranged from small sites accommodating only a few hundred to the massive northern prisons such as Camp Douglas and Rock Island in Illinois and Johnson's Island in Ohio. The Confederate counterparts were located in Richmond and Danville, Virginia, in Charleston, South Carolina, in Salisbury, North Carolina, and elsewhere. By far the most infamous Confederate prison was at Andersonville, Georgia. Built in early 1864 and dubbed Camp Sumter, the hastily constructed and unprotected enclosure built for at most 10,000 Federal prisoners held 30,000 by the summer. The final butcher's bill at Andersonville tallied almost 13,000 dead.

Conditions were miserable in most of the prisons. Of the 12,147 Rebels incarcerated at Elmira, New York, almost 3,000 died. Mismanaged and largely run beyond the gaze of public scrutiny, the prisons neglected to care for even the most basic needs of their populations. Unheated buildings were freezing in the winter and broiling hot in the summer. Imprisoned Rebels at Johnson's Island on the shores of Lake Erie nearly froze to death, while Federals consigned to Camp Sumter and other Confederate sites fell ill with malaria and other diseases from the heat and humidity. Every prisoner endured vermin infestation, ill health, and a woefully inadequate diet.

Controversies over prisoner treatment engendered a bitter political debate during the last part of the war. Both sides hurled charges of cruelty and inhumane treatment at the other, especially after the condition of survivors became generally known. The trainloads of "living skeletons" liberated from Andersonville arriving in Washington, D.C., shocked the northern population, while Confederates released from northern camps had a similar impact on southern civilians. The treatment of prisoners remained a powerful source of acrimony between the United States and the former Confederate States of America long after the war's end.

IV. OCCUPATION DURING WARTIME AND BEYOND

Many thousands of citizen-soldiers were engaged as occupying, rather than combat, forces in roughly one hundred cities, towns, and hamlets across Louisiana, Tennessee, Mississippi, and Alabama, as well as in the loyal slave states of Missouri, Kentucky, and Maryland. After falling under Federal control, these communities were transformed into garrisoned sites where U.S. soldiers were expected to govern, to police, and to regulate the surrounding countryside through raids and expeditions. Collectively, the Union occupiers struggled to implement the early version of reconstruction by securing and subduing the defiant Confederate population. In heavily garrisoned cities such as New Orleans, Memphis, and Nashville, soldiers implemented civil order, fought guerrillas and engaged in counterinsurgency operations, destroyed or disrupted disloyal citizens' property, protected supply lines, and managed the consequences of emancipation.

A sizable number of officers and enlisted men developed an antipathy toward occupation. They manifested growing frustration with their exclusion from the battlefronts where, they believed, the great issues of the conflict would be decided. Yet the truth is that "saving the Union" involved not only major battles and campaigns but also the often tedious, occasionally dangerous, and otherwise problematical tasks of occupation. Youthful warriors of all ranks and educational backgrounds voiced serious doubts about whether occupation duties fulfilled the same patriotic ideal of citizenship and military obligation as service in the front lines. Numerous soldiers expressed disgust at the financial corruption and behavioral lapses that seemed to infect some of their comrades in occupied places, recording concerns about what they perceived as a decline in morality. One officer described occupation as "a dirty piece of business" that often seemed to wreak "vengeance on the innocent and defenseless." Sadly, the on-the-ground consequences of U.S. military occupation as it unfolded in conquered Confederate territory too often confirmed and strengthened negative attitudes.

Black soldiers, who after 1863 composed a significant percentage of the occupying forces, displayed strikingly different attitudes than many of their white comrades. Men in United States Colored Troops (USCT) units on occupation duty embraced, and were empowered by, their roles in demolishing the slave system, punishing its perpetrators, and reinventing the South. Although black military service often provoked lively debate among advocates and opponents in the loyal states, the United States government and Union army commanders supported USCT men as occupiers whose presence released white troops for action in nearby theaters of battle. "We are now determined to hold every step which has been offered to us as citizens of the United States," declared a solder in the 35th USCT Infantry. Black volunteers eagerly participated in the activities so loathed by white soldiers, viewing themselves as holding the front lines for a biracial society. African American soldiers knew the presence and pressure of Federal troops helped ensure the protection of black lives, property, and civil rights against transgressions from Confederates who sought to maintain the oppressive slaveholding social structure. In the midst of a violent and destructive conflict, black and white soldiers thus developed radically contrasting stances over issues of federal power, racial status, and the worth of imposing harsh punishments on the people of the Confederacy.

The policies and practices of military occupation during the war foreshadowed the divisive processes of reunion and reconciliation in the postwar era. Following the end of formal hostilities in the early summer of 1865, a clear majority of white citizen-soldiers believed their military obligation had ended with the reestablishment of the Union and the destruction of slavery. They joined most white civilians in the loyal states in desiring to end coercive rule of the defeated Confederates as soon as conditions warranted and to avoid using the army to advance any postwar political agenda. To some extent, this widespread attitude toward postwar occupation explains the failure, during Reconstruction, to construct a reunited nation with equal political and social rights for all black and white Americans. Long-entrenched suspicions about large peacetime military forces led to a rapid postwar demobilization. An army that numbered a million citizen-soldiers in May 1865 was reduced by 80 percent within six months, and a year after that only 11,000 volunteers remained in service. The regular army numbered just 37,000 by 1869, with a large percentage of the troops deployed in the West to deal with Indians. These figures underscore how little support existed to maintain, and pay for, a large army of occupation in the ex-Rebel states. Absent a significant occupying military presence, the bright promise for justice during Reconstruction, which freedpeople and their white allies in the North sought, was dimmed and then denied by the ingrained beliefs of an ideology that accepted only a limited peacetime role for armed forces in a constitutional republic.

V. COMRADES AND VETERANS

Citizen-soldiers bonded in powerful ways with one another in companies and regiments. Individuals occasionally felt estranged from family and friends back home, and fellow soldiers became the most important support group for the duration of the war. It seemed to men in uniform that civilians living in relative comfort and safety on the home front could never appreciate the soldier's sacrifices. Yet despite the horrors of war, many a volunteer remained steadfastly devoted to his country's cause, although the early idealism was replaced with a hard-edged practical side. "If we lose in this war," remarked a New Yorker, "the country is lost and if we win it is saved." Another northerner declared, "I would rather live a solder for life [than] see this country made a mighty sepulcher in which should be buried our institutions, our nationality, our flag, and every American that today lives, than that our Republic should be divided into little nothings by an inglorious and shameful peace." Often men in the same unit re-enlisted late in the war (Rebels by that time had no choice), and when a soldier's family protested that he had done enough for the cause he explained that he wanted to see the thing through to the end.

A young Michigan veteran provided his own common soldier's creed: "The soldier of '61 was full of life and patriotism, his ardor undampened by hardship and adversity. The soldier of '65 hoped less, but fought and accomplished more. The period of romance had changed to a period of system and endurance. . . . The history of these four years of war has its counterpart in our own lives. In our youth, we acted upon impulse regarding loss of consequences, now we think before we act."

Citizen-soldiers became veterans post-1865. After the great conflict, some recalled their experiences with anger or cynicism, but most spoke of their service with pride. Individually, thousands published memoirs or contributed to printed regimental histories. Northern veterans, white and black, supported the Republican Party and joined the Grand Army of the Republic and other associations; southern veterans supported the Democratic Party and formed their own organizations such as the United Confederate Veterans. Together and separately, they frequently visited their former battlefields, raising money to build regimental monuments to commemorate their service. Although resentment remained in the hearts of the men who fought against each other, it coexisted with a desire on the part of many veterans to foster some sense of sectional harmony. This desire was manifested in deliberate gestures of reconciliation such as the well-publicized North-South reunions held at Gettysburg and Chattanooga, Tennessee. A North Carolina veteran remarked that "Some good to the world must come from such sacrifice," and the tenor of many such comments laid the foundation for venerating the courage of both Union and Confederate soldiers. A majority of veterans preferred to sentimentalize the conflict and in their declining years emphasized the positive and patriotic aspects of their experiences. They would never forget the Civil War or allow others to forget their collective sacrifice. For them, the famous utterance of Union soldier Oliver Wendell Holmes was apt: "In our youth, our hearts were touched with fire."

Plate 8. Twenty-three black refugees near Cumberland Landing, Virginia, in May 1862. A year earlier, Union general Benjamin F. Butler proclaimed that African Americans who reached Union military lines would be treated as "contraband of war" and not returned to Confederate control. "Contrabands" became an almost universally accepted term in both the United States and the Confederacy.

CHAPTER 5

THE PROCESS OF EMANCIPATION

THE LIBERATION OF four million slaves was a major achievement of the American Civil War. The presence of slavery in the South marked the fundamental difference between it and the North in 1861. At first, the North fought to preserve the status quo—that is, the Union "as it was," which meant with slavery intact. In the 1860 election, the Republican Party pledged to keep slavery out of the western territories but to protect it where it existed in the South. A substantial number of northern whites were anti-slavery but also anti-black. As the war dragged on unexpectedly, and as Confederate resistance grew stronger, emancipation for the slaves became both a military necessity to save the Union and, for a sizable minority of the loyal populace, a moral imperative for freedom.

Free African Americans, enslaved people, and black and white abolitionists realized from the beginning that the war brought an opportunity to end slavery. Both slaves in the South and free African Americans in the North agitated, lobbied, and fought for freedom, and in doing so they challenged northern leaders to end the institution of slavery. The strong actions of black people to use the conflict to their own advantage surprised white citizens in both the United States and the Confederacy. Taking up the challenge in order to preserve the Union, Abraham Lincoln issued the Emancipation Proclamation on January 1, 1863. Slavery's doom was ensured when the U.S. Army put force behind the proclamation by defeating the Confederacy on the battlefield. In December 1865, the Thirteenth Amendment accomplished the final destruction of slavery in the United States.

The movement toward emancipation in America represented part of a broader change in the Atlantic world. In 1834, after passage of the Slavery Abolition Act the preceding year, Great Britain ended slavery in its Caribbean colonies, while in 1848 France did the same with its colonial possessions. Since the 1830s, and entering into the Civil War, the United States had ranked as the largest and most powerful slaveholding society. Within the span of a few decades after 1865, the remaining slave regimes of the Western Hemisphere, in Spanish Cuba and Brazil, also toppled.

1. STEPS TO EMANCIPATION: CONTRABAND AND CONFISCATION

The story of wartime emancipation is full of uncertainty and drama. Of the four million slaves in the United States in 1860, approximately 3.5 million lived in the Confederacy, while the remaining 500,000 resided in the loyal Border States. At first, it was truly a white man's fight to restore the Union with as little conflict and property damage as possible. President Lincoln's position at the time of Fort Sumter was that the Civil War would be waged only to restore and preserve the United

States, not to destroy the constitutionally protected slave system. The last thing most northerners wanted was to encourage a slave insurrection in the South. Union officers were ordered to return runaway slaves to their masters according to the Fugitive Slave Act of 1850. Black men were explicitly excluded from volunteering their services to the Union army. As so often happens in wars, a reality unfolded that bore little resemblance to the easy, painless path to victory initially envisioned by both sides. In fact, shortly after the war commenced, a significant number of slaves began to flee from bondage. From 1861 until the end of the war, wherever the Union army moved, slaves flocked to its lines seeking protection and freedom. Others experienced emancipation simply by living in areas brought under the control of U.S. forces.

The march of congressional legislation, military actions, and proclamations regarding slavery began in May 1861 when three Virginia slaves building Confederate fortifications near Hampton Roads, Virginia–Frank Baker, Sheppard Mallory, and James Townsend–escaped to Union-held Fort Monroe at the tip of the Virginia Peninsula. They asked U.S. military officers for asylum. On May 24, after considering the three men's request, Union general Benjamin F. Butler declared the fugitive slaves "contraband of war" and refused to send them back to Rebel lines. Under international law, enemy property that could be used against the United States fell under the category of contraband and could be seized or destroyed. Butler's decision raised some controversy within the Lincoln administration. His actions reflected the feelings of a growing number of military officers who realized that slave labor built Confederate fortifications and provided many other essential services for the enemy's army. To return fugitive slaves, they believed, aided the Rebel cause and thus hurt the Union. Secretary of War Simon Cameron announced a change in policy on May 30, advising Butler to provide safe haven for black people helping the Confederate war effort and put them to work as laborers. Nearby slaves took advantage of this policy immediately. Within a month, more than 900 refugees escaped from their masters' control, and by the end of the war 25,000 freedpeople lived in so-called "contraband camps" surrounding Fort Monroe.

This situation soon demanded that political and military leaders address the issue of contrabands with a more coherent policy. The Republican-dominated 37th Congress moved rapidly, passing twenty-six laws that struck at the heart of slaveholders' power and simultaneously advanced the emancipationist cause. The First Confiscation Act, approved on August 6, 1861, authorized Union troops to seize any private property held by Confederate citizens that was used to promote "insurrection or resistance to the laws," including slaves who worked directly to support the Confederate military effort. Although the First Confiscation Act did not define precisely the legal status of "forfeited slaves," it definitely increased the likelihood of freedom. In addition, the act left substantial doubt as to whether "loyal" versus "disloyal" owners would have their property returned or reimbursed. If Union victory had been secured quickly, these issues may have been more easily addressed, but the war dragged into a second summer, with the United States suffering substantial losses at the Seven Days and elsewhere. In response, Lincoln and many Republicans determined that reunion would require a far harder war than previously anticipated.

Congress passed other laws during the first half of 1862 that brought the country closer to declaring emancipation an official Union war aim. On March 13, it forbade the army and navy to return fugitive slaves to slaveholders; on April 16, it abolished slavery in the District of Columbia (with compensation to slaveholders); and on June 19, it ended slavery in the federal territories (without compensation to slaveholders).

On July 17, 1862, Congress passed the Second Confiscation Act, which ventured much further toward explicit emancipation by freeing the slaves of any person who aided the rebellion. Calling the fugitives "captives of war" and declaring them "forever free," the law went on to authorize the seizure and sale of any other property from disloyal citizens. A provision allowed the president to "employ as many persons of African descent as he may deem necessary and proper for the suppression of this rebellion . . . and use them in such manner as he may judge best." Lincoln could now arm former slaves, if he wished. Also on July 17, Congress issued the Militia Act, which stated that any slave who gave military service to the United States would be free, as would his family.

President Lincoln reluctantly signed the Second Confiscation Act, some provisions of which he believed to be unconstitutional and unnecessarily harsh. Lincoln often has been described as a racial conservative, and his speeches, letters, and actions in 1861 and 1862 confirm that judgment. His principal concern remained maintaining national unity, while congressional Republicans, many of them from districts or states that favored strong anti-slavery measures, could afford to push more aggressively for emancipation.

Those frustrated with Lincoln's reluctance to embrace emancipation spoke up loudly and clearly. Northern newspaper editors, politicians, and interest groups visited the chief executive repeatedly to make their case. Lincoln met with notable abolitionists, including black leader Frederick Douglass and Senator Charles Sumner of Massachusetts, who urged him to proclaim a war for black freedom. The president listened to them with respect but still feared a negative reaction toward emancipation among voters. Lincoln made his position strikingly clear in responding to an editorial in Horace Greeley's *New York Tribune* titled "The Prayer of Twenty Millions." Greeley urged the president to make the destruction of slavery his primary aim. Summarizing his thoughts after the summer defeats of 1862, Lincoln replied: "My paramount object in this struggle *is* to save the Union, and is *not* either to save or to destroy slavery. If I could save the Union without freeing *any* slave I would do it, and if I could save it by freeing *all* the slaves I would do it; and if I could save it by freeing some and leaving others alone I would also do that." Despite pressure from critics such as Greeley, Lincoln's administration put forward no specific plan for emancipation during the first year and a half of the war.

Two military leaders provoked widespread controversy by pressing for emancipation in areas under their control. General John C. Frémont, commander of the Western Department, boldly went beyond the Lincoln administration's contraband policy by emancipating the slaves of Missouri's disloyal slave owners on August 30, 1861. The president, worried that residents of the slaveholding Border States, especially Missourians, would be offended by Frémont's unauthorized action, ordered him to revoke it on September 11. Eight months later, Lincoln rescinded General David Hunter's similar proclamation issued on May 9, 1862, freeing slaves in Georgia, Florida, and South Carolina. Federal military forces thus played a vital role in bringing demands for black freedom to public attention in 1861-62, and Lincoln's reaction fueled debates between supporters and opponents of emancipation and highlighted the absence of clarity and unified direction in federal policy.

Nowhere was this chaotic situation more clearly demonstrated than in the refugee settlements. Beginning with Butler's proclamation, a flood of slaves sought refuge with U.S. military forces, which needed help in caring for them. The contraband camps were officially under the supervision of the U.S. Treasury Department because of its responsibility for confiscated Confederate property, but the government had no detailed plan to manage the welfare of thousands of refugees. The camps quickly became overcrowded and filthy, and measures designed to feed and care for the inhabitants proved shockingly inadequate. Black people had their freedom, but conditions were often worse in the camps than on the plantations from which they had escaped.

Fortunately northern missionaries and benevolent associations stepped in to provide much needed humanitarian aid. Agents from the Freedmen's Aid Society and the American Missionary Association brought food, clothing, and other necessities into the camps. In addition, they built schools and churches, often providing the first opportunity for large numbers of African Americans to be educated and to conduct their religious services in the open. These contraband–or more properly, refugee–camps eventually numbered more than one hundred and dotted the landscape from Washington, D.C., to Hampton, Virginia, and across Tennessee to Vicksburg, Mississippi.

Recognizing the enormity of the refugee problem, the American Freedmen's Inquiry Commission, established in 1863 by the government, called for the creation of a permanent agency to meet the urgent needs of contrabands, later resulting in the Freedmen's Bureau. Able-bodied men among the refugees soon found work as laborers for the military or enlisted in the Union army after January 1, 1863, which meant that the large majority of people in the camps were women, children, and old men. Reforms were needed in every area—health, welfare, and even to stop the looting of camp supplies by Union soldiers. While there were improvements, the refugees continued to suffer from filthy living conditions and exposure to harsh weather. The average mortality rate in the camps soared to 25 percent, higher than that suffered by Confederate soldiers. To some extent, these places could be considered "schools for freedom" where former slaves responded to their new surroundings with admirable resolve and determination. They stretched the boundaries of their emancipated status by seeking paid employment and creating a network of family and friends who could help them prepare for a future suddenly filled with hope.

II. COMPENSATION AND COLONIZATION

Lincoln's greatest fear in 1861 and most of 1862 arose from the possibility that emancipation would provoke the loyal Border States to join the Confederacy and anger the 45 percent of the northern citizenry who voted Democratic. Union military defeats and the fact that so many slaves willingly sought freedom combined to change his mind. Privately, by the time of the passage of the Second Confiscation Act he had come to believe the war could not be won without freeing the slaves. Hoping to soften the blow and to stake out a gradualist, constitutional approach to emancipation, Lincoln invited Delaware, Kentucky, Maryland, and Missouri to formulate plans for compensated emancipation (paying owners for their loss of property in freed slaves) and held out the possibility of colonization (the removal of freed African Americans to Africa or some other part of the world). On three different occasions, the last on July 12, 1862, Border State congressmen rejected the president's plea that they embrace compensated emancipation.

Despite a personal hatred of slavery, Lincoln continued to consider colonization. Having spent his prewar years in the intensely racist Midwest, he believed black people would never find equality or respect in the United States. That is why he proposed a voluntary colonization plan in August 1862 at a meeting with African American leaders from Washington, D.C. Lincoln explained what he considered the benefits of sending black colonists to Central America, where they could flourish without the racism and prejudice he thought would forever hold them back in the United States. "You and we are different races," he told his audience, stating that it was "better for us both . . . to be separated." Two important black leaders who were not at the meeting—Frederick Douglass and Philadelphia abolitionist Robert Purvis—denounced Lincoln's racism and called for black Americans to demand their rights in the country of their birth. Lincoln persisted, however, and even supported an expedition that sent 500 black colonists to an island off Haiti in 1863. Miserable conditions at the site and dishonesty among the white people overseeing the effort created a disaster that forced the president, in early 1864, to abandon all thoughts of colonization.

III. THE EMANCIPATION PROCLAMATION

While consistently reaffirming his public commitment to Union, Lincoln drafted an emancipation proclamation he shared with his cabinet in July 1862. Most of the members supported such a proclamation, but a few persuaded the president to wait for a military victory to announce it. The sting of McClellan's recent failure in the Seven Days campaign might make the proclamation appear to be a desperate measure. If issued too soon, from a position of weakness, they argued, emancipation, and perhaps the whole war effort, might fail. Lincoln agreed and got the victory he needed in mid-September at the battle of Antietam. Acting on his authority as commander in chief, he issued a preliminary emancipation proclamation on September 22, 1862. It declared that slaves in states still in rebellion as of January 1, 1863, would be freed. The announcement had a polarizing effect on the northern political nation. Republicans suffered significant losses in the fall elections as Democrats attacked the proclamation as an unconstitutional expansion of presidential powers.

The final Emancipation Proclamation took effect on New Year's Day 1863. It remains an often-misunderstood document. Lincoln had no power to end slavery in states still in the Union because the Constitution protected the institution, and he exempted parts of the Confederacy then under U.S. military control—where, he said, the Constitution applied. These areas included twelve parishes in Louisiana, fifty-three counties in Virginia, and all of Union-occupied Tennessee. "I do order," Lincoln wrote, "and declare that all persons held as slaves within said designated States and parts of States are and henceforward shall be free." His powers as commander in chief, argued the president, allowed him to strike at the institution wherever the Davis administration held sway, as a means of diminishing the capacity of the Rebels to wage war. At the moment Lincoln signed it, the proclamation did not free one slave in the Confederacy. It was a symbolic victory for aboli-

tionists and reaffirmed the military necessity of the act. But the proclamation began to free enslaved people as Union armies moved deeper
into the Confederacy after January 1. Every mile's progress expanded
the area of freedom and weakened the Confederacy.

Despite its limitations, many abolitionists and their supporters
across the country hailed the Emancipation Proclamation as a document of freedom that heralded the end of slavery. For the first time, the
freedom and welfare of enslaved people fell under the national interest.
Lincoln acknowledged the morality of his decision, declaring it "an act
of justice warranted by the Constitution, upon military necessity." As
soon as they heard about the proclamation, many black people took
it upon themselves to take steps toward freedom by refusing to work
for their masters. The Emancipation Proclamation changed the tenor
of the Civil War, even though Lincoln obviously stressed its value to
defeating the slaveholding power of the Confederacy. Instead of preserving the status quo, a Union victory with the proclamation in place
would overturn the existing southern social order to bring what Lincoln called in his November 18, 1863, dedication at Gettysburg "a new
birth of freedom."

The Emancipation Proclamation had little effect on the large portion of the Confederacy where the Union army did not establish a
strong presence. Enslaved people residing in the Trans-Mississippi Theater, particularly Texas, did not hear official news of their liberation
until mid-June 1865. That is why a substantial number of Texas slaves
never recognized January 1, 1863, as their "freedom day" but rather
commemorated it on "Juneteeth" (June 19, 1865). Overall, perhaps
500,000 of the 3,500,000 enslaved people in the Confederacy—one in
seven—had achieved freedom by the end of the war. The Confederate
South, even in the midst of a massively disruptive conflict, proved able
to maintain much of its slavery-based society.

IV. SLAVES IN THE CONFEDERACY

By 1865, while 500,000 former slaves lived under the protection of the United States in contraband camps, worked on confiscated land, or served in the Union army, approximately three million black people still endured bondage across the Rebel states. Even so, there is much evidence that they also fervently wished for emancipation. Studies have shown that enslaved African Americans did not act foolishly to procure their freedom. If the opportunity existed, they chose liberation, but those who lived in the interior areas where the U.S. military presence was rare expressed their discontent in other ways.

Slaves were forced to contribute to the Confederate war effort by providing necessary labor on the home front and on the battlefront. They worked on farms, in factories and mines, and on railroads. Thousands accompanied the armies as personal servants (a part of the war's story that has not been studied carefully). These enslaved people did not "serve" as Confederate soldiers but performed whatever tasks their owners required. They worked in noncombatant roles such as cooks and teamsters and looked after their owners' health and general well-being. Many other thousands were forcibly removed from their domiciles to build fortifications, dig latrines, transport supplies, and bury the dead for the armies. The Confederate military could not exist without their labor on the front, and the civilians could not exist without their labor at home.

Although vital to the Confederate war effort, enslaved people found ways to destabilize southern society and undermine white morale. By acting as if they knew freedom was coming, they helped upend the slavery-based society long inhabited by white and black southerners. The shortage of white men running plantations proved a powerful incentive for slaves to slow down their work pace, disobey orders, ignore sternly given instructions, move freely from one place to another, and engage in other previously forbidden actions. Altogether, this kind of resistance has been described as a massive labor withdrawal, what the black scholar W. E. B. Du Bois termed the "General Strike." It signaled to slave owners that even their most trusted slaves would not remain loyal when freedom beckoned. Beloved house slaves deserted and often provided intelligence to Union soldiers. Many Confederates felt deeply betrayed when confronted with the indisputable evidence that their "servants" did not wish to stay with them. Both blacks and whites suffered together amid severe shortages of food, clothing, and supplies, and slaves sometimes accompanied owners who fled as refugees. The record shows that whether emancipation came early or late, African Americans eagerly embraced the uncertainties of liberation and rejoiced in the defeat of the Confederacy when it finally arrived.

The possibility of arming slaves became a hotly debated issue as Confederate casualties mounted in 1863 and 1864. Although he initially resisted the idea, President Davis gave his approval. Robert E. Lee, hesitant to make his views public, also eventually advocated enlisting slaves. "I think the measure not only expedient but necessary," Lee wrote on February 18, 1865, adding, "I think those who are employed should be freed. It would be neither just nor wise, in my opinion, to require them to serve as slaves." Howell Cobb of Georgia, a political general and opponent of the proposal, got to the heart of the issue as understood by Confederates who sought above all to preserve their slaveholding society: "The day you make soldiers of them is the beginning of the end of the revolution. If slaves will make good soldiers our whole theory of slavery is wrong." That theory, some other Confederates recognized, had been proved wrong by the existing record of black men in blue. The Confederate Congress enacted a bill authorizing slaves as soldiers on March 13, 1865, but did not offer emancipation. The effort came too late to make a difference, but a few black men were mobilized and drilling as the war came to an end the next month.

V. BLACK MEN IN BLUE

In one of its most radical provisions, the Emancipation Proclamation declared the Union's intention to enlist black soldiers and sailors, stating that they "will be received into the armed service of the United States to garrison forts, positions, stations, and other places." Earlier the administration refused to consider abolitionist and Radical Republican arguments to arm African Americans, although there were a few specially raised "colored" regiments in Louisiana and South Carolina in 1862. In addition, the ranks of the wartime U.S. Navy always included black sailors, whose numbers during the course of the war swelled to approximately 20,000. Most white northerners held powerful negative racial stereotypes regarding black abilities and were horrified by the thought of white and black troops fighting together. An editorial in the *New York Times* expressed this majority sentiment. "Better lose the War," it cautioned, "than use the Negro to turn it."

But the Union needed more men, and after the devastating losses in the 1862 campaigns white volunteers were not coming forth in large enough numbers to replenish the fallen. Driven by the urgency of winning the war, Lincoln bore the inevitable criticism as he authorized active efforts to form black regiments in early 1863. By war's end, recruiters had enrolled 180,000 African Americans in the army, the majority of them former slaves. With military service came a chance to secure their individual freedom, their family's freedom, and their rights to equal citizenship. Beginning in 1863, the Federal army was *explicitly* one of liberation. The mobilization of formerly enslaved men into U.S. armed forces converted part of the Confederate slave labor force into an advantage for the Union.

The support of many government officials helped make the controversial policy turn out well. To facilitate recruiting, the War Department created the Bureau of Colored Troops. This bureau coordinated the formation of 166 black regiments and their deployment in various military theaters. Most of the regiments were formed under the auspices of the federal government and designated USCT. A few units were raised by states, including Massachusetts, Connecticut, Pennsylvania, and Michigan. Brigadier General Lorenzo Thomas spearheaded recruiting along the Mississippi River valley. Recommended to Lincoln by U. S. Grant, Thomas was sent to enlist contrabands, and his efforts accounted for roughly 40 percent of the total USCT forces. He raised units filled with ex-slaves who, by putting on the uniform of the United States, proved to doubters that black men were prepared to fight, kill, and die for their freedom.

Abolitionists lamented that USCT soldiers suffered from a number of discriminations. Their segregated units often received inferior arms and equipment. Perhaps no discrimination cut deeper and caused more disciplinary trouble than the issue of unequal pay. African American soldiers earned less than white soldiers—$10 per month, from which $3 was deducted for clothing, versus $13 per month with no deduction—until Congress corrected this injustice, with back pay for veterans, in 1864. The extreme prejudice typical of the era dictated the units be led by white officers, at least until those restrictions were slightly loosened. By 1865, a few more than one hundred black officers had been appointed, along with roughly 7,000 noncommissioned officers. On the other hand, white officers of black regiments were required to pass a rigorous examination before their appointments. This generally resulted in able and experienced leadership.

The USCT regiments were routinely used as labor battalions, and indeed, Lincoln had this type of duty in mind for black troops. "Sable" soldiers, as they were often called, would build fortifications and work as teamsters, in essence providing the muscle while leaving the fighting to white men. Two assumptions guided Lincoln's decision: African American men were better adapted physically for hard labor than whites, and they were not mentally capable of performing the duties of a citizen-soldier. These assumptions proved wrong almost immedi-

USCT Recruitment
( ) No./State, 1863–65
Hal Jespersen

States of origin for recruits in United States Colored Troops units. This map shows the high percentage of African American soldiers who came from areas, especially along the Mississippi River, where Union military forces established a major presence during the war.

ately, as black units performed ably in numerous engagements. In May 1863, black troops led the assault at Milliken's Bend, Louisiana, retaining their composure under heavy fire and earning admiration from white witnesses. Most famously, on July 18, 1863, the men of the 54th Massachusetts Infantry participated in the unsuccessful assault on Fort Wagner, South Carolina, where they lost 272 of their 650 men. Other black units fought at battlefields such as Olustee, Florida (February 20, 1864), the Petersburg Mine assault (July 30, 1864), and New Market Heights, Virginia (September 29, 1864), where fourteen USCT men won the Medal of Honor.

Confederates complained vociferously that the Emancipation Proclamation and the enrollment of black troops represented an incitement to "servile rebellion" by the United States. Many plantation owners commented on the visible change, for the worse from their perspective, in their slaves' behavior after hearing of the opportunities for liberation promised by the Union. Outraged, the Richmond government announced that black soldiers and their white officers would not be treated as prisoners of war—the officers could be executed, the men in the ranks re-enslaved. In response to that proclamation, President Lincoln issued an executive order announcing that for every Union officer executed, a Rebel officer held prisoner by the United States would be killed; for every black Union soldier enslaved, a Confederate soldier would be sentenced to hard labor. No official executions took place on either side.

In practice, African American troops and their white officers had a variety of experiences, and Confederates applied their draconian policy inconsistently. Some captured black soldiers were treated as prisoners of war, while others were re-enslaved. Still others were executed summarily in the heat of battle or while trying to surrender. The most notorious incident occurred at Fort Pillow, Tennessee, on April 12, 1864. Confederate general Nathan Bedford Forrest and 1,500 men attacked the fortification, and when the Union commander refused a demand to surrender the Confederates seized the fort and overwhelmed the garrison composed of white Unionists and almost three hundred black soldiers. One Confederate soldier recalled that "The poor deluded Negroes would run up to our men, fall upon their knees . . . for mercy, but they were ordered to their feet and then shot down." At the finish, 64 percent of black and 33 percent of white Union soldiers had been killed (Confederates also executed many white unionists in the garrison). Although many other such incidents took place, Fort Pillow particularly outraged northerners, and the phrase "Remember Fort Pillow!" became a familiar battle cry for both black and white soldiers.

Despite a notable fighting record compiled by many black units by the end of the war, USCT men overall experienced far less combat than white soldiers. A significant number performed occupation duty, which seldom included pitched battles or even significant skirmishes. They suffered a 1.5 percent killed-in-action rate compared with 6 percent for white soldiers. Death rates from disease in black units exceeded those in white units. Many white soldiers expressed a new respect for the courage and perseverance of their black comrades-in-arms—though others clung to old stereotypes. Like the inhabitants of the contraband camps, black soldiers were demonstrating the justice of the bloody war in which they served a powerful role in ending slavery.

VI. FREE LABOR, PROPERTY, AND EDUCATION

The unfolding story of emancipation deeply affected efforts at wartime Reconstruction. Defined as the military, political, and constitutional process of bringing the country back together, Reconstruction started when the Union army began occupying large parts of Confederate territory. By 1863, military rule prevailed in substantial portions of Tennessee, Mississippi, and Louisiana, with more to come in the next two years. The question of what a reunited America would look like *with emancipation* complicated an increasingly difficult task. A number of Unionists, however, had a ready vision for emancipated African Americans based on the three interrelated pillars of northern society: free labor, property, and education.

According to sympathetic Republicans and friends of the enslaved people, free labor for southern blacks would resemble the system that prevailed for most ordinary white northerners. Free labor ideology envisioned citizens who planned and worked to own their own farm or business by saving enough money to become independent. They initially earned wages at a job and were free to come and go at will. The goal for the freed men and women would be to profit from their labor while hoping to join the property-owning class at some point. This process would assist in the transition from slavery to freedom. By existing, even flourishing, within the market system, black people would prove their dependability as workers and educate themselves to be free citizens.

The results were mixed and revealed the complexities of trying to conduct a social revolution in the middle of a violent war. If a slave had been trained in a skilled occupation, he or she probably could find a decent-paying job in Washington, D.C., Nashville, Tennessee, or some other places. Often a portion of their small wages would be deducted for expenses, and the army issued regulations that defined "work" for all able-bodied freemen as a "public duty." The freedman could choose his employer but had to sign a contract stating he would remain for a year. These stringent labor regulations were enforced by a system of martial law. For example, General Nathaniel P. Banks used force to compel black workers to accept labor contracts on plantations or public works projects that sometimes included wages but more often just offered room and board. This system displayed racism, but it also operated on the assumption that the notion of contractual labor and wages was completely new to a recently enslaved people who would need to be educated in stages as to its benefits. Suddenly shifting from slavery to free labor during the chaos of war—with a majority white population that held racist views of African Americans—unsurprisingly proved to be problematical.

Military officers allowed private contractors, including some northern speculators and southern planters who took the oath of allegiance to the United States, to hire freed people. The best situation for contrabands usually existed on government-run plantations, the worst on those privately run. The freedmen's colony at Davis Bend, Mississippi, was widely advertised as a hopeful sign for the future of emancipation and free labor. Joseph Davis, the wealthy older brother of Jefferson Davis, abandoned his prosperous plantation as the Federal army advanced through Mississippi. His former enslaved workers, now freed men and women, were assisted by Union military leaders and the Freedmen's Bureau in a transitional experiment to free labor. They leased the land from the government, raised cotton, and began turning a tidy profit.

Sadly, the success at Davis Bend was not replicated in other areas that offered "rehearsals for Reconstruction." At other experiments, like the one in Port Royal, South Carolina, freed people often experienced conditions uncomfortably close to slavery. At Port Royal, earnest teachers, military officials, and businessmen learned that blacks did not want to pick cotton, even for wages, and resisted harsh discipline to make them bring in the crop. They desired to live the life of an independent yeoman farmer, like the majority of their fellow white southerners. Possessing a small piece of property, the second pillar of northern society, became the dream of many former slaves.

To a limited extent that dream existed—or at least drew tantalizingly close in the war years. Former slaves independently farmed approximately 20 percent of the agricultural land occupied by the Union army at venues such as Davis Bend and abandoned plantations in Louisiana. "Forty acres and a mule!" became a familiar demand of the freed people, especially after General Sherman's Special Field Orders No. 15, issued from Savannah, Georgia, on January 16, 1865. During Sherman's famed "March to the Sea," his soldiers freed slaves while destroying the plantation economy's cotton gins, agricultural equipment, and other trappings. Thousands of African Americans followed this Union army, experiencing both kindness and cruelty from Sherman's white troops. Special Field Orders No. 15 removed the followers by designating a large area of land in South Carolina for their use, resettling the contrabands by providing heads of families with a "possessory title" to forty acres of land. Final disposition of the land, Sherman explained, would have to be made by the federal government. By the end of June 1865, 40,000 freedpeople occupied some 400,000 acres.

While freed people eagerly welcomed the opportunities for the life of an independent property owner, the legality of wartime land seizure by the government for the use of contrabands remained uncertain. The president and Congress would have the final authority regarding ownership. Abolitionists and some others strongly urged that freedpeople be given permanent title to confiscated or abandoned Confederate lands. Only by owning and working on their own piece of land, these advocates reasoned, could former slaves truly become independent and realize the American dream. Indiana congressman and chair of the Committee of Public Lands George W. Julian recommended that the 1862 Homestead Act should apply to Rebel lands. Opponents included the usual suspects—speculators who stood to profit from selling confiscated land for profit and northern Democrats who opposed all such schemes for the benefit of freedpeople. Also skeptical were some moderate and conservative Republicans, who already were considering the problems of reunion after a bitter war.

President Lincoln tried to maintain some flexibility, as he did with many other divisive issues. The prospect for long-term black ownership of confiscated land dimmed in 1863, however, when the president announced his Reconstruction plan for Louisiana. The proposal included an offer for any Rebel who took the loyalty oath to recover all property except slaves, promising a major confrontation with the radical wing of the Republican Party. After Lincoln's assassination, Andrew Johnson carried on this policy through executive orders restoring to original owners all property given to freedmen during the war.

The Bureau of Refugees, Freedmen, and Abandoned Lands, established for one year on March 3, 1865, took an active role in the question of landownership. Typically called the Freedmen's Bureau and initially focused on relieving hunger among both black and white refugees (it distributed twenty-one million rations), the bureau also tried to oversee the introduction of a free labor system in the postwar South while adjudicating the expected clash between ex-Confederate plantation owners and their former slaves. A symbol of the federal government's determination to provide for the general welfare of the freedpeople, the understaffed and underfunded bureau did admirable work until it was shut down in 1872.

The Freedmen's Bureau achieved its greatest success in overseeing and extending ongoing efforts for black education, the third pillar of northern society. Even before the Emancipation Proclamation became law, a crusade was underway to plant schools in the occupied lands of the Confederacy. During the war, hundreds of northern teachers went south to help in the contraband camps and at special schools for black soldiers. After the war thousands more, including many women, traveled to teach in newly established freedmen's schools. The teachers hailed from New England, New York, and Pennsylvania, and some were themselves African American. Black or white, one of their purposes in educating ex-slaves—children and adults—in the rudiments of reading and writing was to bring the Protestant work ethic to the freed communities. They taught and preached values such as order, self-discipline, and the Christian faith, while stressing the need to uphold and honor the free labor ideal. Sometimes their methods and messages were resisted or even rejected by their students, causing resentment on both sides.

Working with the cooperation and resources of private charities and state governments, the Freedmen's Bureau founded and funded 3,000 black schools for 150,000 students. Clearly freedpeople yearned for the education that had been so long denied to them under slavery. The Freedman's Bureau also helped establish colleges to train African

American teachers for the new schools. One of the most important legacies of these early schools was in paving the way for the southern public school systems established during Reconstruction from 1865 to 1877.

VII. THE THIRTEENTH AMENDMENT

Neither the advance of Union armies nor the efforts of enslaved people had killed the institution of slavery by 1865. Slaves did much to force the issue of emancipation and its ramifications on the North, but the fact remained that the vast majority could not, and did not, free themselves. Although Union military power shrank the size of the domain controlled by the Confederate government, many Rebel areas remained largely unaffected. In short, the system of slavery was badly destabilized but not entirely destroyed. The final blow would come through constitutional action.

Three of the loyal slave states—Maryland (new constitution, 1864), Missouri (convention vote, 1865), and West Virginia (legislative action, 1865)—abolished slavery before the end of the war. Kentucky and Delaware refused to do so. Unionist minorities in three Confederate states—Arkansas, Louisiana, and Tennessee—took advantage of Lincoln's wartime reconstruction plan and abolished slavery as a condition of readmittance to the Union. These states, however, formally remained in the Confederacy until the surrenders in 1865.

The election of 1864 featured a Republican platform committed to a constitutional amendment that would achieve abolition everywhere in the United States. An amendment was necessary, Lincoln and the Republicans believed, because Congress might not possess the legal authority to make emancipation stick once the war ended. Propelled to victory by a string of recent military successes, Republicans rejoiced in the fact that the northern people voted, by a margin of 55 to 45 percent, not just for Lincoln but also for the Union's twin goals of reunion and emancipation. The election's mandate meant that Lincoln would prosecute the war until all the Confederate armies capitulated. The Thirteenth Amendment, passed by the Senate on April 8, 1864, received the necessary two-thirds majority vote in the House of Representatives on January 31, 1865. The first of the three "Reconstruction amendments," it read in part: "Neither slavery nor involuntary servitude . . . shall exist within the United States, or any place subject to their jurisdiction." Ratification by the necessary three-quarters of the states was secured on December 18, 1865, and on that day slavery ceased to exist across the United States. In four years, freedom had become nationalized.

The ratification of the Thirteenth Amendment did not end the story of black emancipation because its meaning beyond the ending of slavery had not yet been agreed upon. When the surrender document was signed at Appomattox Court House on April 9, 1865, the guns had fallen silent, but both reconstructing the nation and defining freedom remained deeply problematical. A revolution bringing emancipation to enslaved peoples emerged from the bloody battlefields of the Civil War. Freedpeople of the South, African Americans living in the North, and white people across the country had very different ideas about what black freedom should entail. In the decades following emancipation, the outward signs of freedom—civil rights, citizenship, suffrage, and economic independence—would become battlegrounds of a different kind.

Plate 9. "Charge of the Police on the Rioters at the 'Tribune' Office." The war produced considerable internal dissent in both the United States and the Confederacy. No single incident exceeded in scale or violence the New York City draft riots of July 1863.

CHAPTER 6

HEAVY BLOWS BUT NO DECISION:
THE WINTER OF 1862 TO THE SPRING OF 1864

FIFTEEN MONTHS OF campaigning after the failed Confederate offensives in the autumn of 1862 included successes for both sides but ended with Union victories in every major theater. After a winter and spring marked by humiliating defeats for the Army of the Potomac at Fredericksburg and Chancellorsville and inconclusive action in Tennessee and along the Mississippi River, U.S. forces triumphed at Gettysburg and Vicksburg in early July 1863 and at Chattanooga in late November. Those three great victories seemingly foreshadowed the Confederacy's destruction, an outcome the northern populace thought all the more likely when U. S. Grant was promoted to general in chief of all Union armies in March 1864. Indeed, many generations of Americans have looked to Gettysburg and Vicksburg as the war's decisive military events, after which it was only a matter of time before Rebel forces would capitulate. This interpretation, although beguiling for those who seek conclusive turning points, oversimplifies a very complex period of the war. Significant turmoil relating to conscription and emancipation remained part of the political landscape in the United States, while a majority of the Confederate people, though battered by dire news from several battlefronts, remained determined to establish a nation that would preserve their slavery-based social and economic system. "We are in the midst of a desperate and bloody war," wrote a South Carolina farmer at the end of December 1863. "How it will terminate none of us can tell." He added, in language echoed by many across the Confederacy: "But surely this is the time that every man should do all he can for our suffering country."

I. TWO WINTER CAMPAIGNS

Union failures to pursue retreating Confederate armies vigorously after the battles of Antietam and Perryville created widespread dissatisfaction across the North and led to a pair of unusual winter operations. For the most part, the logistical challenges of moving and supplying armies during winter months prevented such action, but President Lincoln, who believed aggressive maneuvers necessary to bolster confidence in the war effort and improve prospects for Republicans, chose two new army commanders in Virginia and Tennessee. In the East, General Ambrose E. Burnside, who had won early victories along the coast of North Carolina and later served loyally under McClellan, took charge of the Army of the Potomac. In the West, General William Starke Rosecrans, a veteran of fighting in both the East and the West and the most prominent Catholic officer in the Union high command, replaced Don Carlos Buell at the head of what soon would be designated the Army of the Cumberland. Rosecrans's orders left no doubt about why he (and Burnside) had been put in charge, emphasizing "the necessity of giving active employment to your forces. Neither the country nor the government will much longer put up with the inactivity of some of our armies and generals."

Burnside took the stage first. With the Army of Northern Virginia spread out between Culpeper, a town on the Orange & Alexandria Railroad in the Piedmont, and the lower Shenandoah Valley, he planned to move the 120,000-man Army of the Potomac to Fredericksburg, cross the Rappahannock River, and interpose his force between Lee and Richmond. The plan started well, but when Burnside reached Fredericksburg during the third week of November he lacked the materials to build pontoon bridges to get across the river. By the time he was able to cross, Lee had placed the Army of Northern Virginia, numbering 75,000, on a series of high ridges west of the old colonial town. Burnside persisted in his original intention, however, and Federals crossed the river under fire on December 11, supported by artillery on high ground east of the river that pounded Fredericksburg.

The main fighting took place on December 13 and featured a series of piecemeal Union assaults into the teeth of Lee's line on Marye's Heights. Traversing an open plateau and raked by musketry and cannon fire, the attackers fell in profusion. Not a single U.S. soldier reached the Rebel lines before nightfall brought the slaughter to a merciful close. A survivor from the Irish Brigade recalled a "blinding fire of musketry" from Confederates sheltered behind a stone wall at the foot of the heights and admitted that the battle rendered much of the Union army "a defeated, dejected and demoralized mob." Casualties exceeded 12,500 for Burnside and almost 5,500 for Lee. Confederates hailed an easy victory after Burnside retreated across the river on December 15, while anger rippled through a northern citizenry sickened by the pointlessness of the frontal attacks. When Lincoln received news of the debacle, he knew opponents of the war would pummel him and his party, sadly remarking, "If there is a worse place than hell, I am in it." A Republican editor in Chicago described how Fredericksburg contributed to a "state of despondency and desperation," a widespread perception that "the war is drawing toward a disastrous and disgraceful termination."

Events on Rosecrans's front offered the Union a slender reed of hope at the end of the year. Federals marched southeast from Nashville on December 26 to strike Braxton Bragg's Army of Tennessee, which was positioned behind Stones River near Murfreesboro. Encamped within a few hundred yards of one another on the night of December 30, soldiers in the two armies listened to the other side's bands play patriotic airs. The next morning, Bragg orchestrated a series of heavy—and costly—assaults that broke part of Rosecrans's line but could not deliver a knockout blow. After a relatively quiet New Year's Day, the fighting resumed on January 2, after which Bragg withdrew thirty-five miles farther south. The carnage at Stones River (Confederates called it Murfreesboro) had been appalling: 13,000 of Rosecrans's 42,000 men (31 percent) and 12,000 of Bragg's 36,000 (33 percent) were casualties—bloodier than Shiloh and the highest combined rate of loss for any battle during the war. Although Rosecrans reported to Washington that the Confederates had "fled with great precipitancy," the victorious Federals failed to pursue the enemy. But at least "Old Rosy" had not lost the battle, and Lincoln responded warmly to the news from Tennessee: "God bless you," he wrote Rosecrans, "and all with you! Please tender to all, and accept for yourself, the Nation's gratitude for yours, and their, skill, endurance, and dauntless courage."

II. A SPRING WITH NO UNION VICTORY

An absence of significant victories during the spring of 1863 created one of war's worst crises for Lincoln and his administration. In Virginia, morale in the Army of the Potomac eroded steadily after Fredericksburg, and soon a cabal of officers worked to displace Burnside. By the end of January, Lincoln decided that a change was necessary, naming Joseph Hooker as the new commander on the twenty-sixth.

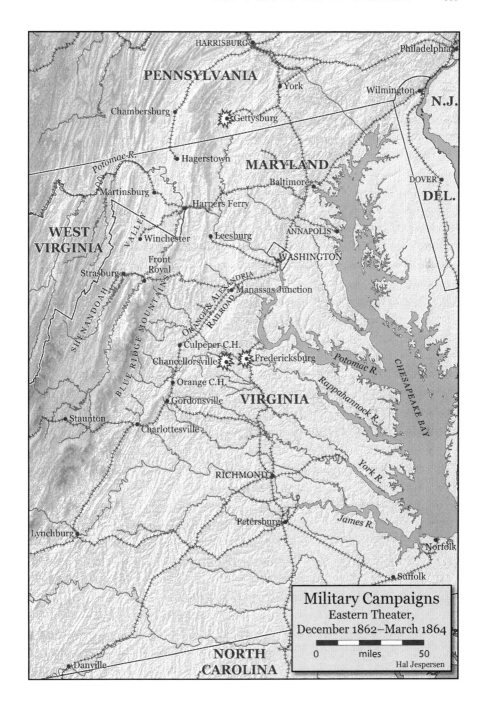

Military Campaigns
Eastern Theater,
December 1862–March 1864

0   miles   50

Hal Jespersen

Nicknamed "Fighting Joe," Hooker rivaled McClellan in his relentless self-focus. He uttered a number of rash statements, even suggesting at one point that the nation might need a dictator to win the war (the implication being that he would make a fine one). Lincoln knew all this but took the risk that Hooker might transcend the cautious culture McClellan had nurtured in the Army of the Potomac. "I have heard . . . of your recently saying that both the Army and the Government needed a Dictator," the president wrote Hooker, "Of course it was not *for* this, but in spite of it, that I have given you the command. Only those generals who gain successes, can set up dictators. What I now ask of you is military success, and I will risk the dictatorship."

Hooker proved adept at restoring morale and improving many aspects of the army's administration—but failed miserably in the ultimate test against Lee and the Army of Northern Virginia. The military front remained at Fredericksburg, and Hooker made an excellent start in late April by moving the bulk of his 130,000 men up the Rappahannock, around Lee's left flank, while leaving a strong force to hold the Rebels' attention. On April 30 he had reached the crossroads of Chancellorsville, ten miles west of Fredericksburg, whence he issued a bombastic order predicting that "our enemy must either ingloriously fly, or come out from behind his defenses and give us battle on our own ground, where certain destruction awaits him." Hooker almost certainly expected, and surely hoped, that Lee would retreat toward Richmond. Instead Lee divided his army, reduced to 65,000 because a quarter of his infantry had been deployed to southeastern Virginia, and took the offensive.

The next four days highlighted a stunning contrast between the two commanders and yielded the most storied of Lee's victories. At first contact on the roads from Chancellorsville to Fredericksburg on May 1, Hooker lost all thought of pressing the offensive, dropped back into a gloomy region of second- and third-growth woods called the Wilderness of Spotsylvania, and failed to use thousands of his troops as the fighting developed. Lee divided his command yet again, sent Stonewall Jackson on a daring flank march on May 2, and committed virtually every man in his army to the desperate combat. Hooker's timidity and superb conduct by the Confederate infantry and artillery, especially during the heaviest action on May 3, allowed Lee to prevail. Hooker retreated from the battlefield on May 5 following a performance that, much like McClellan's at Malvern Hill, frittered away an opportunity to deal a crushing blow to the Army of Northern Virginia. Losses were gruesome for both sides but relatively much worse for Lee than for Hooker—nearly 13,000 Confederates (including Jackson, mistakenly shot by his own troops on May 2 and dead eight days later) and more than 17,000 Federals.

News of Chancellorsville reverberated through the United States and the Confederacy. Within Lee's army and across the South, it completed the process by which Lee assumed an unequaled position as the polestar for belief that victory and independence were possible. Jefferson Davis thanked Lee and his men "in the name of the people . . . for this addition to the unprecedented series of great victories which your army has achieved." For Lincoln and the North, glum tidings from the Rappahannock theater intensified the backbiting and despondency stoked by Burnside's defeat five months earlier. The president took word of the failure very hard. "My God! My God!" he moaned while pacing nervously, "What will the country say?" Horace Greeley, the influential editor of the *New York Tribune*, struck an almost identical note, pronouncing it "horrible—horrible; and to think of it, 130,000 magnificent soldiers cut to pieces by less than 60,000 half-starved ragamuffins."

Union operations in the West did not counter the effects of failure in the East. The Tennessee front remained quiet for months after Stones River, as neither Rosecrans nor Bragg instigated any notable action. Attention in the United States as well as in the Confederacy focused most closely on the Mississippi River, where the Rebel stronghold at Vicksburg had been Ulysses S. Grant's target for many months. Vicksburg remained the principal obstacle to opening the entire river to Union control—a goal prominent in the minds of northern political and military leaders, as well much discussed by newspapers and the public, since Winfield Scott's Anaconda Plan had become widely known in the war's first months.

In late 1862, Grant initially had intended to menace Vicksburg from three directions, but none of the elements of his plan succeeded. Throughout the winter, he sought some means to bypass powerful Confederate artillery positions along the river at Vicksburg—either by finding an alternate water route through marshes, lakes, and streams to the west or by digging a canal—so he could transfer troops to the east side of the Mississippi and then advance against the city. Every attempt failed, prompting Grant to settle on a desperate gamble. He ordered supporting naval vessels stationed above Vicksburg to run past the Confederate batteries while Union infantry marched southward on the west side of the river. Naval officers and Grant's own subordinates, including William Tecumseh Sherman, had serious doubts about the plan, but it went forward successfully between April 16 and 22. By May 1, the navy had ferried 23,000 infantry across the Mississippi at a point approximately forty miles south of Vicksburg. "I felt a degree of relief scarcely ever equaled since," Grant later wrote. "I was on dry ground on the same side of the river with the enemy. All the campaigns, labors, hardships and exposures from the month of December previous to this time . . . were for the accomplishment of this one object." But no one in Washington or elsewhere in the United States knew precisely what was happening, or what would happen, with Grant's campaign. As a consequence, defeats in the East continued to depress national morale.

III. THE UNION IN CRISIS

The spring months of 1863 illuminate how events on the battlefront

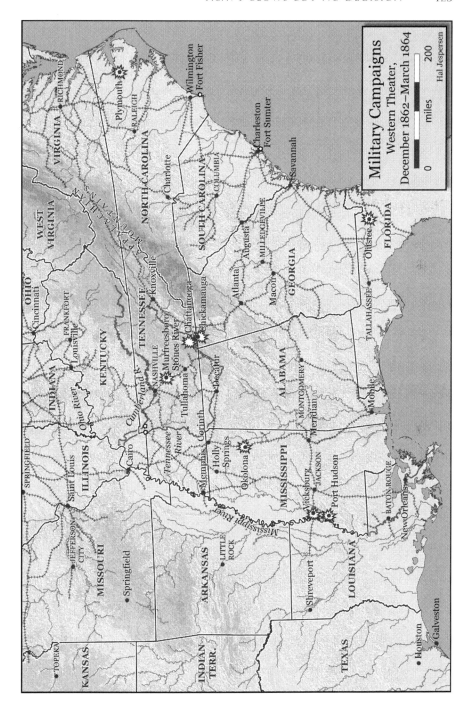

Military Campaigns
Western Theater,
December 1862–March 1864

0   miles   200

Hal Jespersen

and home front intersected and affected one another. On the Union side, intense disagreements about emancipation and, a bit later, federal conscription heightened arguments about the Lincoln administration's conduct of military affairs. A war for Union had been widely supported across political boundaries since the late spring of 1861, but Lincoln's final proclamation of emancipation, issued on New Year's Day in 1863, alienated huge numbers of Democrats already upset with what they considered heavy-handed governmental actions against anyone who voiced opposition to Republican policies. The proclamation, claimed its opponents, changed the war's purpose from saving the Union to freeing black people—something few white people in the loyal states, whether Republican or Democratic, considered worth donning uniforms and risking lives to achieve. Eventually most white citizens would accept emancipation for a combination of three reasons: first, to deny the Confederacy black labor essential to its war effort; second, to punish slaveholders whom they saw as responsible for the war's carnage; and third, to remove the only internal threat to a stable Union in the aftermath of victory. Only abolitionists, white and black, and a few others supported emancipation as a moral goal worth great sacrifice.

In the first six months of 1863, opposition to emancipation undercut morale in the Union armies. On January 17, a soldier in the Army of the Potomac reported that "troops are loud in their denunciation against the President and the Abolition Cabinet generally." Desertion had increased, he claimed, because many men said they would not fight to place African Americans "on a par with white men, that they had been duped and that they only enlisted for the preservation of the Union and nothing else." A few weeks later, an Illinois soldier stationed in North Carolina recorded that the "soldiers, generally have a bitter enmity towards the negroes. Any, that plead for even the most common rights of the negro, do so at the risk of their popularity with their comrades. . . . This is true, not of any particular regiments only, but generally so far as my observation extends, which has by no means been limited." An officer who later supported the Thirteenth Amendment thought pro-emancipation agitation in early 1863 proved doubly detrimental because it "has united the South and has divided the North, it has induced to vote with the democrats many men as patriotic as any in the country and who would have fought as long as any for the proper object of the war."

The proclamation certainly boosted support for the antiwar Copperhead wing of the Democratic Party. Many Democratic newspapers claimed that Lincoln cared less about salvaging the work of the Founders than about killing the institution of slavery. In April, *The Old Guard*, a virulently anti-administration publication, put it this way: "There is not a single supporter of this Administration who is not bent on the everlasting destruction of the Union in order to destroy the institutions of the southern half of it. That is the difference between Democrats and Republicans."

Congressional passage of the Enrollment Act on March 3, 1863, fueled increasing discontent. The first national draft in U.S. history, it mandated that all male citizens between the ages of twenty and forty-five were liable for three years' service. Those wishing to avoid military duty could either hire a substitute, which would exempt them for the entire war, or pay $300 to escape induction in a particular draft call (there were four calls during the war—though no one knew what the number would be in March 1863). As when Confederates opposed their national conscription act the previous spring, the Enrollment Act provoked howls of dissent from those who insisted that it abridged fundamental personal liberties. Poorer men also charged that it favored the wealthy, a complaint that led Congress to abolish commutation—but not substitution—in 1864.

Coupled with emancipation, the draft proved especially toxic. Now, complained unhappy Democrats across the United States, men could be forced into service to free enslaved black people. Violent opposition occurred in many places, most notably in New York City on July 13-16 where mobs of predominantly working-class men took to the streets. Initially an expression of anger over the draft, violence in New York turned into an ugly race riot that targeted black men, women, and children. More than one hundred people died during the four days, casualties of a conjunction of bitter unhappiness with conscription and emancipation.

Difficulties also bedeviled the Confederacy in the spring of 1863, though they proved less disruptive to national morale. Food shortages sent women into the streets of various cities and towns, including Richmond, where the "Bread Riots" of April 2 provoked wide comment. "It is the first time that such a thing has ever darkened the annals of Richmond," wrote one woman, who feared "that the poor suffer very much" and blamed their distress on heartless speculators. Needy wives and widows of soldiers touched a special chord among fellow citizens, and government—at the local, state, and national levels—took measures to alleviate hardships. No politician could remove the sting of Stonewall Jackson's death, which elicited anguished reactions from many Confederates. "The great and good General Stonewall Jackson has fallen," wrote a nurse in Chattanooga. "When I first heard of it I was speechless, and thought, with the apostle, 'how unsearchable are His judgments, and His ways past finding out.'"

Overall, Confederates took heart not only from Lee's victories but also from the obvious political factionalism in the United States. Increasingly Confederates compared Lee to George Washington, as when a Georgia woman expressed thanks that "in this great struggle the head of our army is a noble son of Virginia, and worthy of the intimate relation in which he stands connected to our immortal Washington." A diarist in Richmond, like many others, savored stories in northern newspapers about unrest tied to emancipation. "We see accounts of public meetings in New Jersey," wrote John B. Jones on January 20, "wherein the government at Washington is fiercely denounced, and peace demanded . . . . Some of the speakers openly predicted that the war would spread into the North, if not terminated at once, and . . . the emancipationists would have foes to fight elsewhere than in the South."

The Emancipation Proclamation unquestionably bolstered Confederate determination to resist Union military incursions. It raised the specter of slave revolts, of John Brown at Harpers Ferry, and even of a racial bloodbath of the type that had established the black republic of Haiti. Although often cast as a proslavery moderate, Robert E. Lee denounced the proclamation in language that reveals the depth of southern feeling. On January 10, 1863, he insisted, with obvious anger, that the proclamation laid out "a savage and brutal policy, which leaves us no alternative but success or degradation worse than death, if we would save the honor of our families from pollution, our social system from destruction." The use of "degradation," "pollution," and "social system"—words often deployed by white southerners in antebellum discussions about the possible consequences of abolitionism—highlight the degree to which Lincoln's policy convinced most Confederates that the stakes of the war had been raised immeasurably.

IV. A LANDSCAPE CHANGED—HUMAN, ANIMAL, AND ENVIRONMENTAL DISLOCATION

By the summer of 1863, the war's profound impact on environmental resources stood out across much of the Confederacy and in loyal states subject to military activity. The mere presence of an army disrupted agricultural patterns and rhythms. Wherever an army camped for any length of time, thousands of campfires resulted in the destruction of many acres of forests, substituting moonscapes for previously lush vegetation. Even one night's appearance by an army, either friendly or hostile, could bring the loss of a farm's fencing, crops, and animals. As the war progressed, much of the Confederacy's heartland experienced catastrophic damage from armies bent on destruction or simply seeking food and fodder for soldiers, as well as for thousands of horses and mules. When armies went into winter quarters, the environmental dislocation escalated.

Three witnesses provide graphic testimony about the physical changes wrought by the war. In late June 1863, a British officer named Arthur James Lyon Fremantle traveled through central Virginia with Lee's army. He wrote in his diary about the countryside around Sperryville, a village near the eastern slope of the Blue Ridge Mountains. The nearby presence of two armies for more than a year had left the region "completely cleaned out." Many acres lay "almost uncultivated, and no animals are grazing where there used to be hundreds. All fences have been destroyed, and numberless farms burnt, chimneys alone left standing." Fremantle concluded, "It is difficult to depict and impossible to exaggerate the sufferings which this part of Virginia has undergone." Two Union accounts demonstrate that Middle Tennessee presented a comparably bleak picture. The area, known in the prewar years for its agricultural bounty, had been overrun by Federal armies in 1862 and subjected to intense foraging. "This is a dreary, desolate, barren and deserted looking country," stated an officer well before the midpoint of the war. A cavalryman, writing in April 1863, adopted language similar to Fremantle's: "It is really sad to see this beautiful country here so ruined. There are no fences left at all. There is no corn and hay for the cattle and horses, but there are no horses left anyhow and the planters have no food for themselves."

The cavalryman in Tennessee would have been particularly alert to the absence of horses. The contending sides probably used close to 1,100,000 horses and 750,000 mules—for the cavalry and artillery—to pull supply wagons and ambulances, and to support construction or repair projects associated with campaigning. Losses among horses and mules cannot be determined with precision, but they were terrible. Diseases swept through horse depots and armies, and the plague of equine glanders claimed tens of thousands of victims. In the fall of

1863, the Army of the Cumberland alone, while besieged in Chatta-nooga, lost 10,000 animals dead or so disabled they could no longer work. The following spring, Union armies ordered that all livestock abandoned on the march should be shot to prevent Rebels from cap-turing and returning them to service. Charles Francis Adams, Jr., a Union cavalryman whose great-grandfather and grandfather had been presidents of the United States and whose father was ambassador to Great Britain, spoke to one of the outcomes of this policy. "[T]he air of Virginia is literally burdened today with the stench of dead horses, federal and confederate," he informed his mother: "You pass them on every road and find them in every field, while from their carrions you can follow the march of every army that moves."

The built environment inevitably bore the marks of military dis-ruption. Private homes and outbuildings, as well as mills, factories, railroad facilities, and other structures more directly tied to the war ef-forts, suffered damage or destruction. Among the first was Judith Hen-ry's modest home on the battlefield of First Bull Run, which stood near the center of combat on July 21, 1861, and by the summer of 1862 had been reduced to a crumbling chimney and fragments of wood fram-ing. Fredericksburg, Charleston, Petersburg, Vicksburg, Atlanta, and other Confederate towns and cities endured artillery bombardments that left many dwellings in ruins—and north of the Potomac River, Confederate cavalry burned hundreds of structures in Chambersburg, Pennsylvania, on July 30, 1864. Guerrilla depredations in every mili-tary theater took a toll on private as well as public buildings and oth-er property, most notoriously when Confederates under William C. Quantrill sacked Lawrence, Kansas, in 1863.

A visitor to Fredericksburg, Virginia, in late 1864 captured the degree to which a protracted military presence affected many areas. By that time, the Army of the Potomac and the Army of Northern Virginia had waged four huge battles within a few miles of Fredericks-burg, and many smaller actions and periods of Union occupation had further affected the local population and environment. The visitor saw "no crops now but crops of luxuriant weeds. . . . There are no hands at work in the fenceless fields—no signs of animated life about the deserted houses . . . the neighing of the horses, the cawing of the crow, and the laughter of the children in the yard . . . are no longer heard in this blasted region." Around Fredericksburg, he summed up, "All is still as death for miles and miles under the sweet autumnal sun." That person could not know that Fredericksburg, whose residents white and black were buffeted by the war, would not return to its 1860 population until 1900.

V. A SUMMER OF CONFEDERATE FAILURE

The pendulum of high national morale swung sharply toward the Union cause in June and July 1863. In the Eastern Theater, Lee once again crossed into U.S. territory, while in the West, Bragg and Rosecrans resumed operations in southeastern Tennessee and Grant engaged with General John C. Pemberton, who led an army defending Vicksburg. Secondary Union forces, naval and army, operated against Charleston, South Carolina, and Port Hudson, a heavily fortified position on the Mississippi River a short distance upriver from Baton Rouge, Louisiana. A feverish period of campaigning delivered a series of hammer blows against the Confederacy, as U.S. forces, on every front but Charleston, achieved signal victories.

The most famous of these campaigns pitted the Army of Northern Virginia against the Army of the Potomac and culminated in the largest and bloodiest battle of the war. After Chancellorsville, Lee opted to march northward into the United States. He hoped to keep the Federals off balance by taking the strategic initiative, to secure supplies for his army in the rich farming areas of Pennsylvania, and to encourage Democratic opposition to Lincoln—as he put it, "to repress the war feeling in the Federal States" by maneuvering on Union soil for several weeks. His 75,000 men, remarkably confident after their recent victories, marched through western Maryland in mid-June and spread across southern Pennsylvania before colliding with the Army of the Potomac at Gettysburg on July 1-3. The Federals, 90,000 strong and led by General George G. Meade, who had replaced Hooker on the eve of the battle, defended high ground against attacking Confederates. Fighting swirled across the undulating countryside—in the Peach Orchard, the Wheat Field, Devil's Den, and on the slopes of Little Round Top and Cemetery Ridge, previously forgettable places that assumed long-lasting importance in historical memory. The failure on the third day's battle of Pickett's Charge, easily the most famous infantry assault in American history, settled the issue and led to Lee's retreat on July 4. Meade pursued cautiously, and by July 14 the Army of Northern Virginia had recrossed the Potomac and taken up a position in northern Virginia.

The victory at Gettysburg inspired people across the United States and chastened those in the Confederacy. Although casualty figures remain somewhat in dispute, each side lost at least 22,000, and some reckonings put the total cost at more than 50,000. Particularly hard hit on the Confederate side were North Carolina units (nearly 45 percent of all Tar Heel soldiers became casualties), a phenomenon that fed war weariness on that state's home front. Tellingly, the defeat did almost nothing to compromise Lee's high reputation in the Confederacy. As after Antietam, Lincoln expressed disappointment with his commander's failure to harass a battered enemy. On July 14, he composed a letter to Meade—which he never sent, though Meade learned of its sentiment. The president acknowledged "the magnificent success you gave the cause of the country at Gettysburg" but lamented the "misfortune involved in Lee's escape." Because of Meade's inaction, Lincoln predicted, "the war will be prolonged indefinitely." Others in the United States reached similar conclusions, a fact at odds with the now popular idea that Gettysburg turned the war decisively toward ultimate U.S.

victory.

The outcome of the Vicksburg campaign resonated more powerfully than Gettysburg in both the United States and the Confederacy. Between May 1 and May 18, Grant executed a remarkable series of movements, won five victories, and pinned Pemberton's 32,000 men inside the defenses of Vicksburg. A six-week siege ensued, during which civilians as well as Confederate soldiers in the city suffered terribly under round-the-clock bombardment. On July 4, with the investing Union army swelled to 70,000, Pemberton surrendered his soldiers. Five days later, the smaller southern garrison at Port Hudson also capitulated. Practical Confederate control of the Mississippi had ceased with the loss of New Orleans many months earlier, but the river now lay completely open to Union naval vessels, allowing Lincoln to observe in August that "The Father of Waters again goes unvexed to the sea."

For Confederates, the loss of Vicksburg touched a despairing nerve. They had lost an entire army and a stronghold that, during the preceding months, had assumed tremendous psychological importance. A woman living in South Carolina's upcountry voiced a common reaction on July 9. "There seems no doubt that Vicksburg has fallen after all our sanguine hopes and expectations," she recorded in her diary. "It is a terrible blow to our cause and will prolong the war indefinitely— oh, how much depended on its salvation."

U. S. Grant's stock rose dramatically after Vicksburg, separating him from all other Union officers. One newspaper reporter linked the capture of Port Hudson to Vicksburg's surrender and affirmed that all credit for both "is honestly due to General Grant." Another applauded Grant's "invincible perseverance, endurance and determination," informing readers that Union soldiers seldom saluted the general but rather watched him "with a certain sort of familiar reverence." The person who mattered most revealed his opinion of Grant on July 5, two days before word about Vicksburg's fate reached the capital. If the city fell, pledged Lincoln while speaking with a general wounded at Gettysburg, "Grant is my man and I am his the rest of the war." Eight days later the president wrote directly to his victorious general in "grateful acknowledgement for the almost inestimable service you have done the country."

Activity in one last theater completed the string of Union successes in June and July. Chattanooga remained the most important Tennessee city still in Rebel hands, a center for transportation and communications that linked the northeastern Confederacy to the interior of the Lower South. In late June, Rosecrans, whose Army of the Cumberland had spent the winter near Murfreesboro, inaugurated what became known as the Tullahoma campaign. He employed a series of deft flanking moves to press Bragg's Army of Tennessee toward the Tennessee-Georgia border. By July 7 and at a cost of fewer than 600 casualties, Rosecrans maneuvered Bragg across the Tennessee River into Chattanooga—presenting the northern public with a third notable Union success in a single week.

VI. CLOSING ONE YEAR AND BEGINNING ANOTHER

Chattanooga and Grant dominated military headlines for the remainder of 1863. In early September, Rosecrans forced Bragg out of Chattanooga and into northwest Georgia. The Confederates responded by sending reinforcements to Bragg from Lee's army and elsewhere, which enabled the Army of Tennessee, numbering 66,000, to turn the tables on Rosecrans's 58,000 Federals. The resulting battle of Chickamauga, waged on September 19-20 a few miles south of Chattanooga, exceeded all other engagements but Gettysburg in sanguinary fury. Serendipity and hard fighting allowed Bragg's army to drive a significant percentage of the Federals, including Rosecrans, from the field on the second day. Only a stubborn defense by General George H. Thomas, a Virginian who had remained loyal to the Union, averted complete disaster and allowed the Army of the Cumberland to gather itself in Chattanooga, which soon was besieged by the victorious Confederates.

Unhappy with Rosecrans, whose behavior he described as "confused and stunned like a duck hit on the head," Lincoln approved sending Grant to salvage the situation at Chattanooga in late October. On November 24-25, the Army of the Cumberland, together with reinforcements from Mississippi under General Sherman and from Virginia under Joseph Hooker, attacked along the length of Bragg's lines, carrying positions on Lookout Mountain and Missionary Ridge in fashioning a sweeping victory. The previous month, Lincoln had proclaimed the third Thursday of November a day of national Thanksgiving, a gesture given added meaning by Grant's victory at Chattanooga. "This has been the perfection of a thanksgiving day," wrote Elizabeth Blair Lee, the sister of Lincoln's postmaster general and wife of a Union admiral. " . . . The good news from Grant just overflowed the cup of thanksgiving which was already made full—."

As the armies hunkered down in winter quarters until spring brought a renewal of operations, people on both sides could assess the state of the war. Considerable optimism pervaded the North, where antiwar sentiment hovered well below the high point after Chancellorsville. Lincoln believed the time had come to lay out a blueprint for bringing wayward states back into the Union, which he did in his "Proclamation of Amnesty and Reconstruction" issued on December 8 (the Radical faction of his party denounced the proclamation as too lenient on Rebels). Grant's promotion to general in chief on March 2, 1864, garnered enthusiastic praise. The *New York Herald*, a widely-read Democratic paper, termed him the perfect commander because "He has, above every man of this generation, the confidence of the American people." The Republican *New York Tribune* averred that "no military order has been issued in this war so universally satisfactory as that which we print this morning, appointing Lieut.-Gen. Grant to command all the armies of the United States." Moreover, added the *Tribune* in a jab aimed directly at McClellan, "he never runs away from a less number of Rebels than the force he commands, whether before or after a battle."

Still, it is important to recognize that many people in the United States remained cautious or even pessimistic. William O. Stoddard, one of Lincoln's private secretaries, articulated ideas prominent among the former. The "rebels are to have a long winter in which to recuperate their failing energies," he observed, and history showed "that a nation . . . will endure a vast amount of mere everyday hardships and privations." Union soldiers had seen Confederate resiliency up close. "They will no doubt," an officer in the Army of the Potomac grimly predicted, "fight to the death, in the last ditch." The most pessimistic voices emerged from the ranks of Democrats, with Copperheads predictably taking the lead. Lincoln remained a lightning rod for criticism from all elements of the opposition party, labeled a failed executive, as the *New York Herald* asserted, whose decisions and policies had visited "desolation and mourning" on the nation. Copperheads went much further, furious with what they perceived as Republican eagerness to shed white blood to bring equality for black people. One editor blamed the "reckless, piratical" Republicans in Washington for creating a bleak picture in which "the people are blindly drifting through blood and horrors unparalleled, into social anarchy and utter ruin."

Perhaps more surprisingly, the defeats of the second half of 1863 did not convince most Confederates that their quest for nationhood was doomed. They coped not only with news of Gettysburg, Vicksburg, and Chattanooga but also with severe material shortages, terrible inflation, and intrusive governmental measures designed to tighten conscription, limit antiwar activities, and muster all possible resources. Many undoubtedly lost heart, and anti-Davis administration activists whipped up considerable opposition. Mountainous regions and uplands harbored the most serious disaffection, which sometimes generated spasms of violence. But a series of small, and seldom remembered, victories—at Olustee, Florida, on February 20; Okolona, Mississippi, two days later; Plymouth, North Carolina, on April 20; and else-where—buoyed spirits. More important by far, trust in Lee and his army remained apparently unshakable. Finally, the specter of emancipation hardened resolve. Newspapers used volatile images of enslaved white southerners to paint a chilling portrait of the consequences of defeat. Richmond's *Dispatch*, for example, spoke of Federal plans "to rob us of all we have on earth, and reduce our whole population to the condition of beggars and slaves." The question, insisted this editor, no longer was whether enslaved black people would remain in bondage but whether Confederates and their children "shall be slaves" and become "hewers of wood and drawers of water for their Yankee masters."

Most Confederates likely indulged a cautious optimism as they looked toward the next round of military campaigns. A refugee in Richmond accepted that God had tested the southern people, and she expected a large army under Grant to menace the Confederate capital. But "with the help of God," she wrote, "we hope to drive them back again. . . . I don't think that any one doubts our ability to do it; but the awful loss of life necessary upon the fight is what we dread." Neither the large number of Confederates who would have agreed with this woman nor the mass of northern people who anticipated victory with Grant in overall command could know that nothing in three years of war had prepared them for what would come in 1864.

Plate 10. "Uprising of the North." Civil War armies were national institutions composed of men from each republic's constituent states. Artist Charles Parsons created "Uprising of the North" to show volunteers advancing under their state flags to create a "mighty current . . . bearing aloft in irrepressible might the Stars and Stripes in defense of Liberty and Union!"

CHAPTER 7

A STRUGGLE BETWEEN NATIONS

THE PEOPLE GIRDING themselves for another year of struggle in 1864 understood that they were engaged in a contest between two mid-nineteenth-century nation-states. This goes against the popular image of a fratricidal struggle between reluctant opponents who thought of themselves as American brothers, or the more ubiquitous conception of a conflict between the North and the South. The latter formulation is fundamentally flawed because four southern states—Kentucky, Missouri, Maryland, and Delaware—remained loyal to the Union, and a large portion of the most important southern state broke away to form West Virginia in the midst of war. It is most accurate to think of two nations: the United States, seeking to safeguard the political entity born in the blood and sacrifice of the Revolution and more fully realized by the Constitution, versus the Confederacy, a short-lived republic whose entire history unfolded against a background of all-encompassing warfare. How the contending populations conceived of their nations, how the war affected the growth of central power and influence in relation to the states, and how the warring republics presented themselves to the rest of the world (primarily to the Atlantic world) form important elements of two gripping national sagas.

I. LOYALTY

National sentiment and identity in both the United States and the Confederacy formed part of numerous overlapping and often mutually reinforcing loyalties—including, but not limited to, family, state, religion, region, and country. Depending on the time and situation, different loyalties could emerge as most important. War on an immense scale understandably could intensify feelings of national loyalty, creating a dynamic sense of collective striving to protect what each side valued in its society. It was seldom a question of whether people were loyal to their state or to their nation but rather how those two loyalties, each firmly in place in federal systems of government, intertwined. The armies represented the perfect expression of these combined loyalties, composed of regiments raised in the states for service in a national cause. The soldiers of the 20th Maine Infantry and the 15th Alabama Infantry who fought on the slopes of Little Round Top on July 2, 1863, for example, carried national battle flags that indicated how their efforts far transcended the boundaries and needs of their respective states.

In the United States, longstanding identifications with state and region carried through the war. Colonel Joshua Lawrence Chamberlain, who commanded the 20th Maine at Gettysburg, spoke to the former shortly after the battle when he affirmed his men's affection for "the state whose name we are proud to bear, & which, we believe, we have not dishonored." Chamberlain's soldiers also likely thought of themselves as New Englanders, just as those from the West (the modern Midwest) embraced a sense of regional pride. People attributed distinct characteristics to residents of the various regions—such as flinty self-reliance to New Englanders and less dependence on formality and rules to westerners. Many observers of the Grand Review of Union armies in Washington at the end of the war remarked on regional contrasts. The poet Walt Whitman watched the passing units, later describing the westerners in Sherman's armies as "larger in size" but "more slow in their movements, and in their intellectual quality also" than eastern men in the Army of the Potomac. Geographic pride shone through the comments of an Illinois soldier in the parade, who claimed that a newspaper "speaks very highly of our review and acknoladges [*sic*] . . . that Sherman's Army went far a head of the Army of the Potomac."

Loyalty to state and region supported a mighty effort to protect the integrity of the nation. *Harper's Weekly* published a large woodcut in April 1862 that showed a mass of men rallying to the cause under various state flags. Artist Charles Parsons explained the scene: "The hardy sons of New England swarm over the hills, joining their brothers of the Middle States—swelling, as they meet, the mighty current setting in from the far-off States of the Pacific and glorious West—bearing aloft in irrepressible might the Stars and Stripes in defense of Liberty and Union!" An officer in the 7th New York State Militia created a similar image for his mother on April 18, 1861, yoking determination to crush the rebellion to the work of the founding generation. "The Massachusetts men passed through N. York this morning," he wrote from Staten Island, " . . . Won't it be grand to meet the men from all the States, East and West, down there, ready to fight for the country, as the old fellows did in the Revolution?"

No matter whence they hailed, loyal citizens typically linked what was best about their society and lives to maintenance of the republic. They often used "country," "nation," "the United States," and "Union" interchangeably, something evident in a Republican broadside from

Michigan during the 1864 presidential election: "To-day is to be decided whether this Nation *lives, or dies* at the *hands of traitors*! . . . Be sure and vote for the UNION, GOVERNMENT AND COUNTRY. If the Union and government is not maintained, the nation is disgraced before the CIVILIZED WORLD." Most people who sought to save the Union, including those in Michigan who agreed with the ideas in the broadside, subscribed to a vision built on free labor, the chance to rise economically, and by far the broadest political franchise in the western world. Victory over the slaveholding Rebels would confirm the nation, make it stronger in the absence of slavery's cancerous effect on politics, set the stage for continuing national growth and vitality, and allow a democratic beacon to keep shining in a world dominated by aristocrats and monarchs.

Confederates exhibited a comparable array of state, regional, and national attachments—in their case, substituting loyalty to the Confederacy for an earlier one to the United States (genuine Unionists in the Confederacy, who constituted a small minority of the white population, did not experience this shift in national focus). Generational differences mattered a good deal in shaping Confederate loyalty, with younger people, who always had known sectional divisiveness, proving more eager to embrace secession than those who had spent much of their lives before the rise of virulent discord in the late 1840s and 1850s. As committed to their states as anyone in the North, most white southerners during the prewar decades also had developed a deep-seated devotion to the slaveholding South—a feeling of southern community that abetted a smooth transition to an equally impressive feeling of Confederate community. During the course of the war, escalating violence and material loss across the Confederacy dramatically increased antipathy toward the United States and the Yankee citizenry.

Slavery and race lay at the heart of Confederate loyalties. Fear of Republican threats to the institution of slavery had fueled secession, and a desire to preserve the social and economic structure that guaranteed white control over millions of black people and their labor helps explain the tenacious struggle for Confederate nationhood. In a speech in Richmond on January 5, 1863, Jefferson Davis mocked northern claims to be fighting "to preserve the Union." Lincoln's "brutal soldiery" sought to establish "dominion over you," Davis told his audience, "to disturb your social organizations on the plea it is a military necessity." The enemy, he added in words certain to bolster determination to win southern nationhood, hoped "to reconstruct the Union by striking at everything which is dear to man."

In terms of protecting a slavery-based social structure, state and regional interests aligned perfectly with national ones. Robert E. Lee drove home this point to Governor Henry T. Clark of North Carolina in August 1862. Clark had complained of Union "outrages and depredations" in North Carolina and asked for more military protection. "The safety of the whole State of North Carolina," Lee asserted from Army of Northern Virginia headquarters, "as well as of Virginia, depends in a measure upon the result of the enemy's efforts in this quarter, which if successful, would make your State the theater of hostilities far more injurious and destructive to your citizens than anything they have yet been called upon to suffer." In other words, the Army of Northern Virginia, waging a defense of the whole nation, acted on behalf of the parts, including North Carolina, which required national protection of local institutions.

II. CENTRALIZING POWER

The governments in Washington and Richmond grew exponentially during the war. Ironically the Confederacy, though a republic many people still associate with the doctrine of state rights, developed the most intrusive national government in American history between the era of the founding and the mid-twentieth century. This growth of central power in both nations departed dramatically from the antebel-

Plate 11. The sheet music for *Our National Confederate Anthem* linked loyalties to the slaveholding South and to the Confederacy held by most of the breakaway republic's white citizenry, while also acknowledging the centrality of soldiers to the national project.

lum experience of most Americans, for whom the federal government remained a distant presence. Except for the postal service, regulations and taxes regarding importing and exporting goods, and bonuses of federal lands bestowed on veterans for national military service, the work of lawmakers and bureaucrats in Washington seldom touched people's daily lives. Perhaps most notable was the absence of direct national taxes levied on property or income. The war's voracious demands for men and matériel spawned contentious debates about the limits of central power, but most citizens, whether in the United States or the Confederacy, accepted greater governmental intrusions as the price for achieving widely agreed-upon national goals.

The two most obvious examples of governmental expansion—direct taxes and conscription—already have been discussed, but they were only part of a much larger phenomenon that took somewhat different forms in the contending nations. In each case, opponents of increased national power stepped forward, with Democrats offering blistering critiques of the Lincoln administration and Republicans in Congress and advocates of state rights assailing Jefferson Davis and those who supported his effort to bring many facets of the war effort under central governmental control. These opponents failed, for the most part, as both the executive and legislative branches in each nation pursued centralizing policies.

In the United States, two factors encouraged the growth of Washington's power. First and most obvious, the scale of the effort to defeat Confederate military forces demanded unprecedented actions. Conscription (or the threat of being drafted, which encouraged "voluntary" enrollment) kept armies up to strength, and federal taxes helped defray ballooning costs. The Lincoln administration and Congress also engaged in various activities that encroached on civil liberties in the name of furthering the effort to defeat the Rebels. For much of the war, Republicans actively used their federal power—military and otherwise—to influence elections in the Border States and elsewhere, intimidate Democratic newspaper editors, and otherwise suppress opposition. Lincoln suspended the writ of habeas corpus in different places at different times, which led to imprisonment of thousands of persons considered disloyal without bringing formal legal charges. "I can touch a bell on my right hand and order the imprisonment of a citizen of New York," Secretary of State William Henry Seward bluntly told a British diplomat, "and no power on earth except the President can release them."

Democrats disagreed among themselves about how and how long to prosecute the war—most of them argued that they, rather than the Republicans, stood for true Union principles—but presented a united front regarding the central government's abuse of civil liberties. In their 1864 national platform, they charged Republicans with, among other transgressions, "the administrative usurpation of extraordinary and dangerous powers," "the subversion of the civil by military law," and "the suppression of freedom of speech and of the press." The intensely racist language Democrats deployed in opposing emancipation throughout the war often has diverted attention from their claims that the Lincoln administration, by running roughshod over state and local authority, violated the spirit of federalism and endangered fundamental civil rights.

The departure of southern members of Congress following secession was the second factor that encouraged growth of central power. Reconfiguration of the Senate and House of Representatives opened the way for Republicans to overcome remaining Democratic opposition and enact legislation that took federal influence into previously uncharted territory regarding western settlement, education, and economic development.

Three notable pieces of legislation emerged from Congress in 1862. The Homestead Act, signed by President Lincoln on May 20, offered 160 acres of federal land to anyone who would settle on it for five years, thus supplying the critical asset necessary for success as a small farmer. This carried through on the old free soilers' agenda, prominent in the late antebellum years, of conveying western lands to white laborers or landless farmers who would populate, and render productive, immense stretches of the trans-Mississippi region. On July 1, the Pacific Railroad Act provided a combination of federal land grants and loans to fund construction of a transcontinental line with an eastern terminus at Omaha, Nebraska, and a western one at Sacramento, California. Initially companies would receive 6,400 acres of land and $16,000 in government bonds for each mile of track (more bonds per mile were earmarked for construction across the major mountain ranges). The Union Pacific and Central Pacific railroads grew out of this legislation, which sought to encourage more efficient travel and commercial activity between the East and West, as well as to promote development of the lightly populated western hinterlands.

The third act from 1862 ranks among the most important examples of federal aid to education in U.S. history. The Morrill Land-Grant Act, named after Congressman Justin Smith Morrill of Vermont, was first passed in 1859 but vetoed by Democratic president James Buchanan. Signed by Lincoln on July 2, it shifted the focus in higher education from classical curricula "to such branches of learning as are related to agriculture and the mechanic arts." The new type of education, believed the act's supporters, would benefit a far higher proportion of the population and train graduates who would enhance various sectors of the national economy. Under the act, every state received 30,000 acres of federal land for each of its senators and representatives, the sale of which would be used to establish at least one college. A number of great universities, most of them public, originated from this legislation.

Republicans in Congress also pressed for a national currency that would serve the needs of a burgeoning economy. When the war began, a welter of notes issued by state chartered banks circulated in the country. The National Banking Acts of February 25, 1863, and June 3, 1864, provided for federally chartered banks that could issue notes printed and guaranteed by the U.S. government. In the spring of 1865, a 10 percent tax on state bank notes hastened their demise, and by the end of that year less than 20 percent of the nation's assets lay in state banks. Together with the Legal Tender Act of 1862, which had created the greenbacks, the banking legislation of 1863-64 introduced a more stable currency. This Republican success also signaled a victory for those who, since the struggles between Hamiltonians and Jeffersonians in the early republic and Andrew Jackson's supporters and Whigs in the 1830s and 1840s, had called for greater centralization of banking and currency.

The Freedmen's Bureau provides a final example of groundbreaking federal activity that anticipated many government agencies of the twentieth century. The bureau assisted freedpeople in their transition

from slavery to freedom, with its agents, who were part of the Department of War, performing a range of activities. They distributed food
and clothing, worked to improve medical care (an effort that witnessed
more frustration and failure than success), provided legal assistance,
oversaw labor contracts, and set up schools. Headed by General Oliver
Otis Howard and renewed by Congress in 1866, the bureau lasted
until 1872, though decreasing budgets and heightened opposition by
former Confederates compromised its work.

The story of central power in the Confederacy highlights the transformative effects of a great war. The magnitude of the military and
economic challenge confronting Jefferson Davis and the Confederate
Congress quickly exposed the insufficiency of a strident state rights
approach. Devotion to state rights theory—the preamble to the Confederate Constitution stipulated that each state acted "in its sovereign
and independent character"—foundered on the rock of wartime necessity. Thus did the government in Richmond turn to conscription a year
before the United States did, enact national income taxes and the tax-
in-kind, and resort to impressment of goods, livestock, and enslaved
labor. Like Lincoln, Jefferson Davis also suspended the writ of habeas
corpus, but negative reaction to this drastic measure in the Confederacy, though thousands of people became political prisoners, never
equaled the fury of the Democratic response in the United States.

The Confederacy constructed a central bureaucracy that controlled
diverse elements of the economy and impinged dramatically on people's
daily lives. By the end of the war, the government employed 70,000
civilians, who labored in defense industries and managed tax-related
issues and the draft. Unlike the United States, which generally relied
on contracts with private companies to produce war-related material,
the Confederacy set up its own system of textile mills, arsenals, and
factories to produce much of what its military forces required. Near
the end of the war, at least 10,000 workers, all exempt from conscription, labored in ordnance and other war-related industries in Selma,

Alabama, and during three years of activity the massive government powder works in Augusta, Georgia, manufactured 2,750,000 pounds of high-quality gunpowder. The government also controlled much of the mining of niter (saltpeter), salt, and other crucial resources.

Transportation and civilian travel also came under government regulation. Although the state never formally took control of private railroads, legislation from May 1863 and February 1864 permitted the Richmond authorities to wield considerable influence over schedules and to impress rolling stock and railroad employees. In February 1865, as Union armies squeezed the Confederacy from several directions, the secretary of war received congressional approval to take charge of all railroad operations. The people who traveled on trains had long since been subject to close scrutiny. Government agents and military guards could question passengers about their identity, destination, and reason for their trip. In many parts of the Confederacy, all except very local movement required government documents—a system justified on the grounds of internal security and mobilization. Even members of Congress were subjected to checks that reminded them, uncomfortably, of the documents African Americans needed to travel. In 1863, Senator Williamson S. Oldham of Texas groused that he "was not allowed to go from [Richmond] . . . to North Carolina without going to the Provost Marshal's office and getting a pass like a free negro."

Because the Confederacy lacked formal political parties, there was no institutional opposition to growing central power comparable to the Democratic challenge in the United States. Instead, coalitions in favor of and against the Davis administration's policies developed. The former reached consensus on the need for at least temporary centralization to achieve independence; the latter decried substantive accretions of federal power as a violation of principles that had guided secessionists in 1860-61. Robert E. Lee stood among the nationalists who supported Davis, arguing in 1864 that the government should be empowered "to impress when necessary a certain proportion of everything produced in the country." The railroads, thought Lee, should be devoted exclusively to military transportation, "even should it be found necessary to suspend all private travel for business or pleasure upon them for the present." On the other side, Vice President Stephens deprecated everyone such as Davis and Lee who, he insisted, would subordinate individual liberties and all else to winning the war and independence. In a speech delivered during the spring of 1864, Stephens summoned memories of Patrick Henry in urging the Confederate people never to view liberty as "subordinate to independence." The call for "independence first and liberty second," he averred, was nothing but a "fatal delusion." Only by maintaining liberty would Confederate independence mean anything—the two were "co-ordinate, co-existent, co-equal . . . and forever inseparable."

III. TWO AMERICAN NATIONS IN A TRANSATLANTIC WORLD

Leaders in Washington and Richmond closely monitored European reaction to the war. Because all Americans understood that French support had been crucial to colonial victory during the Revolution, the prospect of European intervention shaped diplomatic endeavors that centered on the question of whether the Europeans, and most particularly the British and the French, would extend formal recognition to the Confederate nation. For their part, European leaders considered the conflict an unnecessary and uncivilized bloodbath that exposed the weakness of American democracy and threatened transatlantic economic stability. Many assumed the Lincoln government could not force the Confederate states, with millions of residents and an economy that ranked among the largest in the western world, back into a Union so fragile it had collapsed after a divisive presidential election. Readily accepting the reality of a Confederate nation, many Europeans imagined a postwar North America in which one sprawling democratic republic had been replaced by two weaker ones.

The Lincoln administration adamantly denied the existence of Confederate nationhood and put Europeans on notice regarding recognition. Secretary of State Seward raised key points in a dispatch to Charles Francis Adams, the U.S. ambassador to Great Britain, in June 1861. The Confederacy was not "*de facto* a self-sustaining power," he wrote, and thus did not deserve to be considered a nation. "British recognition," he added forcefully, "would be British intervention to create within our own territory a hostile state by overthrowing this Republic itself." The United States might have to go to war, he concluded, with any European powers that "fraternize with our domestic enemy."

During the first year of the conflict, Confederates provided growing evidence that they had become, in Seward's language, a "self-sustaining power." In his message to Congress on November 18, 1861, Jefferson Davis mentioned First Bull Run and other military successes, concluding that the enemy's effort to restore the old Union "by arms becomes daily more and more palpably impossible." Moreover, remarked Davis, the Confederate citizenry believed that living in the same country with Yankees was unthinkable: "[T]he separation is final and for the independence we have asserted we will accept no alternative." Having foreclosed the option of reunion and demonstrated self-sufficiency, Davis continued with an eye toward Europe, noting that Confederates "asked for a recognized place in the great family of nations." Victories at the Seven Days and Second Bull Run buttressed the idea of a Confederate nation among many British observers. At Newcastle on October 7, 1862, Chancellor of the Exchequer William E. Gladstone famously observed, "We may have our own opinions about slavery, we may be for or against the South; but there is no doubt that Jefferson Davis and other leaders of the South have made an army; they are making, it appears, a navy; and they have made more than either—they have made a nation."

The ability to envision a Confederate nation never translated into formal recognition. European powers issued proclamations of neutrality in the first months of the war (Great Britain on May 13), which, under international law, permitted the Confederacy to contract for foreign loans, purchase supplies from neutral nations, and commission privateers and otherwise exercise belligerent rights at sea. But these proclamations also officially accepted the U.S. blockade of the Confederacy, even though a legal blockade ostensibly had to be effective (a condition the Union blockading squadrons, even at their peak strength in 1865, never fully satisfied). In August and September 1862, impressed with Lee's victories and horrified by the war's continuing carnage, Lord Palmerston, the British prime minister, and Lord Russell, the foreign secretary, agreed that with one more Confederate success Britain and France should "recommend an arrangement upon the basis of separation." If mediation failed, they agreed, "we ought ourselves to recognize the Southern States as an independent State." News of Lee's retreat from Maryland caused them to hold off on proposing mediation—though the topic continued to generate discussion during the succeeding months.

The United States weathered several diplomatic crises with Great Britain and France. In November 1861, Captain Charles Wilkes and the USS *San Jacinto* stopped the British vessel *Trent* 240 miles east of Havana, Cuba, and removed James Mason and John Slidell, Confederate diplomats bound for London and Paris respectively. Outraged at this clear violation of their neutrality, the British deployed naval strength and several thousand troops to North America. Only an apology and the release of Mason and Slidell eased tensions by January 1862. A second confrontation arose in 1863 when the United States learned that two ironclad warships were being built for the Confederate navy at the Laird shipyards near Liverpool (the same company had constructed the Confederate commerce raider *Alabama* in 1862). Despite a series of protests from Ambassador Adams, the British government waited until the last moment, in early September, to seize the vessels and lower tensions.

Napoleon III of France took advantage of U.S. preoccupation with the Civil War to set up a puppet regime in Mexico. This direct challenge to the Monroe Doctrine involved the overthrow of Benito Juarez's Mexican government and installation of Ferdinand Maximilian, younger brother of Austrian emperor Franz Josef, as Maximilian I of Mexico. The Confederacy offered to recognize the regime in Mexico in return for French recognition, but Napoleon III, though openly sympathetic to the Confederacy and eager to join Britain in negotiating an end to the American war, declined to act unilaterally. He came closest to intervention in early 1863, when he thought it might block a Union invasion of Mexico and protect his imperial interests. Just after Appomattox, the United States conveyed an unmistakable message to the French by sending 50,000 veteran troops near the Mexican border. Napoleon III realized that the United States, whose armies numbered a million men at that point, could crush French forces in Mexico, abandoned his expansionist plans for Mexico, and began a phased withdrawal.

In the end, European policies regarding the United States and the Confederacy turned on self-interest. It was not a matter of Europe's refusing to consider the Confederacy a potentially viable nation. In the summer of 1862, Napoleon III told Confederate diplomat John Slidell that U.S. military forces likely would fail to restore the Union. The emperor expressed admiration for the Confederacy's efforts to establish national sovereignty, but, when Slidell argued for French recognition, he replied: "The policy of nations is controlled by their interest and not by their sentiments, or ought to be so." Acceptance of the blockade and other policies essentially framed the conflict as a struggle between opposing republics. Antislavery sentiment in both Great Britain and France seemingly tipped the balance in favor of the United States, but emancipation, though often described as the crucial factor, by itself did not prove decisive. Similarly, southern cotton, which had fed Britain's critical textile industry for many years before the war, proved not to be indispensable when the English developed alternate sources in Egypt and India. "King Cotton," as antebellum southerners had labeled it, thus failed to prod London into active support of the Confederacy. Final decisions regarding formal recognition hinged on the fact that nothing the Rebels could offer overcame fears in London and Paris of possible war with the United States. The strength of the United States, formidable both economically and militarily, could be turned against any nation that actively intervened to assist the Confederacy.

So Confederates were left on their own, dependent on armies to win enough victories to depress morale behind the lines in the United States and force Lincoln's government to concede southern independence. They were in the ironic position of needing European help but having to prove they could succeed without it before London and Paris would extend recognition. Robert E. Lee had predicted such an outcome during the *Trent* imbroglio in December 1861. Responding to a letter from his oldest son, who expressed hope that anger over the *Trent* might lead Britain to declare war on the United States, Lee advised: "We must make up our minds to fight our battles & win our independence alone. No one will help us."

Whatever the ebb and flow of diplomatic negotiations, Confederates did not need European affirmation to think of themselves as citizens of a nation. For them and their counterparts in the United States, the great North American war promised to shape two national destinies. A pair of officers manifested common aspirations for their respective countries. "I am deeply impressed with the vast importance of success in this campaign," wrote Lieutenant Colonel Walter H. Taylor from Lee's headquarters on May 1, 1864. "If Grant's army is demolished, I don't think there is a doubt but that peace will be declared before the end of the year. . . . Oh, how joyful to both nations will be the tidings of Peace!" Five days earlier, Elisha Hunt Rhodes of the 2nd Rhode Island Infantry had expressed his determination to see the war through to Union victory. "I hope Gen. Grant will be as successful in the East as in the West," he wrote, adding that some officers whose enlistments were drawing to a close "are already talking of home, but as I am in for the war I am not interested. I want to see the end of the war as I saw the beginning." Both men would see the end of the war, though only one would emerge with his nation intact.

Plate 12. "Our Women and the War." This double-page illustration from the autumn of 1862 paid tribute to women who supported the Union war effort through nursing, sewing uniforms, and working with soldiers in the field.

CHAPTER 8

WOMEN AND THE WAR

WITH IMPORTANT EXCEPTIONS, most women stayed at home during the Civil War. Their encouragement of their male relations to enlist, and then to stay in the army and fight, was critical to the war effort, as was their willingness to assume the work burdens of their absent husbands or fathers and brothers on countless farms and plantations, and in businesses, across the country. In addition, thousands of women stepped outside of domestic boundaries, finding employment as nurses, factory workers, teachers, and government clerks. Their initial entrance into the public arena caused controversy, but wartime necessity diminished concerns regarding the dangers of "unladylike" behavior.

While southern women shared many similarities of wartime life with their northern sisters, the differences were more striking. Confederate women, white and black, coped with invasion, occupation, and destruction on a scale not experienced by Union women. By 1865, women's lives were changed in profound ways not anticipated or dreamed of in 1861.

I. WOMEN AT THE HOME FRONT

The lives of most women in the nineteenth century took place within a domestic setting. Marriage and family life represented the stability anchoring a dynamic and fluid society. Moreover, law, custom, and religion protected and nourished the institution of marriage. The home, represented as a "haven in a heartless world," was summed up perfectly in a favorite melody of the era, "Home Sweet Home": "Mid pleasure and Palaces though we may roam; Be it ever so humble there's no place like home!" Although the family was not strictly "political," it was considered the main foundation for sustaining the unique American democratic republic. It makes sense that the war had a huge impact on those women who stayed at home, as well as on the soldiers who emerged from that home.

From this ideal of middle-class domesticity, men were expected to be courageous on the battlefield and women courageous on the home front. The home was positively portrayed in sentimental songs, books, magazines, and newspapers of the era. Men missed the warmth and security of family when they were mustered into service. Mothers, daughters, lovers, and sisters embodied the home for which the soldiers fought.

The patriotic fervor that infused the early months of the Civil War stirred women as well as men to action. "We never knew before how much we loved our country," an eighteen-year-old northern girl declared. "To think that we suffer and fear all this for her! The Stars and Stripes will always be infinitely dear to us." White women across the South, married and single, offered up their vigorous support for secession. A young South Carolinian welcomed the breakup of the Union, rejoicing that it severed "the hated chain which linked us with Black Republicans and Abolitionists."

Enthusiastic support sometimes wavered when the costs of the conflict became apparent to people on the home front following the ups and downs of the respective armies. Many northern women bitterly opposed their sons' or husbands' re-enlistment. Letters from desperate wives and mothers begged Confederate menfolk to come home to save their families from starvation and poverty. Women's letters written early, middle, or late had a direct impact on the morale of soldiers. Indeed, when women North or South withdrew their support of the war, when they wrote sad and frightened and angry letters to their men, letters of protest against the sacrifice of the war, desertion rates rose notably. Alternatively, when times got tough for the Union cause, anti-slavery northern women founded the Woman's Loyal National League to support the Republican Party's policy of emancipation. Philadelphia-based Anna Dickinson, a young and passionate speaker for abolitionism, made a sensational appearance before Congress in 1864, defending President Lincoln's handling of the war. Female writers, poets, social reformers, and orators made their pro-Union voices heard across the United States in journals, books, and speeches delivered in crowded auditoriums.

Most of all, women feared their menfolk would be added to the casualty lists. Deeply held religious and cultural traditions mandated what can be summed up by the phrase "a good death"—traditions violated when soldiers who died in military service were often buried in hastily dug graves in local cemeteries or near battlefields. In July 1862, the United States authorized a permanent national cemetery system for soldiers, but the act did not comfort the majority of mothers and fathers who could not afford to bring their sons' bodies back home. Thousands of Confederate soldiers were buried anonymously in huge cemeteries outside the major hospitals in Virginia, Tennessee, Mississippi, and Louisiana. Mothers and wives were especially vulnerable, emotionally and economically, to the loss of sons and husbands. People on both sides turned to popular songs such as "The Vacant Chair," "Just Before the Battle, Mother," and "Somebody's Darling" to help ease their sorrow. Many also found solace in their faith's creed, summed up in the phrase "awaiting the heavenly country." Henry Wadsworth Longfellow's "Killed at the Ford," a poem aimed at a northern audience, illuminated the sad stories of both sides: "That fatal bullet went speeding forth, / Till it reached a town in the distant North, / Till it reached a house in a sunny street, / Till it reached a heart that ceased to beat, / Without a murmur, without a cry; / And a bell was tolled in that far-off town, / For one who had passed from cross to crown, / And the neighbors wondered that she should die."

II. LADIES' AID ASSOCIATIONS

In 1861, a teenaged girl living in Boston wondered aloud how she and her friends could possibly contribute to the war effort in a way that echoed men's sacrifices. She answered her own question: "We can work though if we can't enlist, and we do. It is very pleasant to see how well the girls and women do work everywhere, sewing meetings, sanitary hospitals and all." An impressive number of women volunteered to help the war effort. Without these activities supporting their governments, it is doubtful that the war would have commanded the support of the people for as long as it did. Ladies' Aid Societies flourished in tiny rural villages, small towns, and middle-sized to large cities in the United States and the Confederacy. Ladies' Aid Societies included members from the upper to middle class of all ages and totaled an estimated 20,000 in the North. There are no precise numbers for the southern societies, but records show they were strong in every state. The societies turned women's private domestic duties into public, politicized roles. The grassroots groups originated in response to shocking accounts of government incompetence in providing basic medical care, clothing, food, and supplies for the volunteers. Women responded with a patriotic passion, and Ladies' Aid Societies from Springfield, Illinois, to Philadelphia, and from New Orleans to Atlanta, donated clothing, gloves, blankets, bandages, and food for their soldiers.

Northern Ladies' Aid Societies divided into local and regional branches led by an umbrella organization named the Women's Central Relief Committee. The Women's Central, as it came to be called, created a very efficient system for transporting and distributing tons of supplies to soldiers. The Women's Central, and the Ladies' Aid Societies it represented, became a part of a larger national organization called the U.S. Sanitary Commission. A quasi-government agency headed by prominent men, the Sanitary Commission worked very closely with the Lincoln administration to bring reform to the Union's medical and supply delivery system. Confederate relief organizations remained local and decentralized, and a substantial number of northern women preferred to donate their time to the United States Christian Commission's (or their own church's) cause of providing soldiers with spiritual guidance in the form of free Bibles, religious tracts, and the efforts of ministers, along with medical and food aid.

Northern towns and cities staged "Sanitary Fairs" to support the goals of the Ladies' Aid Societies. Citizens attended the fairs in great numbers, contributing food, clothing, and toys for sale. The festivities of the multiday fairs included concerts by church groups and schoolchildren, as well as splendid displays of historical artifacts and relics from the American Revolution and the present "Rebellion." Many Sanitary Fairs featured appearances by famous generals and politicians, and by 1865 the events had raised more than $4 million for the Union war effort. From their new public platform, women helped plan and direct numerous fund-raising efforts that lifted morale and provided money for the armies. Sanitary Fairs in Chicago, New York, Boston, and Philadelphia highlighted the successes of female volunteerism for the Union cause. Southern women also held fund-raising events, but they never reached the number or scope of those in the United States.

III. FEMALE NURSES

Most paid nurses before the Civil War were male, a phenomenon that continued during a war that nonetheless laid the foundation for a woman-dominated nursing profession in postwar America. Two leaders of the Women's Central of New York, Dr. Elizabeth Blackwell, the first woman to receive her medical degree in the United States, and Louisa Lee Schuyler, daughter of a prominent New York family, headed efforts to identify the army's nursing needs. Their reports assisted in creating a bureau for examining and registering nurses and coordinating medical relief for the 15,000-20,000 women who served the Union as nurses. In 1861, the U.S. government appointed Dorothea Dix, a well-known mental health reformer, to create and run a federal nursing program. Dix set strict qualifications for becoming a nurse, including an age requirement that the women be over thirty, and by the end of her tenure in 1863 successfully established the program. Others such as New Jersey's Cornelia Hancock and Massachusetts-born Clara Barton saw a great need for volunteer nursing care and deliberately avoided bureaucratic red tape. Energetic and ambitious, Barton assembled her own team and with privately raised money traveled to many battlefields, including Antietam and Fredericksburg, bringing desperately needed relief.

Other women also rose to the challenge. A nurse and field agent for the Western United States Sanitary Commission, Mary Ann Bickerdyke worked tirelessly among the hospitals in Illinois, Mississippi, and Tennessee, raising health and sanitary standards for soldiers of the western armies. Often crossing swords with the male medical establishment, "Mother Bickerdyke" earned the respect and appreciation of legions of grateful soldiers who benefited from her hard work. Dr.

Mary Edwards Walker volunteered her services as a contract surgeon to the U.S. Army but was refused because of her gender. While working as a nurse, Walker kept petitioning until her persistence paid off with an appointment as the first female surgeon in 1863. Later, Walker was awarded a Medal of Honor for her contributions in the Civil War. The majority of black women working in Union hospitals were cooks and laundresses, but they also served as nurses and matrons (senior nurses responsible for nurses and domestic staff). A freed slave, Susie King Taylor, worked as a nurse for the 33rd USCT Regiment in North Carolina. Married to a soldier in the regiment, Taylor expanded her duties from nursing to teaching the men to read and write.

Confederate states sponsored organizations to supplement the armies' medical delivery system, such as the Georgia Relief Hospital Association. As in the North, many notable female leaders emerged to organize desperately needed medical services. From Alabama, Kate Cumming volunteered along with forty other women to go to Corinth, Mississippi, to tend to the casualties of the bloody battle of Shiloh in 1862. Her diary, published after the war, provides the most detailed and insightful record of Confederate nursing. Responding to the inadequate medical care of the early battle casualties, the Richmond government began hiring female nurses in 1862. Wealthy Savannah socialite Phoebe Yates Levy Pember was the matron of Chimborazo Hospital in Richmond, the Confederacy's largest medical facility. Enslaved women, often the personal servants of white volunteer nurses, and poor whites performed the most menial tasks in the southern hospitals.

In all, thousands of women, including Catholic nuns, performed nursing duties during the Civil War. Typical female nurses on both sides were white, middle class, and single or widowed. Northern nurses earned $12 a month, their southern counterparts as much as $40 a month, although rampant inflation soon made their larger salaries a pittance. Other northern hospital workers, such as cooks and laundresses, received $6 to $10 a month. A large number of women also served as unofficial volunteers, simply leaving their homes for the battlefront upon hearing of a husband's or son's injury. Many Confederate women, and a smaller number of Union women, had little choice but to demonstrate their nursing skills because the battlefield and the home front collided so often. Houses, churches, barns, and city halls were commandeered by military authorities for use as hospitals in places such as Winchester, Virginia, Atlanta, Vicksburg, and Gettysburg.

What was life like for the majority of female nurses? They faced many obstacles, performing under new and difficult conditions whether they toiled in field hospitals, Union army naval transports, or in large urban hospitals. Their tasks were largely custodial and involved taking care of hospital wards, cleaning wounds, and distributing medicine and food. Louisa May Alcott, later the author of *Little Women*, volunteered as a nurse for the Union Hospital in Georgetown, D.C. She recorded her tasks on a typical day in January 1863: "Till noon I trot . . . giving out rations, cutting up food for helpless 'boys,' washing faces . . . dusting tables, sewing bandages . . . rushing up and down after pillows, bed, linen, sponges, books, and directions." Alcott lasted only six weeks before contracting a serious case of typhoid fever. Like other nurses, Alcott often spent her evenings helping wounded or dying soldiers compose letters to anxious families. Nurses generally eased soldiers' pain by praying with them, perhaps administering the last rites, and witnessing agonizing deaths.

Women faced resistance, especially at first, from their families for exposing themselves to potentially "immodest" situations with male patients. A young Alabama woman asked shyly whether young ladies would be required to bandage abdominal injuries or to be present at amputations. The answer was yes. Kate Cumming, who served as a matron in a Georgia hospital, exhorted the available women of the Confederacy to do their duty "to relieve suffering" as only they knew how to do. After all, she reasoned, women's caregiving role in their families prepared them for such work. Their domestic skills, along with special training, would blunt male criticism of potentially unacceptable behavior. The most powerful argument in favor of female nurses came from the universally embraced notion that women added a needed humanitarian element—sympathy, kindness, spiritual guidance, and maternal love—to caring for both nations' soldiers. In 1892, the U.S. government declared Union female nurses true veterans of the war and rewarded their service with a modest monthly pension.

IV. FACTORY WORKERS, PROSTITUTES, SPIES, AND SOLDIERS

The wartime expansion of the economy combined with the absence of men brought women of all income levels and classes into the workforce and into the public sphere. Northern women increased their already established presence as teachers, textile workers, and shoe factory workers by 100,000. The enlargement of the federal government created a need for "government girls" in Washington and in Richmond. Working as clerks for the Patent Office, the Departments of War and Treasury, and the Post Office, young unmarried or widowed women crossed the boundaries of previous "ladylike" actions and set the stage for a postwar advancement into white-collar positions.

A significant number of working-class women in the United States and the Confederacy filled factory jobs producing ammunition, clothes, and other military-related products. By 1864, more than 4,000 southern women toiled as seamstresses making clothes for soldiers. Replacing men at half the salary, women worked at ordnance factories and arsenals producing minié balls, paper cartridges, percussion caps, and artillery fuses and shells. Dozens died in explosions caused by unsafe working conditions—more than forty in a single accident at the Brown's Island ordnance facility in Richmond in March 1863. In the United States, women participated in strikes for higher wages, and female employees on both sides consistently petitioned for improved safety standards. Although most strikes during the Civil War were unsuccessful, these and other actions demonstrated women's collective awareness of their rights as citizens to be respected. They, too, were contributing to the nation's survival.

Northern women also participated in overtly anti-government actions. As hatred of Lincoln's emancipation policy swept the heavily Democratic areas of Indiana, Illinois, and Ohio in late 1862, some women with Copperhead sympathies aided a growing network of opposition to the "Republican War." Irish immigrant women joined in the New York City Draft Riots over three violent days in July 1863, protesting both their husbands' draft into military service and Lincoln's emancipation policy. Police arrested several hundred women who were later convicted and jailed. North and South, working-class women scrambled to make ends meet in more traditional ways, such as taking in boarders, doing piecework sewing at home, earning pennies in a local laundry, and cleaning homes.

Less well-known were the thousands of lower-class women working as prostitutes. They flocked to cities such as Washington, D.C., and Richmond, as well as to smaller military depots such as Keokuk, Iowa, and Sewanee, Tennessee. A largely female profession, prostitution can be defined as women who engaged in sexual intercourse for money. Between 1861 and 1865, prostitution increased, flourishing wherever soldiers congregated. Sexually transmitted diseases posed a major risk for prostitutes and their soldier-clients, particularly given the fact that some, such as syphilis, could be fatal. One private described Nashville's red light district: "[T]here was an old saying that no man could be a soldier unless he had gone through Smokey Row. They said Smokey Row killed more soldiers than the war." A move to decriminalize prostitution in Memphis and Nashville gained traction by placing the sex trade under military licensing to control disease. A wave of negative public reaction killed the short-lived experiment.

Hundreds of women on both sides served as spies, couriers, guides, and smugglers. The exact number cannot be calculated because of the necessity for secrecy, but doubtless more worked for the Confederacy than for the Union. Three female spies achieved considerable notoriety during and after the war: Rose O'Neal Greenhow, a Washington society hostess whose warnings to Confederate officers prior to First Bull Run contributed to southern victory; Belle Boyd, who while still a teenager aided Stonewall Jackson's Shenandoah Valley campaign in 1862; and Sarah Edmonds Edwards, who provided valuable service to the Union. The importance of famous female spies paled in comparison to the activities of numerous unidentified southern white women, who were rarely searched, as they moved between battlefield and home front transporting valuable supplies—including medicine, gold, guns, and food—underneath their voluminous hoopskirts. A few female spies were caught and punished—Boyd and Greenhow served jail terms—but most suffered little more than a stern warning from Federal authorities.

Union forces received indispensable help from black women wherever they went in the Confederacy. One of the most famous was Harriet Tubman, a former slave called the Moses of her people for spiriting three hundred slaves from Maryland to Philadelphia. Tubman served as wartime spy for Federal officers in the Sea Islands off the coast of Georgia and South Carolina. White women with Union sympathies were also active. Alvira Smith, an Alabama Unionist, worked behind the lines as a scout and courier, and northern-born Elizabeth Van Lew, a wealthy resident of Richmond, developed an elaborate network to inform Union military forces about the number, conditions, and movements of Confederate troops. So valuable was Van Lew's contribution that U. S. Grant singled her out for warm praise.

None of the many thousands of women who stepped outside of traditional domestic boundaries transgressed gender norms more profoundly than the small group who enlisted as soldiers in the Union and Confederate armies. Estimated to number at least 400-500 (the precise total can never be known), the majority were the wives, lovers, or sisters of male soldiers. Their identities usually were discovered fairly swiftly, leading to immediate removal from the field because only men could enlist or be drafted into Union or Confederate military forces. Some were bold adventurers, such as Sarah Emma Edmonds, also a nurse and spy, who claimed to have served as a private under the name Franklin Thompson in a Michigan regiment in the Army of the Potomac. Mrs. S. M. Blalock volunteered as Samuel Blalock and fought alongside her husband in the Rebel forces. Others successfully hid their gender for a while but were exposed through pregnancy, injury or death. Clara Barton tended to a wounded woman in blue on the battlefield of Antietam; a dead female Confederate was discovered at Gettysburg after Pickett's Charge; and yet another woman soldier was injured at the battle of Chattanooga, captured by the Confederates, and later returned by them to the United States.

A number of women combatants escaped notice altogether during the war, only to have their secret uncovered decades later. Private Albert D. J. Cashier—an Irish immigrant named Jennie Irene Hodgers—fell into this category. Hodgers enlisted and served for three years in the 95th Illinois Infantry, fighting at Vicksburg. Returning to Illinois after the war, she took up farming, living as a man until an injury exposed her true sex in 1911. A former comrade in the 95th asked to comment on the surprising news described the five-foot-tall Hodgers/Cashier as a "brave little soldier." The most famous "recovered" female soldier is Sarah Rosetta Wakeman, who served as Private Lyons Wakeman in Company G of the 153rd New York Infantry and whose letters came to light in the 1990s.

Although other women soldiers left little or no record explaining their motivations for enlisting or descriptions of their experiences in camp and battle, surviving evidence allows a few generalizations. Women who disguised themselves as men to fight in the war—cutting their hair short, wearing pants, binding their chests, changing their names—shared many characteristics with their male comrades. They were young, single, and largely from rural families. They enlisted for many reasons: patriotism, a desire to travel, a romantic notion of combat, or the prospect of bounties and monthly pay. Female soldiers probably resented gender restrictions and longed for the kind of independence that could only be achieved through changing their sexual identities. Thus the opportunity for escape presented by the war's chaos and excitement was too good to pass up.

The ones who escaped detection by the authorities shared every challenge of soldierhood. They learned how to fire a rifle and endured the many discomforts of camp life, patiently joining in the endless marches, risking disease and injury, and most of all confronting the hard reality of battle. "I don't know how long before I shall have to go into the field of battle," wrote Wakeman to her parents shortly before her death in the 1864 Red River campaign. "For my part I don't care. I don't feel afraid to go," she said, adding, "I don't believe there are any Rebel's bullets made for me yet."

The relaxed standards of the volunteer army made it easier to avoid discovery at every stage of service. Physical exams were superficial, the training period short, and living outdoors much of the time offered privacy for intimate functions. At least a few known cases suggest the complicity of male peers in keeping the women's secret. Most important, common social beliefs blinded most men from "seeing" a female comrade until presented with strong evidence. Women wore skirts, had long hair, acted feminine, and were not capable physically or mentally of handling warfare. Then too slight, short, beardless, high-pitched-voice teenaged boys were common enough in both armies, making genital scrutiny as unnecessary as it was unlikely.

Women fought as combatants in a number of Civil War battles and skirmishes. Like their male counterparts, they often performed bravely under fire, and some sacrificed their lives for their country. They were neither lauded openly for their service nor rewarded afterward with a veteran's pension, unless they kept their male identity. After the war, a handful of women published accounts of their military experiences. The majority simply blended back into mainstream society, their anonymity frustratingly secure from the scrutiny of historians.

V. REFUGEES, "SHE-DEVILS," PLANTATION MISTRESSES, AND BREAD RIOTERS

Much more than the majority of U.S. citizens, Confederate women on the home front had their world violated by the war's turmoil. The middling to elite white plantation mistresses lived before the war within a firmly fixed, socially conservative society. The South's overwhelmingly rural character also ensured that these women enjoyed a much less public presence than did their northern sisters. White plantation women, however, did receive protection and respect for their status as wives, mothers, and helpmeets. They, in return, cherished and depended on this identity. At first, women gladly sent their sons, husbands, and brothers off to fight. They, too, raised money and established or participated in ladies' aid societies, and a good number served as nurses.

But as the war continued, and with four out of five of their men serving in the military, a new and unfamiliar role was thrust upon them. White women had to run the plantations and the farms, or, if they lived in a city, they had to manage the large houses and the businesses. From 1862 through 1865, northern armies occupied large areas in the Confederacy, with ever-growing parts of Virginia, Tennessee, Louisiana, Mississippi, and Georgia coming under Union military rule. This occupation took effect across the Confederate countryside but also in cities such as New Orleans, Memphis, Nashville, Vicksburg and Natchez, Mississippi, Atlanta, and Columbia, South Carolina. Some had no option but evacuation; others faced a difficult decision: stay and protect their property, or flee to a safe place where the war would not find them.

Under these circumstances, tens of thousands of white women, their children, and elderly relatives became refugees. Historians have estimated the number may have approached 200,000, excluding those who chose to remain and take their chances with the Yankees. Mary Anna Custis Lee (Mrs. Robert E. Lee) was among the first of the coming wave of Confederate refugees when she and her daughters left their home, "Arlington," in Virginia just across the Potomac River from Washington in the spring of 1861. Moving several times during the war, Mrs. Lee fortunately found other residences when her family's safety was threatened. In contrast, an unlucky South Carolina woman declared, "Show me a safe place and I'll go tomorrow, but no such happy valley exists in the Confederacy!"

White women leaving their homes faced the prospect of a hurried, nightmarish journey on overcrowded roads and dirty trains to what they hoped would be a destination free from the long reach of Federal forces. The experience threw together all classes and conditions of women, sparing no one in the process. Refugees from the eastern states often fled to cities, most obviously Richmond but also to Raleigh, North Carolina, and Columbia, South Carolina. Residents of the Deep South found Georgia a refuge in 1862 and 1863, while those living in Louisiana and Tennessee sought out Texas. Although a few found a pleasant welcome with relatives or friends, most at some point experienced hunger, joblessness, poverty, isolation, and disease. The huge wave of refugees strained city and state budgets and often prompted a backlash from the current residents. A disappointed woman who left Louisiana for Texas exclaimed sadly, "It is strange the prejudice that exists all throughout the state against refugees." Both the move and the resettlement proved deeply traumatic for women and children. Among the white Confederate population, refugees probably suffered the most, many never recovering their footing economically, socially, or psychologically in the postwar period.

Those who did stay at home in occupied areas, whether on plan-

Plate 13. Confederate refugees, as presented in this wartime sketch of women and children encamped in woods near Vicksburg, Mississippi, experienced a type of dislocation virtually unknown on the Union home front.

tation or farm or in city, became unwilling captives of enemy troops. Male citizens took loyalty oaths and, because of the expectation of harsh punishment, generally controlled their open hostility toward the occupying troops. Women, on the other hand, felt freer to express their hatred of Yankees. In 1862, the ladies of New Orleans exceeded the limits of Union commander Ben Butler's patience when their defiance toward Union soldiers reached epic proportions. Public taunts and insults, chamber pots emptied on the heads of Federal officers walking on the streets, and flaunting the Confederate battle flag pushed Butler to issue General Order No. 28, commanding the ladies to cease and desist their vicious attacks or "be regarded and held liable to be treated as a woman of the town plying her avocation." "Beast" Butler's threat to punish white women of New Orleans as prostitutes outraged Confederates but had its desired effect of restoring civil order.

This kind of action was not widespread, but the affected Union soldiers began referring to southern women as "she-devils" who did not match up with the "southern belle" image they had carried southward with them. It is important to know, however, that white elite and middle-class southern women felt protected by powerful Christian Victorian gender ideas that distinguished between "good" and "bad" women, allowing them to commit hostile acts that were only rarely punished. White mothers, sisters, and wives were generally respected, even if they were the enemy. While violence against white women by soldiers, including rape, did occur during the Civil War, it was relatively rare. Acting in ways that would have been unthinkable for ladies before the war illuminated the severe and sudden loss of white women's previously protected status.

While death, destruction, poverty, and humiliation increasingly stalked the Confederacy, women still had to manage plantations and farms, often sharing the field labor with their slaves. Plantation mistresses dreaded the responsibility of taking charge of enslaved labor just as the system was crumbling. A despairing mistress wrote of her slaves: "We cannot exert any authority; I beg ours to do what little is done." Many women who lived within reach of the Union army felt betrayed when supposedly devoted house servants deserted. Yet food crops were grown and harvested, cotton picked, property protected, homespun clothing produced, sacrifices made, families raised, and loyalty sustained even in a wildly unpredictable environment. A young woman's letter to her soldier sweetheart described the feeling held by most at home for the troops, who could rely on "loving hearts and busy hands . . . praying and toiling for their preservation and success." Overall, these women demonstrated a fortitude and faithfulness to the Confederate cause that commanded respect during the war and veneration by succeeding generations of white southerners.

From the beginning of the conflict, the rumors—and then reality—of emancipation changed the nature of slavery in the Confederacy, bringing enslaved women freedom and opportunity. Most slaves stayed on the plantations during the war, but in many places the relationship between white and black people reflected a shift in power. Enslaved people's workload increased and their responsibilities grew, but they also became restive, often demanding better treatment from their owners. And for thousands of slave women the war brought freedom *and* opportunity—freedom from their masters and mistresses and freedom to move about freely and worship as they wished; opportunity to protect their children and to reunite with family members. Their freedom was not firmly secured, and it came accompanied by grave dangers and uncertainties. Enslaved and contraband women routinely faced dangers such as vulnerability to rape or beatings from either Confederates or Union soldiers.

By the end of 1864, large numbers of white women abandoned their support of the Confederacy. Too many lives had been lost, too much land and property destroyed, too much sacrifice demanded. They began hiding youngest sons and begging husbands to come home. This sentiment echoed across class lines as the war's hardships multiplied. Yeoman farming families, representing the majority of Confederate people, struggled in the best of years. During the war, as soldiers fought for the nation's survival, women wrestled with expanded responsibility for raising and feeding their typically large families for an indeterminate time. They got by trading for food, selling crops (sometimes impressed by the government), and striving not to lose their land to debt or Union occupation. Increasingly, their men read plaintive letters such as this: "Bill, I don't want to make you desert, but if you don't come home your child is going to starve."

Crowds of angry women asserted their rights as citizens through wartime protests, taking to the streets. Poor women in urban areas suffered the most from the food shortages and the extreme inflation

Plate 14. *Frank Leslie's Illustrated Newspaper* offered this unflattering view of women in Richmond who took to the streets in April 1863 to protest sharp increases in food prices. The caption delivered an anti-Confederate editorial message for readers at the time: "Southern Women Feeling The Effects of Rebellion, And Creating Bread Riots."

that made feeding their families a daily chore. Women mobilized to demand a fair price for flour and other basic necessities in 1863, leading to the famous food riots in Richmond as well as less well-known disturbances in Virginia, Alabama, North Carolina, and elsewhere. These same women also wrote thousands of letters to state governors demanding aid on the basis of their shared sacrifice for the war. Confederate governors such as Joseph E. Brown of Georgia and Zebulon B. Vance of North Carolina responded to the pleas from female citizens. Politicians knew that desperate times required desperate measures, and a rough but effective welfare system eventually diminished the worst of the suffering. The war's end brought a great relief for all women that the killing and destruction had ended. For white women living in the defeated areas, feelings of despair and shock overwhelmed hopes for a peaceful future. For freedwomen, joy at their oppressors' utter defeat contrasted with their former mistresses' desolation. Women of the loyal states shared in the victory celebrations, while mourning the loss of so many young men.

VI. CONCLUSION: A WOMAN'S CIVIL WAR

Women's voluntary participation on the home front showed their desire to sustain their nation's survival even if it meant shouldering huge burdens. More than a few anticipated that their stellar record of sacrifice and volunteerism during the Civil War would assist them in the fight for woman's suffrage and citizenship as Congress debated the Fourteenth and Fifteenth Amendments. This was certainly the case with the well-known feminists Elizabeth Cady Stanton and Susan B. Anthony, whose strenuous wartime efforts in the Women's National Loyal League and other aid societies buoyed their expectation that the government's efforts for emancipation and full citizenship for the freedmen might be extended to women as well. That hope would be deferred for over fifty years. A new woman did, however, emerge from the Civil War. How could it be any other way? Millions of destinies were changed, whether mother, wife, daughter, or sister; whether living on a farm or laboring in the factory; whether serving as a nurse, soldier, secretary, teacher, or spy. Overall, women gained a new confidence in working, speaking, and participating in the public sphere. After the war, it was no accident that women's volunteer groups, whether conservative or liberal, whether in charity, temperance, moral reform, home mission societies, education, or political reform had their biggest impact ever on American society and culture. When war came, "a woman's courage" earned them a vital part in the epic story of the American Civil War.

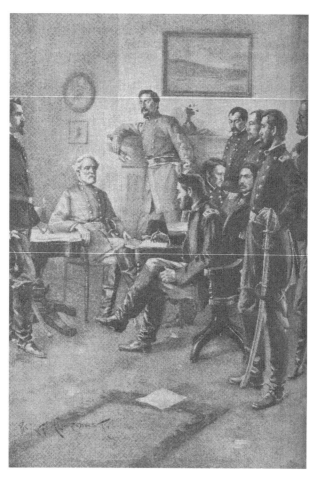

Plate 15. "The Surrender at Appomattox." For most observers in the United States, the Confederacy, and abroad, R. E. Lee's capitulation to U. S. Grant marked the effective end of the war.

CHAPTER 9

PRESSING THROUGH TO UNION VICTORY: THE SPRING OF 1864 TO THE SPRING OF 1865

ULYSSES S. GRANT'S ascension to general in chief of U.S. armies in March 1864 placed at the helm the kind of officer Abraham Lincoln had sought for three years. The two men, president and general, ultimately most responsible for Union victory agreed on the need to apply the nation's formidable human and material resources relentlessly. Yet Rebel resistance continued for another fourteen months, a period of dramatic changes in military momentum that witnessed the nadir of Union civilian morale, the possibility of a Democratic resurgence that would have undermined emancipation, and, finally, the war's most compelling example of how the battlefield's verdict dictated political outcomes. People in both nations focused on the northern elections of 1864, with Confederates, who contended with growing economic and social dislocation, pinning hopes on the possibility of a Democratic victory that might presage peace negotiations. A bookseller in Atlanta expressed a common sentiment on July 3, 1864, when he tied the operations of invading Federal forces to Democratic prospects in the November elections: "The Democratic Convention that was to have met tomorrow at Chicago has been postponed until August 29th probably to see the result of the present campaigns in Virg[inia] and Georgia. It is hoped that if these great efforts prove abortive that a *peace* candidate will be nominated by that assembly." Two months later, after Atlanta had fallen to Sherman, a bureaucrat in Washington took up the same subject from a different vantage point. Sherman's success, he wrote sarcastically, "will be a bitter pill to the *patriotic* Democrats . . . . Now let us have Mobile, Petersburg & Richmond, Charleston and Wilmington, and *the jig is up* with Treason in the South." Even after Republican success in the elections, fighting dragged on for almost half a year, ending in April and May with Confederate surrenders, Lincoln's assassination, and the imprisonment of Jefferson Davis.

I. GRANT'S GRAND PLAN: MAY–JULY 1864

The new general in chief called for five simultaneous advances in three theaters. Nathaniel P. Banks would take 30,000 men from Louisiana into the Alabama heartland, then turn east toward Georgia. William Tecumseh Sherman, with a force of more than 100,000 opposite Joseph E. Johnston's 65,000-man Army of Tennessee, would strike southward from Chattanooga to Atlanta, after which he would move farther into the interior of Georgia. In Virginia, three armies confronted the Rebels: Meade's Army of the Potomac, numbering 120,000 and accompanied by Grant, faced Lee's 64,000 along the Rappahannock River frontier; Benjamin F. Butler's Army of the James, 30,000 strong, would advance up the James River against Richmond; and General Franz Sigel would lead a small force into the Shenandoah Valley to deprive the Confederacy of that region's logistical bounty. "The armies were now all ready to move for the accomplishment of a single object," Grant later explained in his memoirs: " . . . Lee, with the capital of the Confederacy, was the main end to which all were working."

As with many plans, Grant's quickly ran into problems. Banks got bogged down in an operation along Louisiana's Red River and never mounted a campaign into Alabama. Sigel and Butler similarly failed in Virginia, leaving just Grant and Sherman to achieve success. By the middle of May, people in both the United States and the Confederacy devoted most of their attention to Richmond and Atlanta, the former anticipating word of the cities' capture and the latter clinging to the hope that both would hold out until after the fall elections.

Between the first week of May and mid-June, Grant and Lee traded powerful blows in what came to be called the Overland campaign. Unlike previous military operations, when one army would retreat after an engagement and it might be weeks or even months before the next clash, the Overland campaign subjected soldiers to a form of continuous combat that featured massive battles separated by brief interludes of skirmishing. On May 5-6, the battle of the Wilderness cost Federals 18,000 and Confederates 12,000 casualties, after which the contestants marched southward for a single day before commencing the battle of Spotsylvania, which between May 8 and 21 exacted a toll of another 18,000 U.S. and 12,000 Confederate soldiers killed, wounded, or missing. Subsequent fighting at the North Anna River (May 23-26), Cold Harbor (heaviest fighting on June 1-3), and outside Petersburg (June 15-18), together with smaller actions, pushed losses during the six weeks to approximately 60,000 for Grant and more than 35,000 for Lee. Even veterans of sanguinary combat at places such as Antietam or Gettysburg found the new pattern of action deeply disturbing. Early in June, for example, a staff officer quoted General Gouverneur K. Warren, head of the Fifth Corps in the Army of the Potomac, who lamented, "For thirty days now, it has been one funeral procession, past me; and it is too much! . . . The men need some rest."

The Overland campaign taught Grant and Lee about the other's tenacity and skill—though neither ever fully acknowledged that fact. By the time they reached Petersburg, their battered armies scarcely resembled the ones that fought in the Wilderness during the first week of May. The second largest city in Virginia, Petersburg held the key to control of Richmond—a series of roads and railroads that kept Lee's army supplied—and became the focal point of operations in the Eastern Theater. On June 19, Grant inaugurated the siege of Petersburg, ushering in a more static form of warfare that would drag on for many months.

Operations in Georgia also garnered wide attention between May and July. Neither the mercurial Sherman nor Johnston relished the prospect of large battles, and their campaign played out in a series of Federal maneuvers that forced the Confederates to abandon one defensive line after another. Clashes at Resaca (May 13-15), New Hope Church (May 25-26), and Kennesaw Mountain (June 27), among others, fell far short of the Overland campaign's bloody benchmark, as Johnston skillfully responded to Sherman's flanking movements. But the overall thrust of the campaign favored the Federals, and Johnston, widely criticized in the Confederacy for giving up too much ground at too little cost (a South Carolina woman later described him as an "arch-retreater"), allowed Sherman to reach the outskirts of Atlanta by mid-July. On the seventeenth, Jefferson Davis, who knew how devastating the loss of the city would be strategically and to Confederate civilian morale, replaced Johnston with General John Bell Hood. Sherman had little knowledge of Hood, but one of his subordinates remarked that the new Rebel chief was "bold even to rashness, and courageous in the extreme." From this, remarked Sherman drolly, "I inferred that the change of commanders meant 'fight.'"

Hood understood why he had been placed in charge and immediately took the offensive in the battles of Peachtree Creek (July 20), Atlanta (July 22), and Ezra Church (July 28). His troops suffered more

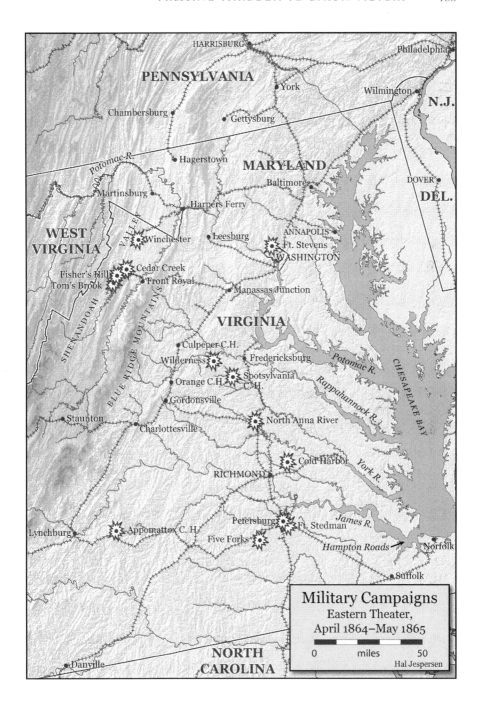

Military Campaigns
Eastern Theater,
April 1864–May 1865

0   miles   50

Hal Jespersen

than 11,000 casualties, Sherman's about half as many, and the armies remained in a stalemate at Atlanta. "I am glad when the enemy attacks," Sherman wrote his wife, "for the advantage then is with us." Although Sherman might be content with the progress of his operations, perceptions behind the lines in the United States took on a very different cast. For many civilians, the most obvious outcome of ten weeks' campaigning in Georgia was continuing Confederate possession of Atlanta.

II. THE DARKEST SUMMER FOR THE UNION CAUSE

Civilian morale in the summer of 1864 presents a fascinating picture. Most Confederates maintained an edgy optimism despite growing material privation in much of their nation attributable to inflation, disruption of the railroad network due to military operations, and the Union naval blockade. Most of Tennessee, the lower Mississippi River valley, parts of Arkansas, and areas along the Atlantic coast effectively had passed under Union control. Guerrilla activity escalated in various areas, and pockets of virulent opposition to conscription plagued Confederate authorities in the uplands of several states. The divide between ardent state rights advocates and those willing to accept greater central authority deepened, with rhetorical fusillades emanating from both camps. From a distance of a century and half, it seems that Confederates, in the face of all these developments, should have been utterly demoralized—yet such was not the case.

Hope for success rested largely on Lee and the Army of Northern Virginia. Neither the defeat at Gettysburg nor the awful losses of the Overland campaign seemed to affect belief in Lee. In early June, the *Richmond Daily Dispatch*—a pro–Davis administration newspaper—observed, "The confidence in Lee and his army is not confined to the ranks of that army and to our fellow citizens. It is as extensive as the Confederacy itself. It pervades every neighborhood and every family

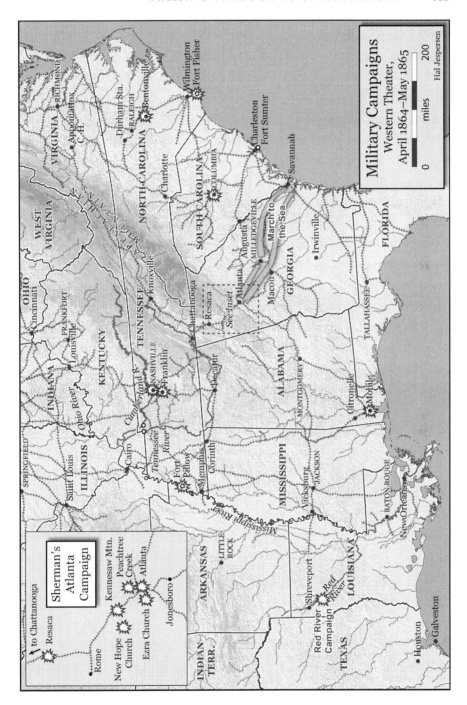

Military Campaigns
Western Theater,
April 1864–May 1865

Hal Jespersen

0   miles   200

Sherman's Atlanta Campaign

circle." Just before the beginning of the siege of Petersburg, Charleston's *Mercury*, an anti–Davis administration sheet, remarked that Grant's "headstrong and persistent and remorseless courage has not achieved the fall of Richmond," prophesying that failure against Lee would defeat Lincoln and the Republicans in November.

Many in the United States had reached a comparable conclusion. Extremely high expectations when Grant took the reins of overall command fell away during May and June. News of unimaginable casualties in Virginia, profound disappointment that neither Richmond nor Atlanta had fallen, and increasing fears that Lee might prove more than a match for Grant raised questions regarding whether it was worth the cost of forcing the Rebels to rejoin the Union. Peace Democrats seized on news from the military fronts to hammer the Republicans. A Copperhead journal pulled no punches in slamming Lincoln, the Republicans, and Grant in one brutal passage: "What is the difference between a *butcher* and a *general?* A butcher kills animals for food. A general kills men to gratify the ambition or malice of politicians and scoundrels." The tag "butcher" was applied to Grant from various quarters, including by a foreign observer in the Confederacy who wrote in his diary, "Grant's soldiers are getting tired of him and call him the butcher, and won't fight."

Most Republican editors tried to bolster faith in the war effort, counseling patience as Grant and Sherman closed in on Richmond and Atlanta. The *Chicago Tribune* urged readers to recognize that "Gen. Grant's operations are making good progress. . . . There is no occasion for disheartenment. . . . The fall of Richmond, when it comes, will stand on record with earth's great sieges, and such are not worked out in a night." The *New York Times* also raised the possibility of a siege that would end the conflict: "If Lee allows himself to be shut up within Richmond, . . . the problem reduces itself to a repetition of Vicksburgh over again. Will he do it? There is a question."

The benefit of a siege might be months away, however, and in

July and August the need for clear Federal victories to buoy spirits became acute. Republicans recognized the crisis, and many in the party thought it best to jettison Lincoln as the party's candidate in 1864. The president survived internal challenges to receive the nomination in early June. But he would not run as a Republican because the party, aware of continuing disagreement among voters about emancipation and other Republican policies, adopted the name Union Party in an effort to attract the widest possible vote. Democrat Andrew Johnson of Tennessee, the only senator from what became the eleven Confederate states to remain in Congress during the secession crisis, joined Lincoln on the ticket. Six weeks after his nomination, Lincoln remained pessimistic. On August 23, he asked members of his cabinet to sign a blind memorandum that revealed the depth of his concern: "This morning, as for some days past, it seems exceedingly probable that this Administration will not be re-elected. Then it will be my duty to so co-operate with the President elect, as to save the Union between the election and the inauguration; as he will have secured his election on such ground that he can not possibly save it afterwards."

III. MOBILE BAY AND THE NAVIES

The day Lincoln passed the blind memorandum around to his cabinet, Union naval vessels and army units captured Fort Morgan. The fall of the fort, which guarded the entrance to Mobile Bay, closed the last major Confederate port on the Gulf of Mexico and left only Wilmington, North Carolina, open to welcome blockade runners. The good news from Mobile, which had begun on August 5 when Admiral Farragut defeated a small Confederate fleet defending the bay, added to an enviable record compiled by Union naval forces throughout the war. Often overlooked or slighted in treatments of the conflict, the U.S. Navy played a major role in defeating the Confederacy. For its part, the Confederacy used technology and a small group of ironclads and commerce raiders in an impressive attempt to offset northern numbers and power.

The U.S. Navy began with just 42 commissioned vessels manned by fewer than 10,000 officers and seamen. Four years later it rivaled Britain's Royal Navy with nearly 700 vessels—about a third of which were steam warships constructed during the war and 70 of which were ironclads—and more than 130,000 sailors served during the course of the war. Northern industrial capacity made this remarkable transformation possible and guaranteed that the Confederacy would steadily lose ground in naval power. Union strategy employed naval strength in three important ways: as a blockading force designed to cut off southern commerce with Europe and thus fulfill part of the Anaconda Plan; in joint army-navy efforts along the Mississippi and other rivers; and as an important element in operations, such as that at Mobile Bay in 1864, directed against key points along the Confederate coast.

The Confederates began the war with no navy and never made it a major priority. They put their limited resources into construction of ironclads capable of destroying wooden blockading vessels (37 were either completed or under construction when the war ended), technological developments designed to protect crucial harbors, and the purchase of several swift commerce raiders that preyed on northern shipping. Construction and deployment of the CSS *Virginia*, which met the USS *Monitor* in a standoff at Hampton Roads on March 9, 1862, heralded the opening of ironclad warfare. The innovative Confederates even built the world's first successful submarine, the CSS *Hunley*, which sank the USS *Housatonic* off Charleston on February 17, 1864 (the crew of the *Hunley* also perished in the effort).

The blockade proved to be the most important element of the naval war. The Union slowly extended its control over the Confederate coastline by sealing ports, closing Wilmington, the last important one to fall, in January 1865. The Union navy never completely cut off commerce between the Confederacy and the outside world; however, it reduced volume to about one-third of its prewar levels and thereby denied the Confederacy precious war-related materials. By the end of the war, the blockade functioned as a notable component of the northern war effort.

The nature of campaigning in the Western Theater afforded ample opportunities for the U.S. Navy. The Union put together a flotilla that included seven ironclads specifically designed for duty in narrow, shallow rivers. The navy cooperated effectively with Ulysses S. Grant's operations against Forts Henry and Donelson on the Tennessee and Cumberland rivers in February 1862 and the citadel at Vicksburg on the Mississippi between December 1862 and July 1863, as well as the capture of Island No. 10 and Memphis in March and June 1862. Without the help of the navy, it would have been far more difficult for the United States to gain control of the Mississippi River and Middle and West Tennessee.

As many weaker nations had done in the past, the Confederacy turned to commerce raiders to combat a much stronger naval opponent. A range of problems convinced the Davis administration that privateers promised more trouble than results, so the focus shifted to cruisers that would act as commerce raiders (privateers typically sold captured vessels, while commerce raiders typically destroyed them). Confederate strategists hoped that these cruisers would accomplish several goals: so damage northern shipping that the Union would have to send its blockading squadrons in pursuit of the raiders; terrorize northern coastal areas; and help induce war weariness among civilians in the United States. Lacking the necessary shipbuilding facilities, the Confederacy purchased several cruisers from British builders. Led by the CSS *Alabama*, CSS *Florida*, and CSS *Shenandoah*, the raiders captured more than 250 American merchantmen and whalers, drove another 700 to register under foreign flags, and kept many of the remainder in port because of skyrocketing insurance rates. Although the northern merchant marine suffered terribly, commerce continued with shippers and companies using foreign bottoms to haul their cargoes.

The raiders failed to achieve any of the broad strategic goals, garnering headlines but making no major contribution to the Confederate war effort.

IV. SHERMAN AND SHERIDAN AND THE ELECTION OF 1864

Abraham Lincoln's reelection depended on the national armies rather than the navy. From a low point in late August, morale across the United States rebounded beginning in early September and reached an ebullient crescendo by late October thanks to Sherman's operations against Atlanta and General Philip H. Sheridan's campaign in the Shenandoah Valley. Between them, Grant's two favorite subordinates sculpted victories that reelected Lincoln, gave Republicans huge majorities in both houses of Congress, guaranteed that emancipation would be part of any peace settlement—and sent waves of disappointment rolling across the Confederacy.

Democrats selected their presidential ticket just before the first good military news created headlines in newspapers across the North. Meeting in Chicago on August 29-31, they chose George B. McClellan to head the ticket and endorsed a peace platform that demanded "immediate efforts be made for a cessation of hostilities, with a view of an ultimate convention of the States, or other peaceable means, to the end that, at the earliest practicable moment, peace may be restored on the basis of the Federal Union of the States." McClellan refused to support the platform, insisting that military victory and restoration of the Union should precede any cessation of hostilities.

Reports from Atlanta broke the grim spell of doubt in the United States. After Hood's aggressive spasm during late July, the Federals sought to sever the city's lines of supply and communication. Sherman also ordered a constant artillery bombardment to "make the inside of Atlanta too hot to be endured." On August 31, a Union flanking force got astride Hood's final rail link, south of Atlanta at Jonesboro, and settled the issue. Confederates abandoned the city on September 1, thereby losing a communications, supply, and industrial hub that also functioned as a gateway to the untouched heart of Georgia. On September 2, Sherman telegraphed Lincoln: "Atlanta is ours, and fairly won." An obviously grateful president responded the next day. "The marches, battles, sieges, and other military operations, that have signalized the campaign," he wrote in words that surely combined feelings of relief and joy, " . . . have entitled those who have participated therein to the applause and thanks of the nation."

Spirits sank in the Confederacy, though many tried to find ways to rally. Speaking in Macon, Georgia, later in September, Jefferson Davis summoned all men to take up arms. "When the war is over," he told the crowd, "and our independence won (*and we will establish our independence*,) who will be our aristocracy? I hope the limping soldier." A woman in Winchester, Virginia, noted on September 5 that Baltimore newspapers carried "Bad news! . . . they [the Federals] have possession of Atlanta. . . . The Yankees are very triumphant of course. This will have an unfavorable effect on the election."

Operations in the Shenandoah Valley took over the spotlight between mid-September and late October. In June, Lee had detached an infantry corps under General Jubal A. Early from the Army of Northern Virginia to operate independently. Over the next five weeks, Early swept Federals from the Shenandoah Valley, crossed the Potomac River and threatened Washington on July 11-12 (Abraham Lincoln briefly came under fire at Fort Stevens, part of the defensive works girdling the city), and then fell back into the northern part of the valley. Irascible and profane, Early provided his summary of the campaign with a typically salty remark to a subordinate: "Major, we haven't taken Washington, but we've scared Abe Lincoln like hell!" Early had somewhat unnerved Lincoln, who suggested to Grant that he bring a significant part of the Union army at Petersburg "with you personally, and make a vigorous effort to destroy the enemie's force in this vicinity."

Grant wisely talked Lincoln out of that idea but determined to end Rebel military activity in the valley and destroy the area's logistical value to the Confederacy. He instructed Sheridan to accomplish these goals by pursuing Early relentlessly and used plain language to explain what lay in store for the economy of the valley. "In pushing up the Shenandoah Valley," the general in chief told Sheridan, "Take all provisions, forage and Stock wanted for the use of your Command. Such as cannot, be consumed destroy."

The protracted drama in the valley came to a rousing climax between September 19 and October 19. During those four weeks, the Shenandoah represented a true second front in Virginia featuring 40,000-50,000 Union soldiers and 15,000 Confederates. Sheridan's striking victories at Third Winchester (September 19), Fisher's Hill (September 22), Tom's Brook (October 9), and Cedar Creek (October 19) broke Confederate military resistance, and "The Burning," a focused assault on logistical capacity, left much of the area an economic ruin. Well before Sherman's March to the Sea laid a heavy hand on Georgia's interior, Sheridan's army applied Grant's strategy of exhaustion—as some historians have labeled the effort to wreck the economic infrastructure that fed, clothed, and armed Confederate soldiers—to the Shenandoah Valley. The campaign also boosted Lincoln's candidacy for reelection. *Harper's Weekly* jubilantly contrasted Sheridan's victories with the Democratic Party's Chicago convention. "That patriotic body . . . pronounced the war a failure," crowed *Harper's*, while Sheridan's men won a triumph "under which Lee must wince and reel, for if he can not hold the Valley he can not hold Richmond."

Voters went to the polls with a stark choice on November 8, 1864. A Republican vote meant the war would be prosecuted vigorously and emancipation completed; a Democratic vote opened the possibility of an armistice that could lead to prolonged negotiations with the Confederacy and the undoing of progress toward ending slavery. With expectations for victory soaring because of what Sherman and Sheridan had accomplished, voters gave Republicans, who ran as the Union Party, an overwhelming endorsement. Lincoln won 55 percent of the popular vote and a 212-21 landslide in the Electoral College (McClellan carried only New Jersey and slaveholding Kentucky and Delaware). Thousands of soldiers cast ballots, and more than three-quarters of those whose votes can be determined supported Lincoln—which means that many Democrats deserted their party to make certain the war would be carried through to restore the Union. Republicans dominated both the new Senate, where they outnumbered Democrats by more than 4-1, and the House of Representatives, where they gained 50 seats and an unchallengeable majority.

V. FINAL MILITARY CAMPAIGNS AND THE SURRENDERS

Three major campaigns remained to be waged. After the fall of Atlanta, John Bell Hood attempted to draw Sherman northward by moving the war out of Georgia into Tennessee, where he hoped to reclaim territory long lost to the Confederacy. In consultation with Grant, Sherman detached George H. Thomas to defend Tennessee. On November 30, Hood launched precipitate frontal assaults against a force under General John M. Schofield at the battle of Franklin, losing more than 6,000 men and 12 generals to Schofield's 2,300, after which the Federals withdrew in good order to join Thomas's force in Nashville. Hood followed and took a position outside the city, where he waited for two weeks. On December 15-16, Thomas crushed the Army of Tennessee in the battle of Nashville. Black troops played a leading role in the victory, a fact that stung the Rebels. "[O]h woeful humiliation," wrote an Arkansan who paused to study pursuing Federals. "The faces of Negroes!" he sputtered. "Pushed on by white soldiers in their rear, but *there*, nevertheless in the front rank of those our men were running from."

Sherman, meanwhile, had left Atlanta in mid-November to make a slashing raid across Georgia to Savannah. Essentially unopposed on this March to the Sea, the Federals implemented Grant's strategy of exhaustion by destroying a vast amount of war-related material on a front sixty miles wide. On December 22, Sherman sent a brief note to Lincoln: "I beg to present you as a Christmas-gift the city of Savannah . . . ." After a period of rest and reinforcement, Sherman marched through South Carolina and into North Carolina in early 1865. His soldiers laid an especially hard hand on South Carolina, which they blamed for causing the war. A cobbled-together army under Joseph E. Johnston tried unsuccessfully to slow Sherman's advance through the Carolinas, fighting a midsized battle at Bentonville, North Carolina, on March 19-21. Sherman's campaigns in Georgia and the Carolinas demonstrated that Union armies could rampage at will through much of the Confederacy. "Savannah was of little use to us for a year past, it has been so closely blockaded," wrote a woman in Richmond who tried, without success, to mitigate the impact of Sherman's campaigning, " . . . but the moral effect of its fall is dreadful. The enemy are now encouraged, and our people depressed. I never saw them more so."

While Sherman and Hood maneuvered and fought across four states, Grant and Lee remained largely immobile outside Petersburg and Richmond. Their armies prepared elaborate fortifications that eventually extended for dozens of miles. A promising opportunity to break the stalemate had come in late July 1864 at the battle of the Crater, when the Federals tunneled under a section of the Confederate line and exploded a powder charge that obliterated several hundred yards of the southern defenses. A mismanaged attack that featured a division of black troops allowed a splendid opportunity to slip through Grant's fingers, after which he relentlessly probed against Lee's supply lines and extended the entrenchments toward the south and west in an effort to stretch the Confederates to a breaking point.

By March 1865, Union movements had restricted Lee's supply lines. Aware of what Grant was doing and desperate to break free of the suffocating siege, Lee launched his final tactical offensive of the war on March 25 in the battle of Fort Stedman. Brief success gave way to bloody failure, and Grant prepared to deliver a final blow. Philip H. Sheridan's crushing victory on April 1 at Five Forks, which anchored Lee's extreme western flank, set the stage for the abandonment of Petersburg and Richmond on April 2-3.

Six days of a fighting retreat brought the Confederates to Appomattox Court House, where Grant's pursuing forces blocked Lee's attempt to turn south and link up with Johnston's army in North Carolina. Convinced there was no possibility of escape, Lee remarked, "[T}here is nothing left for me to do but to go and see General Grant, and I would rather die a thousand deaths." Lee signed papers of surrender for 28,000 troops on April 9, and his veterans formally stacked arms on the twelfth. In line with President Lincoln's wish to begin the sectional healing process as soon as possible, Grant allowed Confederate soldiers to receive paroles and return to their homes. "I felt like anything rather than rejoicing at the downfall of a foe who had fought so long and valiantly, and had suffered so much for a cause," Grant later observed, "though that cause was, I believe, one of the worst for which a people ever fought."

Most people North and South considered Lee's surrender the effective end of the war. Such was the position he and his army held in the Confederacy that few believed the struggle would continue with any prospect of southern independence. As one woman in Georgia put it on April 18, "[E]verybody feels ready to give up hope. 'It is useless to struggle longer,' seems to be the common cry, and the poor wounded men go hobbling about the streets with despair on their faces." Other surrenders followed in rapid succession: Johnston roughly 90,000 men stationed in North Carolina, South Carolina, and Georgia to Sherman at Durham Station, North Carolina, on April 26; Richard Taylor an additional 10,000-12,000 to E. R. S. Canby at Citronelle, Alabama, on May 4; and an array of forces in the Trans-Mississippi Theater under an agreement signed in New Orleans on May 26. All of these Confederates received the same terms offered to Lee by Grant.

Before the last troops surrendered, Jefferson Davis also fell into Union hands. He left Richmond with a small group of advisors and a military escort, proceeding southward with the intention of continuing the war. Stopping briefly in Danville, Virginia, the party went on to Georgia, where on May 7 Varina Davis and the couple's children joined the president. Three days later, at the small community of Irwinville, Union cavalry overtook the fleeing Confederates and apprehended Davis. Sent to Fort Monroe in Virginia, Davis was imprisoned in a casemate and, for a time, had his legs shackled—the latter a gesture that carried immense symbolic importance in the former slaveholding states of the Confederacy.

VI. DID THE WAR END IN THE SPRING OF 1865?

On April 10, 1865, Secretary of the Navy Gideon Welles mused about news regarding U. S. Grant's "capture of Lee and his army" the previous day. "The tidings were spread over the country during the night," noted Welles, "and the nation seems delirious with joy. . . . This surrender of the great rebel Captain and the most formidable and reliable army of the secessionists virtually terminates the rebellion." Welles predicted that there would be some continued "marauding, and robbing & murder . . . but no great battle, no conflict of armies, after the news of yesterday reaches the different sections." Acerbic Richmond editor Edward A. Pollard, whose massive Southern History of the War chronicled the stormy life of the Confederacy as it unfolded, echoed Welles. In the final volume of Southern History, completed in 1865, Pollard remarked, "The surrender of General Lee drew after it important and rapid consequences, and, in effect, terminated the war."

Although these two witnesses anticipated how most Americans would understand the end of the Civil War, a number of scholars have questioned whether Lee's surrender should be reckoned the decisive indicator of the war's end. The onset of the sesquicentennial of Reconstruction in the second decade of the 21st Century inspired a good deal of attention to what some historians have labeled "the long Civil War," a formulation that emphasizes postwar violence in the former Confederacy and the conflict's other enduring consequences. Within this chronological reframing, the war did not close at Appomattox but rather extended through Reconstruction, or through the Jim Crow era, or even down to the present as "the war that never ended."

For far too long, argue advocates of a long Civil War, too many authors and readers have burrowed ever more deeply into the period between Fort Sumter and Appomattox, treating those four bloody years largely in isolation and thereby robbing the conflict of needed context. A longer perspective works against a focus on Appomattox—a focus that, in this view, creates a misleading impression that Grant and Lee's agreement ended fighting and opened the way for reunion and reconciliation.

No serious person can dispute the necessity of placing the Civil War within a spacious 19th-Century landscape. More specifically, any attempt to grasp the centrality of the war to the larger story of American history must engage with its long-term racial, constitutional, social, and commemorative effects. Many of the profound questions with which the Civil War generation grappled remain present, in some form, in the third decade of the 21st Century. Continuing debates about state versus central authority, the difficulty of ordering a biracial (now multiracial) society in a fair manner, the challenges of a military occupation, and wrangling about messy aftermaths of armed confrontations all bring Civil War examples to mind.

But constructions of a long Civil War should not obscure the fact that the conflict did end in 1865. Clear indications of this fact include the surrender of all Confederate military forces, the dismantling of the Confederate state, the restoration of the Union, the destruction of slavery, and the rapid demobilization of a million citizen-soldiers of the United States. These are huge outcomes that underscore the unequivocal termination of a war that, had the verdict on the battlefield been otherwise, would have established a powerful republic devoted to the perpetuation of slavery.

The political and social conflict that followed Appomattox should not be considered an extension of the war by other means. Postwar violence, however grotesque at times, did not approach in scale or fury the military carnage of the war years. The bloodiest incidents during Reconstruction scarcely would have qualified as minor skirmishes during the actual war. Moreover, former Confederates perpetrating the postwar violence had vastly scaled back their goals, from establishing a pro-slavery nation state to regaining local political power and maintaining white supremacy. The Jim Crow South, a reality by the late 19th Century, lasted for many decades and should be viewed as the most obvious expression of the Confederate generation's response to defeat and emancipation.

To describe postwar events as a violent continuation of the military action of 1861-1865 robs the most all-encompassing war in American history of much of its singularity and meaning. Too great an emphasis on the long Civil War, in fact, can reduce the war itself to just one episode or event among many. U. S. Grant, it is worth mentioning, immediately accepted the centrality of what transpired at Appomattox on April 9, 1865. In his Memoirs, he averred that Lee's surrender essentially closed the rebellion. "I determined to return to Washington at once," he explained, "with a view to putting a stop to the purchase of supplies, and what I now deemed other useless outlay of money." For the general in chief, managing the transition to peace already had begun.

VII. THE GRAND REVIEW, THE COST OF THE WAR,
AND WHAT WAS SETTLED

The Grand Review of U.S. forces in Washington, D.C., on May 23-24, 1865, celebrated a military victory that, in the view of the loyal citizenry, had preserved the Union, ensured the viability of democracy, and vanquished forces of a slaveholding oligarchy inimical to the intent of the founding generation. More than 150,000 soldiers from the Army of the Potomac and Sherman's western armies marched up Pennsylvania Avenue to the delight of throngs of onlookers. Their seemingly endless ranks represented the impressive military power of a mobilized populace, citizen-soldiers who had risked all in a brutal war and stood as exemplars of disinterested patriotic sacrifice. The soldiers had come forth in "tribute to free government, and to the democratic institutions under which they were reared," affirmed one newspaper, " . . . representatives of every loyal State, to struggle, shoulder to shoulder, for their common country. They were our friends and brothers and sons, our fellow-citizens, our *people*." A Baltimore paper placed the veterans' work "alongside the events of the Revolutionary generation," attributing "moral sublimity" and overriding importance to one dimension of their work: "It is the significance of the transition from the soldier to the citizen. The soldier of yesterday is the citizen of to-day."

Confederates engaged in no such celebrations. Veterans making their way to homes often far distant from the theater where they served, as well as the civilian populace, had to reconcile to defeat on a monumental scale. Although some white southerners had remained more steadfast than others and a significant number never had given their hearts to the cause, most Confederates knew that as a people they had expended blood and treasure in profusion before ultimately collapsing in the face of Union military power. Most would have preferred to be citizens of an independent Confederacy; all grasped that return to the United States, on terms dictated by the victorious Yankees, would be their reality.

The human and material cost of the war dwarfed that of any other military event in American history. More soldiers died in the conflict than in all other American wars combined from the colonial era through the early twenty-first century. Traditional estimates place dead for the Union army at 360,000 and for the Confederate army at 258,000—a combined total of 618,000. Two-thirds on each side died of disease and one-third from battle wounds. Recent research suggests that overall military deaths may have been between 700,000 and 750,000, with the Confederate proportion higher than originally believed. At least one in four of the white military-age men of the Confederacy perished in the war, a rate far exceeding that of any other war in American history, including the Union side of the Civil War.

Economically, significant parts of the Confederacy lay in ruins. Two-thirds of the region's assessed wealth disappeared during the war, much of it in the form of property in slaves. The presence of massive armies for four years left as much as 50 percent of all farm machinery and 40 percent of all livestock destroyed. Railroads, bridges, levees along rivers, mills, and industrial facilities lay partially or completely in ruins. The war tipped the economic balance decisively in favor of the loyal states. Northern wealth increased by 50 percent between 1860 and 1870, while southern wealth decreased by 60 percent.

Beyond physical damage, the Confederates had lost their slavery-based social structure. This left them somewhat bewildered, deeply angry, and uncertain about the future. A witness from mid-April 1865 tried to articulate the impact of this dimension of defeat. "The *abolition of slavery* immediately, and by a military order, is the most marked feature of this conquest of the South," wrote Robert Garlick Hill Kean while traveling through Virginia. "Manumission after this fashion will be regarded hereafter," Kean predicted with scarcely controlled temper, "when it has borne its fruits and the passions of the hour have passed away, as the greatest social crime ever committed on the earth."

Plate 16. The Grand Review. Soldiers of the Army of the Potomac marching down Pennsylvania Avenue on May 23, 1865, with the completed Capitol dome in the background. The veterans could see a huge banner on the Capitol that proclaimed: "The Only National Debt We Never Can Pay, Is The Debt We Owe To The Victorious Soldiers."

The war settled three great questions. First, the Union was permanent. The actions of great armies had rendered irrelevant all legal debate regarding the constitutionality of secession. Second, the cancer of slavery had been removed, freeing more than 4,000,000 black people from bondage. Third, central governmental authority had trumped state and local authority in fundamental ways, setting precedents that affected the nation's history going forward. Less certain were the legal, social, and economic status of the freedpeople, topics that would be at the center of postwar political discussion.

Survival of the nation towered over all other outcomes of the war. Emancipation certainly loomed largest for approximately 15 percent of the American population, whose emergence from what Frederick Douglass called the "hell-black system of human bondage" marked one of the great watersheds in the nation's history. But emancipation was a largely internal phenomenon that had almost no effect on the actions or standing of the United States on the world stage. For Europeans especially, as well as for others around the globe, the war's greatest legacy was a nation that by 1900 boasted the world's largest economy, was joining the ranks of major imperial powers, and would, throughout the twentieth century and into the twenty-first, wield unmatched economic, military, and diplomatic power.

Plate 17. As with many other places in the Confederacy, the city of Richmond suffered significant damage during the war. This image from April 1865 depicts a group of people amid ruins near the heart of the Rebel capital, among whom is an African American man on the far right. The photographer thus invited contemplation of two important themes of the war—physical destruction in the Confederacy and profound impact on the lives of black people.

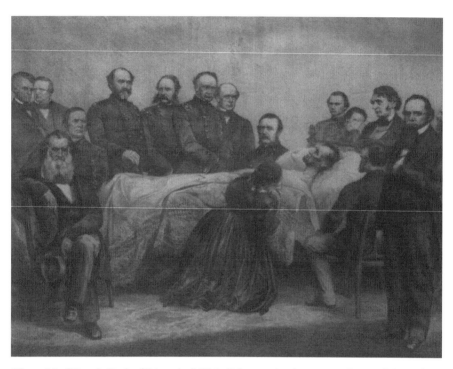

Plate 18. "Death Bed of Lincoln." This lithograph places members of the cabinet and Congress, military leaders, and a kneeling Mrs. Lincoln in the cramped bedroom where the president died. Coming just three days after Lee's army stacked arms at Appomattox, Lincoln's assassination triggered widespread anger across the loyal states.

CHAPTER 10

RECONSTRUCTION AND THE PROBLEMS
OF REUNIFICATION, 1863-1868

THE SURRENDER DOCUMENT signed at Appomattox Court House solidified the two goals of a restored United States: reunion and emancipation. Its generous terms were intended to begin healing the wounds of a tragically bitter and destructive conflict. After the Civil War, the country had to be reassembled to form a whole. A precise definition of "Reconstruction" is necessary, and fortunately it is simple, even if its implementation was not. Reconstruction was the process of bringing the eleven seceded southern states back into the Union. The story of how the nation defined and achieved reunification comprises several compelling elements, including wartime Reconstruction, the Appomattox surrender, the dramatic clash between Andrew Johnson's Presidential Reconstruction and congressional Reconstruction, and the election of 1868. White northerners, white southerners, and freedpeople made up the crucial groups whose different expectations and perspectives are key to understanding the chaotic and fascinating years of Reconstruction.

Many vital questions regarding the U.S. position on reunion and Reconstruction demanded answers in the years from 1863 to 1868. What specific conditions should be set to readmit the eleven seceded states, and what branch of government should be in control of the process? What kind of political rights should be granted to the male freed slaves of the region? What would "free labor" look like for the four million black people in the heavily plantation-based cotton economy? What kind of punishment, if any, should be inflicted on the rebellion's leaders and followers? How much of the country's resources should be deployed in rebuilding the South? A policy for reuniting the country was made more urgent when President Abraham Lincoln's Emancipation Proclamation complicated a future peace agreement. From 1861 to 1863, the major northern goal in the war was restoration of the Union. Lincoln's proclamation added a second goal: freedom for the slaves. Thus an urgent task for lawmakers was that reconstituting the Union had to involve bringing white Confederates back to the national "family" table, while simultaneously setting a place at that table for black people, whose status beyond freedom was unclear.

I. WARTIME RECONSTRUCTION

The fortunes of war fluctuated for the Union, but successive military campaigns brought more and more territory—in Louisiana, Virginia, Mississippi, Tennessee, South Carolina, and Arkansas—within Federal control. Under the circumstances, Lincoln desired to replace military occupation with loyal civilian governments as soon as possible, demonstrating to Confederates that the United States would be forgiving in welcoming back to the fold its "errant children." On December 8, 1863, Lincoln announced a "Proclamation of Amnesty and Reconstruction" (also known as Lincoln's "Ten Percent Plan") that seized control of the process for the executive branch. He based his authority on the section of the U.S. Constitution that states: "the President shall have power to grant reprieves and pardons for offenses against the United States." His proclamation offered a pardon to every former Rebel pledging a simple oath of loyalty to the Union and accepting emancipation. If 10 percent of a state's citizens who voted in the 1860 presidential election took the oath, they could form a government and adopt a constitution. Lincoln required that the new constitutions prohibit slavery.

Lincoln based his plan on a belief that because secession was illegal, the southern states were never out of the Union, and reunion should be straightforward and uncomplicated. Later, Lincoln summed up his feelings, stating, "I want no one punished; treat them liberally all around. We want those people to return to their allegiance to the Union and submit to the laws." By 1864, the former Confederate states of Louisiana, Tennessee, and Arkansas had established functioning Unionist governments under Lincoln's Ten Percent Plan.

This ignited a firestorm of protest from Radical Republicans in Congress. A vocal minority within the party, radicals pushed Lincoln on the issues of emancipation and black troops and sought a postwar South remade in the northern image of democratic capitalism. While most radicals opposed land redistribution schemes for the black masses, they insisted on securing civil and voting rights for freedmen, assuming that those protections would allow the ex-slaves to rise and flourish in a free labor system. To a man, they were opposed to Lincoln's efforts to reunite the sections without forcing major changes on the former Confederacy. Led in the Senate by Charles Sumner of Massachusetts, Benjamin F. Wade of Ohio, and Henry Wilson of Massachusetts, and in the House of Representatives by Henry Winter Davis of Maryland, George W. Julian of Indiana, and Thaddeus Stevens of Pennsylvania, among others, radicals championed the idea that the Confederacy should be treated as a "conquered province" whose re-admittance to the Union would be governed under the authority of Congress.

Congressional Republicans initiated a national debate over Reconstruction policy with passage of the Wade-Davis Bill in July 1864. Dismissing Lincoln's Ten Percent Plan as far too mild, they hoped to prevent official recognition of former Confederate states until 50 percent of the voters took a loyalty oath. President Lincoln's response was swift and sure. He "pocket-vetoed" the bill (he refused to sign or act on it), ensuring its doom. An immediate standoff between Lincoln and Congress was deflected by Union battlefield victories combined with the president's triumphant reelection. Passage of the Thirteenth Amendment in January 1865 further eased tensions between the two branches of government. In his second inaugural address delivered on March 4, 1865, President Lincoln depicted the conflict as the nation's punishment for the sin of slavery, God's justice meted out even if "every drop of blood drawn with the lash, shall be paid for another drawn with the sword." Importantly, Lincoln concluded his speech with a beautifully expressed plea for reconciling the broken country: "With malice toward none; with charity for all."

As he did in his Proclamation of Amnesty and Reconstruction in December 1863, Lincoln insisted that two demands be made of the soon to be former Confederates: they accept emancipation (although his policy on the freedpeople's status beyond freedom remained unclear) and swear a loyalty oath to the United States. Together these demands represented the United States' terms of surrender as the war came to an end in the spring of 1865.

II. APPOMATTOX AND LINCOLN'S ASSASSINATION

Appomattox Court House was a remote community deep in the countryside of Virginia. A peaceful place throughout most of the war, the small village achieved immortality as the site of the historic surrender of Confederate forces to Ulysses S. Grant on April 9, 1865. Grant and his staff rode into the village that afternoon and stopped their horses at the two-story brick house of a man named Wilmer McLean. Awaiting them in the parlor of McLean's residence sat Robert E. Lee and a lone aide. Grant seated himself in front of a small table and, after the exchange of a few pleasantries, began writing out the terms of surrender. "I only knew what was in my mind," reflected Grant later. His terms were magnanimous and showed his and President Lincoln's great desire that the beaten Confederates be neither humiliated nor punished. The Rebels were to "lay down arms," return home as paroled prisoners, and promise to obey the laws of the United States. Breaking with custom, Grant did not require Lee to hand over his sword. Southern officers could retain their sidearms, and both officers and enlisted men could keep their horses and mules. Copies of the surrender were made, and Lee wrote out a letter accepting the terms.

News spread quickly through the Union camps, and soon thousands of soldiers were cheering and throwing their hats into the air. A hundred-gun salute was begun, but Grant immediately stopped it, saying, "The war is over. The Rebels are our countrymen again." Perhaps the most common emotion for the weary soldiers of both sides was a great relief that the war, and the killing, had finally ceased. The gigantic problems of reconstructing the Union and easing the bitterness between North and South lay ahead.

In the hopeful spring days of early April, many northerners expected former Rebels to be reintegrated into the body politic fairly quickly. But less than a week after Appomattox, Abraham Lincoln was assassinated. On April 14, the same day the U.S. flag few again over Fort Sumter, a twenty-six-year-old actor named John Wilkes Booth entered the presidential box during a Ford's Theatre performance of *Our American Cousin*, shooting Lincoln in the back of the head with a single-shot derringer pistol. The mortally wounded president was carried across the street to the Peterson house where he faded quickly and died early on the morning of April 15 without regaining consciousness.

"Now he belongs to the ages," intoned Secretary of War Edwin M. Stanton. A shocked nation mourned its leader. White citizens across the former Confederacy watched and worried, their feelings of elation at Lincoln's murder suppressed by fear of northern retaliation.

The assassin fled Washington, working his way south, where he expected but did not receive a hero's welcome. Slowed by a broken leg sustained during his escape, Booth was eventually trapped in a Virginia barn. After refusing to surrender, he was shot and killed, never to answer for his crime in a court of law. A military tribunal tried eight of Booth's alleged co-conspirators, sentencing four to be hanged. Many in the North thought the assassination a Confederate plot, funded and supported by Jefferson Davis's administration. Others suggested that there was a conspiracy existing within the Union itself. However, no compelling evidence exists linking any person or group to the assassination besides Booth and his accomplices. No doubt the assassination and its aftermath hampered the prospects of a peaceful reunion, but there were no major incidents of retaliation taken by Union armies stationed in the South against civilian or soldiers. The truth is that both sides were ready to lay down arms.

III. NORTHERN WHITES AT WAR'S END

The majority of northern whites fought to preserve the United States, approving of emancipation primarily as a weapon to destroy the power of slaveholders to break up the country. Most people stuck to a very narrow definition of emancipation and freedom that did not include equal rights and suffrage privileges. They overwhelmingly desired a harmonious reunion but thought Reconstruction should be conducted on *northern* terms, that is, preserving the causes of Union and freedom for which they had sacrificed so many lives. This sentiment prevailed as more than a million men of the volunteer army demobilized and returned home. By November 1866, just 11,000 volunteers remained in the U.S. Army. Union soldiers received their final pay and discharge papers, and most proceeded to travel by train to their hometowns, often with their regiments. The returning heroes were greeted by townspeople waving flags and bands playing joyful songs such as "When Johnny Comes Marching Home Again."

Homecoming for northern veterans was relatively easy and fast. One Illinois soldier remembered, "When I returned home I found that the farm work my father was then engaged in was cutting and shucking corn. So the morning after my arrival, I doffed my uniform of first lieutenant, put on some of my father's old clothes, and proceeded to wage war on the standing corn. The feeling I had while engaged in this work was sort of queer. It almost seemed, sometimes, as if I had been away only a day or two, and had just taken up the farm work where it had left off." In contrast to the level of destruction in the Confederacy, northern wartime property damage was limited, and farms and factories flourished. In fact, a large number of Union veterans benefited from the coming three decades of an unparalleled economic boom (and periodic busts) that defined the postwar era.

While Union veterans and their families found an easier transition from military to civilian life than did their former enemies, the suffering inflicted by the war had enduring effects on a significant number of ex-soldiers who struggled to cope with missing limbs, lingering and long-lasting physical issues, and the effects of battle fatigue (now described as post-traumatic shock syndrome) on their mental stability. Thousands of families, too, whose sons, fathers, brothers, or husbands never returned were bereft and faced a shaky future. The U.S. government provided some support for war widows to aid families in need and devoted a growing part of its budget over time to veteran's benefits. (Southern states allocated less in benefits for Confederate veterans.)

IV. SOUTHERN WHITES AT WAR'S END

Homecoming for Confederate veterans offered a different experience. For most Rebel soldiers, forced demobilization began when they received their parole, a check-like piece of paper that served as a passport home. But that home could be hundreds of miles away, and many men took advantage of free railroad passes issued courtesy of U.S. Grant. Most combined different forms of travel on their journey—rail, horse, mule, and foot. Upon their return, the men on the losing side did not find a band playing patriotic airs or a crowd cheering their service. Often nothing was left of their former property, and sometimes they could not find their families. A number spent months after the war searching for their refugee relations, perhaps homeless and in dire circumstances. Undoubtedly the former soldiers in a "Lost Cause" realized the enormous price they had paid for secession, war, and utter defeat. One out of every ten white men lay dead, thousands of acres of formerly fertile land across the Confederate states had been abandoned, and big and small cities and towns had been partially burned or destroyed.

The economic destruction included human property. With slavery gone, millions of human beings who had composed $3 billion of capital in 1860 were free. The white population of the South hated and resented their conquered status. The racial and economic structure may have changed, but fixed ideas regarding race and place remained engraved in their hearts and minds. One white North Carolinian illustrates the dilemma and dangers of assuming a painless reunion between the two sections. He lost everything in the war—his sons, his home, his slaves. How did he bear the tragedy? His answer was that the Yankees had "left me one privilege—to hate 'em. I get up at half-past four in the morning, and sit up until twelve at night, to hate 'em." A few years later a Virginia minister declared his congregation should never "Forgive those people, who have invaded our country, burned out cities, destroyed our homes, slain our young men, and spread desolation and ruin over our land!"

V. FREEDPEOPLE FACE A NEW WORLD

It's not surprising that former slaveholders expressed shock at the reality of freedom for their ex-slaves. A Georgia plantation mistress complained loudly when a former slave refused to let her pass him in the street, stating, "It is the first time in my life that I have ever had to give up the sidewalk to a man, much less to negroes!" In great contrast, former slaves' vision of freedom was expansive and at first simply meant the absence of white control over every part of their lives. Suddenly they could do things previously forbidden such as hold meetings, learn to read and write, celebrate holidays, buy guns, own dogs, marry, and establish churches. Emancipation also meant re-forming broken families. A freedman recalled an emotional reunion with his father: "That was the best thing about the war setting us free, he could come back to us." Ex-slaves eagerly made their unions legal by marrying in great numbers just after the war. By 1870, the two-parent household predominated among a majority of African Americans in the South.

The newfound right to exercise control over one's household was accompanied by the strong desire of the rural black masses to be independent landowners. Freedmen lobbied for land redistribution, realizing that owning a plot of ground provided the best foundation for a better future. They believed emancipation entitled them to break as far as possible from the world of prewar plantations. One sympathetic northern observer wrote: "The sole ambition of the freedman at the present time appears to be to become the owner of a little piece of land, there to erect a humble home, and to dwell in peace and security at their own free will and pleasure."

Intent on restricting black freedom and ensuring the cotton crop would be picked, southern planters desired to return the freedpeople to the fields as gang laborers in an arrangement as close to slavery as possible. Freedmen's Bureau officials tried to balance the interests of both groups, insisting that the planters pay wages and the workers sign contracts for one year. Blacks refused to work under those conditions, and eventually a compromise, called sharecropping, replaced slave gang labor. Over the years, the cotton plantations were cut up into small parcels, usually fewer than forty acres, with many parcels leased by free African American families. The different expectations and interests of the three groups—northern whites, ex-Confederates, and freed men and women—as they sought to navigate and control the new postwar world was taken up by politicians in Washington, D.C. The guns had fallen silent, but the battle for the meaning of the Civil War continued to divide.

VI. PRESIDENTIAL RECONSTRUCTION

Vice President Andrew Johnson, former slave owner, state legislator, Democratic U.S. senator, and wartime governor of Tennessee, assumed the office of president with the strong support of northern leaders and citizenry. Johnson was put on the 1864 ticket to broaden the appeal of the Republicans beyond their base. In other words, Johnson was not a Republican and had no interest in becoming one. His strategy was to build up a Union Party majority, attracting both northern and southern Democrats and middle-of-the-road Republicans. Johnson crafted his prewar political career championing the rights of the plain yeoman farmers of the South. "Treason is a crime and must be made odious," he declared. His deep hatred of the southern slaveholding class proved reassuring to Republicans who considered the South a conquered province. The strong belief held by most Republicans, however, that the federal government, directed by Congress, should protect the civil rights of blacks in the ex-Confederate States (guaranteeing equal protection under the law, for example) promised certain conflict with the new president.

The Republicans did not have to wait long. In May 1865, Johnson announced his Reconstruction plan with Congress in recess. Like Lincoln, Johnson seized the initiative for the executive branch. His program offered pardons to all whites except certain categories of high-ranking politicians, military officials, and wealthy Confederates who were required to apply individually. The seceded states were to hold constitutional conventions and form state governments. The new governments were compelled to repeal secession, abolish slavery, repudiate their debt (rendering debt incurred during the Civil War worthless), and declare their renewed national loyalty for readmission to the Union. Johnson believed his policy followed in spirit and practice his predecessor's Ten Percent Plan that had been firmly rejected by the Radical Republicans.

His turnabout on the planter class he professed to loathe set the stage for fierce conflict with Congress. Finding himself in need of allies to head off a mounting Republican outrage over the summer and fall of 1865, Johnson engaged in a brisk business in pardoning thousands of former Confederate officials. The pardons provided the opportunity for many prominent Confederates to win state elections and be appointed to nonelective offices. By October 1865, all ex-Confederate states but Texas had reestablished a civil government. Trouble was brewing, however, as northerners expressed astonishment when elections for national office not only included the return to the U.S. Senate of the former Confederate vice president, Alexander Stephens of Georgia, but also brought fifty-eight former Confederate congressmen to the House of Representatives.

Johnson's Reconstruction policy failed to include African Americans in any significant role, leaving the details of their condition for the states to work out. A staunch Union man who favored emancipation, Johnson opposed black suffrage and civil rights. His sympathies lay with the poorer white farmers of the South, his beliefs in a small national government and state rights more typical of northern Democrats than of Republicans. During the summer of 1865, a number of southern state legislatures reconstituted under Johnson's plan passed a series of restrictive racial laws known as the "Black Codes." The primary purpose of the codes was to keep African Americans subordinate in order to reassemble coerced labor to harvest the cotton crop. The laws enforced labor contracts requiring African Americans to work a full year, and some permitted whipping as punishment or made black unemployment a crime. Black Codes relied on the power of the state to enforce the laws, and punishment for resisters was administered by an all-white police and court system.

The noxious laws showed an unrepentant southern white citizenry intent on rolling back emancipation and rejecting free labor, which incited indignation on the part of the northern people far beyond the Radical Republicans. Even citizens who did not support racial equality—and most did not—believed that the freedpeople's personal liberty and ability to compete as free-labor workers should be guaranteed and, if necessary, enforced by federal protection. Johnson's unpopularity grew as the northern press reported numerous shocking examples of how ex-Rebels were violating the spirit of Appomattox.

Here was a golden moment for Johnson to adopt a flexible stance and exercise some damage control. He found himself in an incredibly difficult position, and blame for Reconstruction's failures cannot be attributed solely to his blunders. Unfortunately, it is also true that Johnson demonstrated a nearly complete absence of the political skills necessary for compromise. Mocked already by some as the "accidental president," Johnson proved stubborn and needlessly self-destructive. From his viewpoint, he had two choices: admit failure and start his program over or accept the new governments and stand tall for his version of Reconstruction. He chose the latter. Defense of his plan meant that pardoned southerners should control the South, while the president and the executive branch directed Reconstruction and ruled the nation. Emancipated slaves deserved freedom but not suffrage under this model, and Johnson rejected out of hand federal enforcement of civil rights. His forthright stance guaranteed a rocky year ahead as Republicans and Democrats convened for the opening of the 39th Congress in December 1865.

The assembled Republicans detested Johnson's plan. Outnumbering Democrats more than 3-1, they wielded a powerful influence in disrupting or destroying the president's policy. On the first day of the session, they denied admission to all representatives elected from the former Confederate States. Next, they proceeded to set up a Joint Committee on Reconstruction (also known as the Committee of Fifteen) to oversee the process. Republican success depended on unity between the radical and moderate wings of their party. The smaller number of radicals and the majority moderates had many goals in common but also some serious differences. The radicals' ambitious plans for an overhaul of the defeated South depended on establishing Republican-controlled state governments supported by a sizable number of black voters whose civil rights were protected by government.

Moderates, on the other hand, considered themselves practical men who accepted and welcomed the changes brought over the course of the Civil War. They wanted to roll up their sleeves and work with the president, the radical wing of their party, and as many Democrats as possible to get the country back together. They were not enthusiastic supporters of black suffrage for two reasons. They thought it would offend great numbers of northern voters—few states in the North allowed blacks to vote—and knew it would offend southern men who were favorably disposed toward reconciliation. Moderates such as James G. Blaine (Maine) in the House and Lyman Trumbull (Connecticut) and John Sherman (Ohio) in the Senate found agreement with both Johnson and the radicals. For example, they concurred with the president that re-entry should be made as easy as possible and that states should decide themselves whether or not to give the franchise to black men. But they also supported the radicals' demand that the basic civil rights of the freedpeople needed protection and that Congress, not the executive branch, should control Reconstruction policy.

What was the position of the other major party in the country? After the war, the Democratic Party can best be described as "a respectable minority" that still commanded a large number of voters but remained relatively powerless until the mid-1870s. Republicans effectively attacked Democrats for acting disloyal during the war. "Not every Democrat was a traitor," crowed Republicans: "But every traitor was a Democrat." During the first year of Reconstruction, a bitter dispute developed between Democrats and Republicans over the extension of citizenship and the franchise to African Americans. Encouraged by President Johnson, many northern Democrats, such as Ohio's George Pendleton, a congressman who cast his vote against the Thirteenth Amendment, attacked what they called the "Africanization" of the South. Democratic politicians and voters wholeheartedly supported Johnson in his ongoing struggle to sustain the integrity of his policies.

In February 1866, Republicans submitted two important bills for the president's consideration. The first would extend the life of the Freedmen's Bureau; the second was the Civil Rights Act of 1866 that guaranteed black citizens legal protections. If Johnson agreed to sign the bills, Republicans would take it as evidence they could work together. In a message permeated with ill will and racism, Johnson vetoed both bills, claiming that they represented unwarranted expansion of national power. His vetoes ended hope of cooperation between the executive and legislative branches. Congress overrode his veto and in the process made history. The Civil Rights Act was the first major piece of legislation to be passed over a president's veto. A northern newspaper approved, noting that securing civil rights for the freedpeople "follows from the suppression of the rebellion. . . . The party is nothing, if it does not do this the nation is dishonored."

Concern regarding the president's possible sabotage of the Civil

Rights Act through executive proclamations or orders led Republicans to propose the Fourteenth Amendment to the Constitution in June 1866. The amendment defined black people as citizens, assured all citizens equal protection under the law, and declared that a state could not "deprive any person of life, liberty, or property, without due process of laws." Section 3 of the amendment barred some prominent former Confederates from holding high political positions. Congress could (and did) reverse this at a later date. Vigorously upholding Section 3 in 1866 meant that Republicans, who had no strength in the South before the Civil War, could keep many southern Democrats out of positions of power until the region stabilized enough to support a genuine two-party system.

Johnson, stung by heavy criticism, assumed that pervasive racism among whites would protect him from assaults from the Radical Republicans. Instead, freedpeople's status became the focus of concern for a sizable number of northern voters who believed that basic human rights of blacks in the South should be protected. These feelings were caused in part by the founding in 1866 of a secret white organization in Tennessee named the Ku Klux Klan. The Klan and other groups kept African Americans from exercising their civil rights (and later from voting) by harassing and even killing some individuals who presumed to act in ways that suggested equality with whites. Violence against freedpeople and white Republicans in the South received widespread publicity when it spread to urban areas in the form of race riots. Scores of blacks were murdered by white mobs in 1865 and 1866. Two of the largest riots occurred in Memphis and New Orleans. "We are to have the black flesh of the Negro crammed down our throats," declared a Memphis newspaper editorial just days before the rampage took place. The racial incidents demonstrated that the restored civil authorities in the South would not even minimally protect black freedom (no white rioter was ever brought to justice). These disturbances led many to wonder if the rebellion had really been suppressed or if a temporary return to U.S. military authority was necessary to restore order.

The bad publicity following the riots united moderate and radical Republicans against Johnson's Reconstruction program. Both sides took their cases to the voters. In a vigorous campaign leading up to the midterm elections of 1866, Republican speakers urged voters to preserve and protect the aims of the Civil War by supporting the Fourteenth Amendment, reinstituting military rule, and destroying the "Old South" once and for all. Johnson called on Democrats and Republican moderates to rally to his side and stop the radicals' assault on the Constitution. The results of the fall elections produced a resounding defeat for Johnson and delivered to Republicans a rare "veto-proof" majority. Congress now moved to consolidate and extend its power over Reconstruction.

VII. IMPEACHMENT AND CONGRESSIONAL RECONSTRUCTION, 1867-1868

The Joint Committee on Reconstruction passed a series of acts in March 1867 (the Reconstruction Acts) dissolving all the southern state governments formed under Johnson's plan. Tennessee had been readmitted to the Union after ratifying the Fourteenth Amendment in July 1866. Ten ex-Confederate states were divided into five military districts, each commanded by a Union major general responsible for implementing congressional Reconstruction. Federal troops stationed in each district assisted in enforcing the laws. The Reconstruction Acts required that the states register all qualified black and white voters; the voters were to elect delegates to a convention, which in turn had to write a constitution that included black male suffrage. Having done so, the voters could elect a governor and state legislature. The last step was ratifying the Fourteenth Amendment. Predictably, Johnson vetoed the acts. Just as predictably, Congress overrode his vetoes. The president's response remained combative. Although outwardly compliant with the policy,

Johnson issued executive orders to limit the power of the military governors of the reconstructed South and ousted a number of government officials sympathetic to the Radical Republicans.

Next in the unfolding high drama of Reconstruction came passage of the Tenure of Office Act and the Command of the Army Act. The former intended to stop Johnson's ongoing efforts to remove prominent Republicans from government positions by requiring Senate approval and the latter to stop his sacking of friendly generals from overseeing policy in the military districts. President Johnson and his advisors believed both laws to be unconstitutional, and in February 1868 he violated the Tenure of Office Act by firing Secretary of War Edwin M. Stanton, a Radical Republican supporter. Convinced that a defiant Johnson had fatally transgressed the Constitution, Republicans made the grave decision to impeach him. If successful, impeachment by the House of Representatives would be followed with a trial conducted in the Senate resulting in Johnson's removal from office. On February 24, 1868, the House voted 126–47 for impeachment on the grounds of "high Crimes and Misdemeanors." The first eight articles of impeachment represented the heart of the case and focused on the president's alleged violations of the Tenure of Office Act. On February 25, the Senate began proceedings, with the trial commencing on March 30.

Chief Justice Salmon P. Chase presided and, to his credit, struggled to govern the process in a fair and impartial manner. The political subtext of the trial was the fight over the meaning of the war's sacrifice and over Reconstruction. President Johnson's able defenders, including former Supreme Court associate justice Benjamin R. Curtis, argued that the Tenure of Office Act was blatantly unconstitutional. The Republicans, meanwhile, attacked the president's opposition to their plans for Reconstruction. Their primary concern was that Johnson's actions subverted the Union victory in the war, rendering it meaningless. By May 6, the arguments had concluded, and on May 16 the Senate voted 35–19 for conviction, falling one vote short of the two-thirds majority required for removal from office. Seven Republicans voted against impeachment, reflecting a growing moderate disenchantment with the Radicals' strategy. President Johnson had survived, but his administration remained fatally damaged.

"The country is going to the Devil!" cried Pennsylvania's Radical Republican Thaddeus Stevens upon hearing that Andrew Johnson was not to be convicted. Stevens had expected the favorable results of the 1866 elections would lead to the 1868 presidential nomination for a fellow radical such as Senator Benjamin Wade. Other Republicans opposed Wade or any other radical nominee who might alienate and divide northern voters and perhaps bring a Democrat back to the White House. Moderates reasoned that while the country had rejected President Johnson's leadership, most did not endorse a radical agenda, especially in regard to racial relations. Their beliefs would be confirmed by the off-year elections, when northern voters emphatically rebuffed the radicals by returning New York, Pennsylvania, and Ohio to the Democrats. Two states, Ohio and Kentucky, turned down black suffrage amendments. With the radical leadership diminished by the fight, moderate Republicans took control of the party machinery, searching for a winning candidate in the upcoming presidential election.

VIII. ELECTION OF 1868

Since the election of 1864 the people of the United States had witnessed the end of the Civil War, the abolition of slavery, the assassination of one president and the impeachment of another, and a brawl over Reconstruction with no end in sight. The approaching election, which would pit Republican Ulysses S. Grant against Democrat Horatio Seymour, promised to be momentous and offered a continuing referendum on Reconstruction. After Lincoln's death, Grant was the most prominent and revered symbol of Union victory. He believed his reputation was tied to ensuring that Reconstruction did not sacrifice

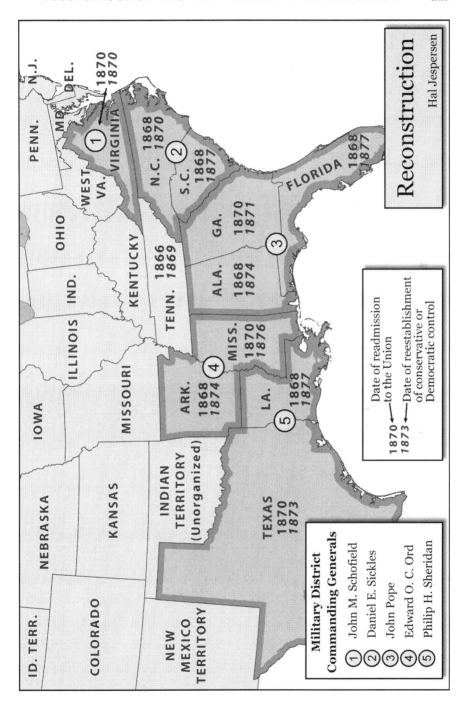

Reconstruction

Hal Jespersen

Date of readmission
to the Union
1870
1873 ⟶ Date of reestablishment
of conservative or
Democratic control

**Military District
Commanding Generals**

① John M. Schofield
② Daniel E. Sickles
③ John Pope
④ Edward O. C. Ord
⑤ Philip H. Sheridan

Plate 19. "The Senate as a Court of Impeachment for the Trial of Andrew Johnson" (the president in left foreground). The trial reflected bitter political division between Johnson and Republicans in Congress and fascinated the American public.

the aims for which the United States had been preserved. Serving as the general in chief of U.S. armed forces overseeing the military part of Reconstruction, Grant became increasingly dismayed by Johnson's policies. He had come to believe that the peace he had forged stood in danger of being lost by, as he put it, "mere trading politicians." Republicans turned to General Grant because he seemed to rise above the nasty partisan politics engulfing the country while advocating using the rule of law against the resurgence of ex-Confederate power. The general in chief was also known as a man who supported congressional Reconstruction without being associated with the radical demands for social equality between the races. On May 20, while the passions aroused by the impeachment trial still ran high, the Republicans met in Chicago. Grant was nominated unanimously on the first ballot, with Indiana congressman Schuyler Colfax selected as his running mate. The historic gathering featured a dozen black delegates to the Republican National Convention including P. B. S. Pinchback of Louisiana and Robert Smalls of South Carolina.

On July 4, the Democratic National Convention opened in New York City. After many ballots, the Democrats selected New York's widely respected governor, Horatio Seymour, for president, with Francis Preston Blair, Jr. of Missouri getting the nod for vice president. At the convention and on the campaign trail, Democrats echoed the sentiments of their constituency in the North but also aimed to lure southern white voters back into the fold. They demanded immediate amnesty for all former Confederates and the withdrawal of Federal forces from the South, ending so-called Republican military rule of the region. Democrats asserted that they constituted the only national party that could bring about a true sectional reconciliation with the white majority of the South. Condemning congressional Reconstruction as "unconstitutional, revolutionary, and void," they championed state rights when it came to "the regulation of the elective franchise" and attacked the looming Republican "Negro supremacy" and the "militarism" of the Grant administration.

As was customary during presidential elections in the nineteenth century, General Grant did not campaign, preferring to remain in his Galena, Illinois, residence and receive greetings from groups of supporters. But thousands of Republican speakers and organizers spoke on his behalf across the country, often quoting Grant's statement that became the Republican campaign slogan: "Let us have peace." The Republicans had a clear message. They were the party that won the war, saved the Union, emancipated the slaves, and were offering an excellent plan for Reconstruction that would be fair to both black and white, saving the peace. Republicans took to "waving the bloody shirt," reminding voters that the Democrats were the party of slavery, secession, and treason. "Scratch a Democrat," charged the *New York Tribune*, "and, you'll find a rebel under his skin." Both parties engaged in character assassination, with numerous Democratic speakers frequently referring to Grant as a butcher, a stupid drunk, a military despot, and a "Negro lover." To the tune of "Captain Jinks of the Horse Marines," Democrats mocked the Union hero: "I am Captain Grant of the Black Marines; The stupidest man that ever was seen." Grant's popularity and stature seemed immune to such slander, and Seymour proved a listless candidate. Favorable results in the early fall elections predicted a strong Republican vote on November 3.

In the end, Grant celebrated a victory in the popular vote, 53 percent to Seymour's 47 percent, while winning by a landslide in the Electoral College, 214–80. Seventy-eight percent of the electorate participated, adding for the first time the votes of 400,000 black men. Their support was crucial to the triumph of the Republicans in 1868. "We have learned of Grant's election," declared a black female missionary, "and all the col'd people's hearts about here have been made glad thereby," to which she added cheerfully, "while on the other hand the Rebs. are quite down in the mouth." The southern white voters flocked to Seymour, and the ticket secured the electoral votes of Kentucky, Maryland, Delaware, New Jersey, New York, and a few other states, proving that the country was almost evenly divided between the two major political parties. While the "unreconstructed" states of Virginia, Texas, and Mississippi could not vote, charges of voter fraud and intimidation against white and black Republicans in the South were reported that fall. But most citizens were relieved and pleased that the election had come off in a mostly peaceful manner.

"I am afraid I am elected," the winning candidate told Mrs. Grant on election night. His inaugural address delivered on March 4, 1869, urged the development of a prosperous economy, advocated reform in Indian policy, spoke of securing respect for the country overseas, and promoted passage of the Fifteenth Amendment, which would enshrine black male suffrage in the Constitution. Grant took some care to stress the urgency for reconciliation between North and South: "I ask patient forbearance one toward another throughout the land, and a determined effort on the part of every citizen to do his share toward cementing a happy union." His coming administration would be charged with, and judged by, implementing the Republican-dominated, interracial governments in most of the ex-Confederate states.

Plate 20. "The Union as It Was, the Lost Cause Worse than Slavery." Published in the autumn of 1874, Thomas Nast's biting cartoon suggested that African Americans faced a perilous future in former Confederate states as Reconstruction drew to a close.

CHAPTER 11

THE END OF RECONSTRUCTION, 1868-1877

"WHAT THE AMERICAN public always wants," a perceptive critic once observed, "is a tragedy with a happy ending." The famous agreement forged at Appomattox yields a tidy and triumphant conclusion to the Civil War, and U. S. Grant's election to the presidency in 1868 seemingly prepared the way for Republicans to solidify their impressive record of legislative accomplishment by fulfilling the promise of emancipation. Yet the final years of the Reconstruction Era—a period as a whole often described as an "unfinished revolution" or a "splendid failure"—unfolded as a tragedy, yes, but without the happy ending. Major issues left unsettled by the war itself, such as self-determination, political democracy, race relations, and state rights, were contested during the final years of Reconstruction, when Republican regimes held sway for differing lengths of time in much of the former Confederacy. The fate of the national two-party system, as well as the structure of state and local politics across the South, hinged, to a significant degree, on how Republicans fared in implementing congressional Reconstruction from 1868 to 1876.

During these years, America's global power expanded, spectacular economic changes reshaped both factories and farms, and the forces of immigration, urbanization, and industrialization brought urgent challenges that demanded new solutions—but no issue commanded more attention than Reconstruction because of its importance to the generation that had fought the Civil War. Northerners wished for harmony with the white southern population, while desiring to define freedom's meaning for the formerly enslaved men and women. Republicans pursued legislative and constitutional avenues to commit the country to equality before the law regardless of race, to define citizenship to include black people, and to enhance the power of the national state to protect the rights of all citizens.

In 1867, Radical Reconstruction awarded black men the right to vote in the South, beginning a momentous experiment in interracial democracy. Appreciating the great importance of the black vote for their party's future, in February 1869 the outgoing Republican Congress strove to guarantee African American suffrage with the last of the three Reconstruction amendments. The Fifteenth Amendment stated that the "right of citizens of the United States to vote shall not be denied or abridged by the United States or by any State on account of race, color, or previous condition of servitude." It passed both houses of Congress and went to the states, where, because Republicans controlled the majority of the legislatures, it obtained the required three-fourths majority for ratification by March 1870. The Fifteenth Amendment represented another huge advancement for black Americans, which, like emancipation, had been unimaginable a short while before.

The final stage of Reconstruction, the "Redemption" of the South, culminated with the contested presidential election of 1876. The compromise that brought Republican Rutherford B. Hayes to the White House is usually credited with ending the northern attempt to remake the former Confederate States so black and white people could coexist peacefully and where black men could vote without fear of violent reprisals. In the end, the Union held. Reconstruction's accomplishments were considerable, but full realization of the potential political and social fruits of emancipation proved too formidable a goal in a nation where most white people never had been primarily concerned with the status of black people. An uneasy white reconciliation in the reunited nation proved easier to achieve than black equality, and by 1876 the northern people, most of whom would have identified reunion as the primary object and success of the war, had withdrawn their support for the Republican version of Reconstruction.

I. THE SOUTHERN REPUBLICAN COALITION IN POWER

When President Grant assumed office in 1869, the majority of the ex-Confederate states had Reconstruction governments in place. Republican rule rested on black votes and restrictions on white suffrage. The Republican vision of Reconstruction—a free-labor society in the South, protection and civil rights guaranteed for its freedpeople, and a competitive two-party system—was ready to be tested in a great experiment in biracial governance. Could African Americans be accepted as one more group of law-abiding citizens who could claim a place beside their former masters in the South? Or would Reconstruction leave them "nothing but freedom?"

Overseeing the critical policy would be a southern Republican Party that had no natural roots in the region. Establishment of these "Black Republican" governments met with immediate opposition from violent white supremacists intent on overturning them and restoring Democratic Party rule. Throughout congressional Reconstruction, the majority of the southern white population viewed the Republicans as an instrument of despised change. Outside the South, the party attracted the most prosperous, educated, and influential elements of the population and was supported by an increasingly powerful block of middle-class voters. In contrast, the party's southern base consisted of the poor, the illiterate, the powerless whites, and the black voters; southern Republicans held power but desperately needed long-term support of the freedmen, of some southern whites, and of northern men who made their postwar careers in the South.

African Americans formed by far the largest—80 percent or more—part of the fragile Republican coalition. With the support of President Grant and the protection of the U.S. Army, the freedmen joined Union Leagues (organized political groups supporting Republicans), voted enthusiastically, engaged in other political actions, and were elected to all levels of government throughout the South. South Carolina and Louisiana had a majority of black legislators, and seventeen African Americans were elected to the U.S. Congress, including the first two to serve in the U.S. Senate: Hiram R. Revels and Blanche K. Bruce, both of Mississippi. The research of modern scholars demonstrates that most black officeholders were competent and intelligent men, and that ordinary black voters cast their votes to uphold the new Republican state governments.

Black leaders came mostly from the elite of the community. A majority were literate and educated, and many had enjoyed free status before the Civil War. Often professionals who worked as ministers, farmers, artisans, and small businessmen, prominent African Americans also included a large number of veterans of the Union army. Francis L. Cardozo from South Carolina, who served as that state's secretary of state and treasurer, attended the University of Glasgow. Hiram Revels was a North Carolina-born minister and educator, while Ben Turner of Alabama, an ex-slave who described himself as "destitute of education," made his reputation in the U.S. Congress as a champion for black literacy. South Carolina congressman Joseph H. Rainey worked as a barber before the war and spent his years as a national legislator urging greater enforcement of civil rights laws.

By the end of Reconstruction, more than six hundred African American men served as legislators. As a group, they contradicted a major myth of Reconstruction promulgated in the early twentieth century by historians who described elected black officials as ignorant or incompetent. A majority of black officeholders managed effectively the duties of their offices. Most ex-slaves were illiterate, but blame for that condition must be placed on a system that denied them access to education. Yet although black men made undeniable political gains, the vast gap between the Republican Party's leadership and its base of illiterate ex-slaves grew ever more problematical.

Indeed, Republican politicians, whether black or white, could offer little hope to freedpeople who were often less interested in advances in the legislature or in demanding their civil rights on public transportation in Atlanta than in improving their economic fortunes. They were engaged in a daily struggle to find a place for themselves and their families in the new South. Black politicians pressed for confiscation and redistribution of land from white planters to freedpeople, but the majority of white Republicans expressed scant support. The entire region suffered from economic depression and looked to reviving the cotton market as a way to brighten prospects. This required adjustments and compromises from the former plantation owners as well as the black labor force. Sharecropping provided the compromise but offered little upward mobility. It brought black laborers, who farmed parcels of a white owner's land in return for a share of the profits, into dependency and debt, making it difficult to live with dignity. Although many black southerners carved out relatively stable lives as property owners, others moved from lives of chattel slavery to lives of debt peonage. No longer enslaved, most sharecroppers nonetheless missed out on the economic benefits they had expected from emancipation. Especially common among African Americans, sharecropping also ensnared many white

Plate 21. "The First Colored Senator and Representatives." In 1872, Currier and Ives offered this group portrait of African Americans who served in the U.S. Congress during Reconstruction.

farmers. Yeomen who sought to participate in staple crop production were caught in the web of debt that merchants could spin. They, too, had hopes for a Republican Reconstruction that would improve their prospects.

"Scalawag," a derogatory term meaning "a low worthless fellow," referred to white southerners who voted with the Republican Party during Reconstruction. The second largest element of the Republican coalition, they welcomed the opportunity to diminish or destroy the power of planters they believed had kept the prewar South backward and dependent. Scalawags tended to be Unionists during the Civil War and lived in the uplands of Tennessee, North Carolina, Virginia, Georgia, Arkansas, and Alabama. Although the scalawags ranged widely in

terms of their social standing, economic background, and political loyalties, they did share common beliefs. First and foremost, they wanted
the South to enjoy a progressive and prosperous economy based upon
the benefits of free labor and industrialization.

James L. Alcorn of Mississippi ranked among the more prominent
scalawags. A former Whig and Confederate officer elected as a Republican governor, he supported both emancipation and the Fourteenth
Amendment and was determined to implement an agenda to bring his
state into the modern world. Scorned by many of their fellow southerners, scalawags such as Alcorn dominated state public offices, working toward a more economically progressive and diverse South. Scalawags welcomed northern investment and technology that promised
new or improved roads and bridges and a substantially enlarged railroad system. They sought opportunities to build or expand businesses
and factories and to raise the standard of living for all, not just the class
of plantation owners who dominated the prewar economy.

Other notable scalawags included Georgia governor Joseph E.
Brown and the former Confederate general James Longstreet, who in
1867 proclaimed that defeated southerners should accept the new order. A supporter and friend of U. S. Grant, Longstreet joined the Republicans and moved to New Orleans, where he worked in a cotton
firm and headed an insurance company. Eventually he held a number
of prominent positions in the federal government, earning the permanent scorn of numerous "unreconstructed" ex-Confederates who
dismissed the fact that he had been one of Robert E. Lee's most trusted lieutenants. The wealthier scalawags of New Orleans and Atlanta
looked forward to, and lobbied for, government-sponsored subsidies
and loans for railroad construction and textile mills.

Most scalawags were neither prominent nor wealthy, and their continued support represented a vital part of the Republican Party's future
in the region. Simply put, the party could not sustain itself without
backing from a diverse and substantial group of white men. The plain,

hardworking farmers of the region—representing the greatest number of the scalawags—expected the Republicans to make good on their pledge for debt relief and cheap land. The yeomanry wanted to put the vestiges of a slavery-based economy behind them, and they looked forward to the material benefits of Unionism for themselves and their children, including increased access to education and better employment.

As the 1860s came to an end and the new decade began, scalawags came under increasing pressure to join a resurgent white Democratic Party. A widely circulated taunt defined a scalawag as "a native born white man who says he is no better than a negro and tells the truth when he says it." Foreshadowing the ultimate failure of the Republican coalition, most scalawags rejected any move toward social or political equality with the former slaves, ultimately adhering to the region's pervasive racism.

The third and smallest part of the Republican coalition was composed of northern whites who came south during the war and settled there afterward. Although tiny in number—perhaps 2 percent of the overall southern Republican vote—they dominated the party's leadership, holding 30 percent of the elected positions. These men were often former Union soldiers, Freedmen's Bureau agents, businessmen, lawyers, doctors, journalists, missionaries, engineers, and educators. Called "carpetbaggers," a term coined by hostile southern whites implying that all their worldly belongings could fit into a carpetbag suitcase, they provided a solid core of leadership for the party. Albion W. Tourgée and Oliver Otis Howard were noteworthy representatives of the group. Tourgée, an author and soldier, moved to North Carolina just after the war and distinguished himself as a superior court judge fighting for black equality and against the Ku Klux Klan. Howard boasted a more celebrated career. A native of Maine, corps commander with the Army of the Potomac who later headed the Army of the Tennessee, and commissioner of the Freedmen's Bureau, he founded Washington's Howard

University, a black college, in 1867. Carpetbag politicians made up a highly educated group who, although often idealistic, also migrated for the South's sunny weather and economic opportunities. As businessmen, judges, or public officials, their collective ambition sought to bring a modern social and economic structure to the region, while at the same time dramatically widening the democratic possibilities for ordinary people. More than sixty northerners served in the U.S. Congress from the southern states, while nine carpetbaggers served as Reconstruction governors, including New England-born U.S. senator and Mississippi governor Adelbert Ames, who fought a losing battle for the political and equal rights of black people in the Magnolia State.

II. REPUBLICAN STATE GOVERNMENTS AT WORK AND UNDER FIRE

Republican governments brought many positive changes to the South in a short period. Several states, including South Carolina with its black-dominated legislature, passed progressive civil rights laws, and in most states the judicial system underwent a needed reorganization. For the first time and with assistance from northern philanthropists, Republicans established public schools for both races. State financial aid supported railroad development and helped rebuild damaged or destroyed infrastructure, while industrial commissions worked to attract northern capital. These Republican reforms were worthy but also expensive. By 1870, tax rates rose to three or four times their 1860 levels. The rising costs of government fell hardest on small white landowners, who responded by forming taxpayers associations in every state to protest. Many withheld their taxes, forcing some state governments into a serious fiscal crisis. The anti-tax movement that swept across the South strengthened the Democrats' argument regarding the general inefficiency, wastefulness, and corruption of Republican rule.

Unfortunately Democratic charges contained considerable truth.

Republican-dominated state houses were notably plagued by violence, corruption, and political turmoil. Opponents accused numerous Republican state legislators of accepting railroad bribes, seizing profits from shady land deals, and awarding business contracts to friends and supporters. Funds for public schools mysteriously disappeared into the wrong pockets. Louisiana's corruption was particularly notorious, and its malfeasance received national press coverage. Inexperienced governments trying to solve longstanding and difficult problems can explain some of the corruption. In reality, this kind of financial and political chicanery was widespread in the decades after the Civil War. The postwar decades featured unprecedented economic growth, with great quantities of cash flowing from big business interests into friendly politicians' pockets. Northern states, including New York, Pennsylvania, Ohio, and Indiana, experienced their own massive corruption stories that reached the federal level when the Crédit Mobilier and Whiskey Ring scandals rocked Grant's administration. The corruption and graft, high tax rates, and wasteful spending allowed Democrats to create and exploit a portrait of a helpless and beaten white population whose fortunes were dependent on the wiles and whims of incompetent blacks, greedy scalawags, and vengeful carpetbaggers. Political attacks on southern Republican governments following this script helped the Democratic Party bring Reconstruction to a thudding halt.

The unexpected success of black officeholders, improvements in literacy among the ex-slave population, and economic advancements by some freedpeople both incited and united a powerful political drive toward instituting a new system of white supremacy. "The great and paramount issue is Shall Negroes or White Men Rule?" cried a Democratic politician. By far the most potent white outrage focused on black suffrage and the presumed racial equality it bestowed. Republican power in the South, made possible by African American voters, had to be smashed and blacks returned to a subordinate position. The political comeback of the Democratic Party relied on, and benefited from, a reign of terror to intimidate black and white Republican leaders and voters.

The most notorious terrorist group, among many, was the Ku Klux Klan. It attracted members from all ranks of southern society, including veterans and dozens of former Confederate officers. The hooded organization caused constant turmoil in numerous election cycles in every former Confederate state. Few in the North imagined the consequences of widespread lawlessness that undermined Reconstruction. KKK-inspired voter intimidation, numerous political murders, and general terror paralyzed Republican governments in Mississippi, Louisiana, Arkansas, and the Carolinas in the late 1860s and early 1870s. A Klan leader, the Confederate military hero Nathan Bedford Forrest, explained the targeting: "I have no powder to burn killing negroes. I intend to kill radicals."

Terrorism did not go unchallenged. Republicans defended themselves by organizing militias to capture Klan members and bring them to justice. Often they returned from their forays to burned-out homes or found their families frightened by threats. Even if Klan perpetrators were caught, white southern juries would not convict. For example, a Mississippi district attorney's case fell apart when five witnesses were killed. This type of occurrence exerted a chilling effect on jurors everywhere. One response lay in the imposition of martial law enforced by local or state militias. Many Republican governors and other officials proved reluctant to take this unpopular step, fearing an even worse backlash from the Klan.

The actions taken in 1869 by one carpetbag governor, Clayton Powell of Arkansas, offered an example of strong state leadership. A Union army veteran who fought guerrillas in Missouri, Powell organized black and white militias under the command of Union army veterans, ordered the militia to capture and arrest Klan members who committed election outrages, and proclaimed martial law in affected counties. Military courts tried the Klansmen, several of whom received death sentences carried out by a firing squad. Powell effectively broke the Klansmen's power in Arkansas, but other states did not fare as well. As the Klan grew ever bolder, beleaguered state and local officials pleaded with the federal government for assistance in maintaining order.

In response, President Grant signed into law three measures known as the Force Acts of 1870-71. These enabled him to use the power of the federal government to restore order by sending troops, imposing martial law, and suspending the writ of habeas corpus. In addition, Grant appointed a proactive attorney general, Amos T. Akerman, and established the Department of Justice as a part of the cabinet. Akerman wielded his power through federal marshals and military forces to arrest thousands of Klansmen in several states. Although only sixty-five Klansmen went to federal prison, Grant's strong response made the presidential election of 1872 the "fairest and freest" in the South until the late twentieth century.

The Force Acts helped smash the KKK, but their negative impact on the fate of Reconstruction among northerners was profound. The actions taken under the law, however justified, violated the cherished American belief in the separation of powers. Most citizens assumed that once the Civil War ended, state rights and a national government whose powers were limited would again prevail. Across the country, Democratic newspapers vilified Grant for imposing a "military dictatorship" on the helpless region. He defended his actions as undertaken only when "acts of violence . . . render the power of the State and its officers unequal to the task of protecting life and property and securing public order therein." This explanation fell on increasingly deaf ears in the North as well as the South.

III. RETREAT FROM RECONSTRUCTION AND SOUTHERN REDEMPTION

Ulysses S. Grant won reelection in 1872 handily, overcoming a serious challenge from anti-Reconstruction Democrats and dissatisfied Republicans. But Republicans, who sustained majorities in both houses of Congress that year, noted that popular enthusiasm for a harsh Reconstruction had waned. In the 1870s, the enormous difficulty of reconstructing the South belied a formerly optimistic vision of an easy reunion. Harmony between the sections clearly could not be achieved quickly. In fact, it had become a huge undertaking that involved not only readmitting the seceded states but also reinventing a South without slavery, restoring a semblance of harmony between former enemies, and rebuilding the Southern infrastructure and economy destroyed by the conflict. As optimism increasingly gave way to a practical desire to let the southern states exercise "home rule," congressional resistance to leniency toward former rebels lessened. In 1872, Congress passed an Amnesty Act that removed officeholding disabilities for everyone except a few of the highest-ranking politicians and military officers of the former Confederacy. (In 1898, Congress issued a universal amnesty for all those who had not been granted it in earlier acts.)

In the 1870s, both the federal government and the northern voters began to tire of the continual fight to reconstruct their former foes. Other issues, such as the Indian wars in the West, began to draw attention and energy away from southern problems. Republicans lost badly at the ballot box in 1874, as negative reactions to the devastating depression of 1873 restored Democratic control of the U.S. House of Representatives for the first time since 1859. Meanwhile, the Republican coalition weakened under relentless pressure from white Democrats in the South, who refused to support what they considered illegally constituted state governments. The Democratic cry that Republicans had denied votes to competent white southern voters while enabling "unfit" African Americans to cast ballots resonated with many northerners. Southerners railed against "Black Republicanism" and fought against "Negro rule." Nothing seemed to stop the crumbling of the Republican Party and the reemergence of southern Democrats. When whites regained control of their state governments, they immediately removed African Americans from office and did whatever possible to deny black voters their voice in politics.

By 1876, southern Republican governments remained only in Florida, Louisiana, and South Carolina. After fraud marred the closely fought presidential election of 1876, backroom deals and a series of compromises allowed Republican Rutherford B. Hayes to take the White House over Democrat Samuel B. Tilden. Despite the fact that the Republican Party relied on African American votes for their power in the South, Hayes ended Reconstruction when he pulled the last U.S. troops out of the region. By April 1877, "Redemption" was complete with all states of the former Confederacy again under Democratic rule.

The election of 1876 and its aftermath solidified a status quo that remained in place for the remainder of the nineteenth century. Republicans controlled the majority of northern voters and held a virtual monopoly on the presidency. Although elections were usually close, every president between 1860 and 1900, with the exception of Grover Cleveland, was a Republican and all but Lincoln a veteran of the Union army. The Democrats, meanwhile, typically controlled the House of Representatives, dominated the "Solid South," and held power in a number of northern localities, particularly New York City. African Americans, most of them still living in the South, were largely denied a voice in politics. It would take another depression, in 1932, to begin the historic transformation of the Democratic Party from its antebellum incarnation as a pro-slavery and state rights political organization to its later liberal incarnation.

One of the most controversial eras in American history, congressional Reconstruction, until the 1960s, was widely depicted in popular culture as well as in textbooks as an experiment gone terribly wrong. According to this interpretation, only when the South's white Democratic "Redeemers" wrested state governments from the clutches of the Republican Party and occupying Federal troops did sanity again prevail throughout the region. Current history books present a far more positive and complex depiction of the era, although scholars continue to debate its successes and failures. Most historians do not find it surprising that the Republican Party's control in the South lasted fewer than ten years, but many do find it surprising that it ever was able to wield any power at all.

Was Reconstruction a success or failure? The overriding goal of the war for most loyal citizens had been restoration of the Union.

IV. WAS RECONSTRUCTION A LOST MOMENT?

Many historians have described Reconstruction as a lost moment when the white loyal citizenry abandoned a commitment to provide full political and social equality to freedpeople. This interpretation generally describes a war that began as a struggle to restore the Union, turned into a fight that elevated emancipation to an equivalent war aim, and, after the Confederacy collapsed, positioned the nation to press on toward racial equality. Failure to fulfill the last of these goals, goes a common argument, allowed a moment of national promise to slip away, doomed formerly enslaved people to decades of brutal Jim Crow governance, and delayed progress toward African American equality until the second half of the 20th Century.

The idea of a lost moment makes sense only if a credible possibility of racial equality existed in the aftermath of the war. Two things would be essential to achieve that end. First, there would have to be widespread agreement among white northerners that only equality for freedpeople would render military victory over the Confederacy and emancipation complete—and that equality would have to include, among many other things, enfranchising black men. Second, success would require an effective, and perhaps prolonged, military occupation of the former Confederate states because ex-Rebels almost certainly would oppose racial equality. Such an occupation, in turn, would rest on public approval of a substantial post-Appomattox military presence in the form of either a greatly increased regular army or a large force of citizen-soldiers.

Most white Americans in the loyal states did not believe the war left any major questions unresolved. First to last during the conflict, they identified restoration of the Union as the war's great objective. Most also came to accept emancipation as necessary to defeat the Confederacy and to safeguard the nation's future because only slavery-related issues, they thought, could trigger another internal rebellion of the sort that erupted in 1860-1861. With the Union salvaged and emancipation accomplished, there was no groundswell to pursue equal rights for freedpeople with a massive military presence in the former Confederacy. White Americans generally saw emancipation as the concluding act in a drama featuring slavery-related issues as a poisonous aspect of political life, not as the beginning act of a narrative leading to full racial equality.

Attitudes regarding black enfranchisement underscore the absence of any sense of urgency about equal political rights. In 1865, only five New England states allowed African American men to vote. That year, referenda to emulate those states' voting laws failed in Minnesota, Wisconsin, and Connecticut. Over the next three years, similar referenda in New York, Ohio, Kansas, and Nebraska Territory yielded the same negative result. By 1868, more than three years after Appomattox, only Minnesota, where a second referendum succeeded, and Iowa had joined the five New England states in extending the franchise to black men.

What about guaranteeing equal rights through a long-term military occupation? In April 1865, huge stretches of the former Rebel states, including virtually all of Texas, contained almost no Union troops. A true occupation would have required massive congressional appropriations that might stretch over many years. It also would have meant abandoning a deep-seated antipathy to peacetime military forces that had been in place since hatred of the Quartering Act of 1765 helped create sentiment for the American Revolution.

In the weeks after Appomattox, both men in blue uniforms and civilians on the home front demanded a rapid demobilization. As already noted in chapter 4, the Union army fielded more than 1,000,000 citizen-soldiers on May 1, 1865, 800,000 of whom mustered out by the end of November. One year later, just 11,000 of the volunteers remained in service. Secretary of War Edwin M. Stanton aptly said of the demobilization: "No similar work of like magnitude regarding its immensity and the small limit of time in which it has been performed, has . . . any parallel in the history of armies." This demobilization reflected nearly universal sentiment among white citizens that the war had accomplished its goals and that no large postbellum force would be necessary.

Congressional actions further highlight the absence of support for a large army of occupation. On July 28, 1866, Congress fixed the size of the regular army at 54,302, a number reduced in 1869 to 37,313 and in 1876 to 27,472. Between 1866 and 1877, U.S. soldiers performed duties related to Reconstruction but also garrisoned coastal installations and conducted operations against Native Americans. In 1866, for example, half of the regulars were stationed in the South and half deployed along the coasts or in the West. Over the next nine years, the contingent in the South dropped from about 45 percent in 1867 to less than 10 percent in 1875. At the peak in 1866, the regular army's strength across the former Confederacy fell short of 30,000—compared to the 1,000,000 citizen-soldiers available in April 1865. By 1871, the midpoint of Reconstruction, just 8,700 regulars were carrying out Reconstruction-related duties. These statistics indicate there never was a real occupation of the former Confederacy—though brutal suppression under the boot heel of Yankee soldiers became a staple of Lost Cause special pleading. Thirty thousand soldiers in a territory covering 750,000 square miles—an expanse larger than all of western

Europe--scarcely rises to the level of an "occupation."

Any claim for a lost moment during Reconstruction runs aground on hard realities: The overwhelming majority of loyal citizens in the United States believed the nation had achieved its wartime goals, cared little about the fate of formerly enslaved people, and had almost no interest in supporting a large peacetime army. Taking these factors into account, Reconstruction should not be considered a lost moment.

But was it a success or a failure? By the measure of reestablishing political, economic, and social relations between North and South, Reconstruction was a success. The nation was stable and strong by 1876. If another goal was to fulfill the promise of emancipation by bringing justice to the freedpeople, then it was a failure. Four million Americans had cast off the shackles of slavery, but poverty and racism severely limited their freedom. Yet the judgment of failure should be qualified. African Americans tested the limits of freedom and found great meaning in their new family and community lives. By late 1866, for example, Charleston's African American community had built eleven churches in the city. By 1869, the Freedmen's Bureau was in charge of 3,000 schools that educated over 150,000 black children throughout the states of the ex-Confederacy. Half of the teachers in those schools were African American. Finally, the Thirteenth, Fourteenth, and Fifteenth amendments provided the foundation for the civil rights movement of the 1960s, when some of the major promises of the Civil War and Reconstruction era were finally fulfilled. The Union had been saved and the seeds for a more just and equitable society sown during the course of a seismic war and its aftermath.

Plate 22. Decoration Day (later changed to Memorial Day) provided an occasion to recall the service of citizen-soldiers during the Civil War. In this engraving from *Frank Leslie's Illustrated Newspaper*, a one-armed veteran instructs a young boy, while his mother and sister place flowers on the grave.

CHAPTER 12

THE WARTIME GENERATION REMEMBERS
THE CONFLICT

AMERICANS WHO EXPERIENCED the Civil War plumbed its meanings in four major interpretive traditions. Three of the four took shape almost immediately after the war—the Union Cause in the North, the Emancipation Cause among some white people in the North and black people in both sections, and the Lost Cause in the South. A fourth, the Reconciliation Cause, appeared somewhat later and won numerous adherents among white people throughout the re-united nation. Each of the traditions embraced a selective reading of events and allowed its adherents to take something meaningful away from the conflict that would remain the greatest event of their lives for most of those who lived through it.

The Union, emancipation, and reconciliation traditions overlapped in some ways, as did the Lost Cause and reconciliation traditions. Yet

each of the four represents a distinct attempt to explain and understand the conflict. For example, Union and emancipation joined in
expressing joy at the destruction of the Confederacy but often diverged
in discussing the end of slavery. For the Union Cause, emancipation
represented a tool to punish slaveholders, undermine the Confederacy,
and remove a longstanding threat to the development of the republic; for the Emancipation Cause, it stood as the most important, and
ennobling, goal of the northern war effort, a signal blow for the advancement of millions of black Americans. Union and reconciliation
similarly lauded the fact that one nation emerged from the conflict,
and anyone who cherished the Union had to welcome, on some level
at least, the reintegration of former Rebels into the national citizenry. Yet unlike reconciliationists, who avoided discussion about which
cause was more just, supporters of the Union tradition never wavered
in their insistence that Confederates had been in the wrong. Adherents
of the Lost Cause and reconciliation could agree to mute emancipation
and the slavery-related politics of secession, but many former Confederates, whatever their public rhetoric about loyalty to the reconstituted
nation, persisted in celebrating a struggle for southern independence
that had gravely threatened the Founders' state-building handiwork.

All four traditions included a religious component. Those who
loved the Union detected a providential hand in the war's outcome,
predicting ever-greater success for a nation that seemed, with God's
approbation, destined to serve as a model of democracy and economic
vitality. For the freedpeople, emancipation provided a joyous ending
to their long and brutal passage through the wilderness of slavery. As
one black woman, filled with emotion, had put it to Union soldiers in
Alabama: "Glory Hallelujah! The Lord's heard our prayers. . . . There's
eight hundred of us praying for you at Mobile!" Former Confederates
necessarily took a very different lesson from the war, interpreting it
as a stern test of their faith and constancy. "It's hard to think that
our glorious old Confederate banner—which we have borne high aloft

unconquered so long—must now be furled," wrote one Confederate cavalryman who hoped white southerners would rebuild their land, "—but I doubt not—in his own good time God will give us a new & more beautiful one which shall float proudly and wide over all of our foes. Let us put our trust in Him." Many reconciliationists shared the idea of God's testing the American people—but with a happier ending than was possible for the Lost Cause—as well as confidence that reunion paved the way for American imperial greatness as a Christian nation on the world stage.

I. THE WINNERS—UNION AND EMANCIPATION

Most of the twenty-two million citizens of the loyal states would have identified restoration of the Union as the conflict's most important outcome—making the Union Cause by far the most widely embraced of the four traditions among the wartime generation. Herman Melville put the case very directly in the dedication for his collection of war poetry: "The Battle-Pieces In This Volume," he wrote, "Are Dedicated To The Memory Of The THREE HUNDRED THOUSAND Who In The War For The Maintenance Of The Union Fell Devotedly Under The Flag Of Their Fathers." On June 18, 1865, Republican politician Roscoe Conkling took more words to render a comparable assessment of the war's meaning in a speech to members of the 117th New York Infantry, who had stopped in Utica on their way home from service in Virginia and North Carolina. He congratulated the "victorious soldiers of the Republic" for their role in defending "the life and glory of your country. . . . a common purpose has inspired you, a common hope has led you on. . . . Peace with the Government and the constitution our fathers established, has been the object of the war, and the prayer of every patriot and every soldier."

The Union Cause lauded U.S. military forces as a powerful instrument that crushed the rebellion and ensured the republic's future.

After the martyred Lincoln, Ulysses S. Grant stood as the preeminent Union idol. His victories at Forts Henry and Donelson, Shiloh, Vicksburg, and Chattanooga had broken Confederate power in the Western Theater, and his decisive confrontation with Robert E. Lee in Virginia had ended triumphantly at Appomattox. William Tecumseh Sherman, the victor at Atlanta in 1864, and Philip H. Sheridan, who that same year thrashed Confederates in the Shenandoah Valley, emerged from the conflict as Grant's premier lieutenants, transcendent war heroes immortalized in art and literature.

Decoration Day (later Memorial Day) began in 1868 and soon became a major holiday that honored the Union dead, more than 300,000 of whom were interred in dozens of national cemeteries created shortly after the war. Speeches on Decoration Day and words engraved on hundreds of monuments erected across the North celebrated the Union Cause. Texts on three of those monuments—one in New England, one in Kansas, and one in the far Southwest—offer sentiments typical of many others. Meredith, New Hampshire, honored its sons in "The Twelfth Regiment New Hampshire Volunteers Who Fought In The War Of 1861-65 For The Preservation Of The Union." In September 1898, the residents of Junction City, Kansas, unveiled an arch commemorating soldiers and sailors, "Who Inspired By Patriotism Freely Offered Their Lives For The Maintenance Of An Undivided Country." Long before the ceremony in Junction City, citizens of Santa Fe had placed an obelisk in the town's plaza, requested by the "people of New Mexico through their legislatures of 1866-7-8," that carries the words "May the Union be Perpetual."

Citizen-soldiers lay at the heart of much of the Union Cause tradition. To them, affirmed countless speakers, writers, and artists, the nation owed undiminished thanks. No one put this sentiment better than U. S. Grant, who in the 1870s distilled into a few sentences what most loyal citizens would have said gave the most meaning to their great internecine conflict. "What saved the Union," Grant told companions at a dinner, "was the coming forward of the young men of the nation. They came from their homes and fields, as they did in the time of the Revolution, giving everything to the country. To their devotion we owe the salvation of the Union. . . . So long as our young men are animated by this spirit there will be no fear for the Union." The nation's preeminent hero had pared the war's triumphal elements down to a single salient point. Citizen-soldiers had saved a democratic republic invaluable not only to its own citizens but also as an example of popular self-rule for the rest of the world.

The Emancipation Cause developed alongside the Union Cause. Among black and white abolitionists, Radical Republicans, and the overwhelming majority of the nation's more than four million African Americans, the end of slavery stood as the war's most consequential outcome. These people, perhaps 15 percent of the whole population, joined Union Cause brethren in laying full blame for the outbreak of war on the seceding states and tying the rebellion directly to a "slave power conspiracy" that had wielded too much influence in the antebellum decades. Those devoted to the Emancipation Cause deeply resented what they saw as a tendency among some northerners, especially Democrats, to forgive ex-Rebels too easily. They also worried that those who trumpeted reunion above all else failed to give due attention to emancipation as a path-breaking accomplishment. In the early 1870s, Frederick Douglass notably lamented what he saw as northern complicity in spreading, or at least tolerating, pro-Confederate arguments. In an address at Arlington Cemetery on Decoration Day in 1871, he urged loyal Americans never to forget that "victory to the rebellion" would have "meant death to the republic." The "unselfish devotion of the noble army who rest in these honored graves," he continued, had yielded "a united country, no longer cursed by the hell-black system of human bondage."

Many white Union veterans felt a bond with their black comrades and held emancipation up as a worthy and necessary element of the war for Union. Thousands joined USCT men in integrated chapters of the Grand Army of the Republic, the largest veterans' organization in the country and the first national political lobby in American history. After noting that the "fixed policy of Lincoln primarily was the preservation of the Union," a white regimental historian from Pennsylvania specifically applauded the president's anti-slavery feelings. The Pennsylvanians in the regiment "sealed their convictions with their blood on the sacred soil of Gettysburg," he wrote, thus giving force to the Emancipation Proclamation, "the most immortal moral edict known to any nation" by which Lincoln "caused the shackles to drop from the arms, intellects and souls of about four millions of American citizens."

African American communities in states of the former Confederacy established traditions, much like Decoration Day, that marked the achievement of freedom. Although often held on January 1 to honor Lincoln's Emancipation Proclamation, these commemorations did not follow a rigid pattern—as the celebration of Juneteenth in Texas demonstrates. Seldom openly antagonistic toward those who praised the Union Cause but scarcely mentioned emancipation, black people argued for the addition of emancipation to Union as an imperishable outcome of the bloody labors carried out by U.S. soldiers and sailors.

The nearly 200,000 African Americans who had donned blue uniforms held a special position in the Emancipation Cause narrative. They had risked their lives to stake a claim for freedom and political and legal equality. "What a picture for the historian's immortal pen to paint of the freemen of America," wrote USCT veteran Joseph T. Wilson, "whose sufferings were long, whose struggle was gigantic, and whose achievement was a glorious personal and political freedom!" Although the Robert Gould Shaw Memorial in Boston included black soldiers, no public monuments commemorated the USCT units (such recognition came in 1998 with the African American Civil War Memorial in Washington, D.C.). But black veterans stood out as exemplary citizens in many of their communities, and their generation always remembered the role they had played in the great drama of emancipation.

II. THE LOST CAUSE

Former Confederates entered the postwar world as losers on a grand scale who remained defiantly unapologetic about their effort to establish a slaveholding republic. Seeking to take something positive away from their catastrophic experiment in nation building, they created what came to be called the Lost Cause school of interpretation. It predominated among the more than five million white people who identified themselves as Confederates during the war, as well as among thousands of Kentuckians and other Border State residents who hated emancipation and other Republican policies during and after the war. Architects of the Lost Cause interpreted the war as an admirable struggle against hopeless odds, played down the importance of slavery in bringing secession and war, ascribed to Confederates constitutional high-mindedness, and celebrated the gallantry of soldiers who followed Robert E. Lee and other Rebel commanders. Such a struggle involved no loss of honor on the part of the vanquished and placed Confederates in the best possible light before the bar of history. Repeated endlessly during the post-Appomattox decades, Lost Cause arguments reached a wide audience through participants' memoirs, speeches at gatherings of veterans, and commemorative programs at the graves of Confederate soldiers. White southerners created their own Memorial Day in 1866—sometimes called Decoration Day or Confederate Heroes Day—and gathered their military dead in special sections of cemeteries in cities such as Richmond, Atlanta, and Petersburg. Various artworks, including prints published in the North, also celebrated the Confederate struggle, as did public monuments on courthouse grounds and elsewhere.

Superior Union manpower and material resources figured prominently in the Lost Cause. The United States had enjoyed an advantage of approximately two-and-one-half to one in soldiers, but Lost Cause advocates typically lengthened even those odds. Few devoted more attention to Union numbers and industrial might than Jubal A. Early, who characterized the campaign Lee and Grant waged in 1864 as "a contest between mechanical power and physical strength, on the one hand, and the gradually diminishing nerve and sinew of Confederate soldiers, on the other, until the unlimited resources of our enemies must finally prevail over all the genius and chivalric daring, which had so long baffled their mighty efforts in the field." An imposing monument on the Capitol grounds in Austin, Texas, told a similar story. Its text underestimated Confederate strength by 250,000-300,000 and overestimated that of U.S. forces by 600,000: "The South, Against Overwhelming Numbers and Resources, Fought Until Exhausted. . . . Number Of Men Enlisted: Confederate Armies, 600,000; Federal Armies, 2,859,132." Contending against odds of almost five to one, as the Texas memorial would have it, set a standard that Lost Cause advocates used to instruct their children and later generations about resiliency and sacrifice (women were especially diligent in monitoring how southern school textbooks dealt with the sectional crisis and the war).

Lost Cause writers knew their slaveholding society had stood outside the mainstream of Western history, and they sought to remove that stigma from their record by presenting slavery as peripheral to secession and the Confederacy. The example of Alexander H. Stephens, the Confederacy's vice president, illuminates how statements in 1861 differed from Lost Cause arguments. As already noted, Stephens's Cornerstone Speech of March 21, 1861, laid out an unequivocal statement of the Confederacy's devotion to white supremacy and the "natural and moral" subordination of enslaved black people, observing that "This, our new Government, is the first, in the history of the world, based upon this great physical, philosophical, and moral truth." Stephens's postwar memoir, in contrast, claimed the "War had its origin in *opposing principles*. . . . a strife between the principles of Federation, on the one side, and Centralism, or Consolidation, on the other. Slavery, so called, was but *the question* on which these antagonistic principles, which had been in conflict, from the beginning, on divers *other questions*, were finally brought into actual and active collision with each other on the field of battle." Jefferson Davis's statements from 1861 and in his memoirs followed a similar trajectory regarding the importance of slavery.

Beyond the battlefield, the Lost Cause generally ignored divisions within the Confederate populace to depict a united people waging a steadfast resistance against Yankee aggressors. Women often received extravagant praise as the staunchest Confederate partisans, while slaves remained loyal to their masters and mistresses. The introduction to a collection of Confederate women's narratives touched key Lost Cause bases: "[I]t may truly be said of the Southern women of 1861-65 that the simple narrative of their life and work unfolds a record of achievement, endurance, and self-sacrificing devotion that should be revealed and recognized as a splendid inspiration to men and women everywhere." Patriotic women thus joined gallant soldiers and loyal slaves as allies in the Lost Cause version of the Confederacy.

Robert E. Lee occupied center stage in much Lost Cause literature. Indeed, he eventually figured more prominently in Confederate memory than did Grant to the Union Cause tradition (Grant always shared the spotlight with the martyred Lincoln). Lee afforded Lost Cause writers their best chance to find a sympathetic audience beyond the borders of the old Confederacy. Widely praised as a self-effacing Christian gentleman, Lee had faced intimidating odds on the battlefield—two-to-one or more in some instances—yet crafted a series of notable victories such as Chancellorsville and Second Bull Run. He and his men fit the template of stalwart heroes engaged in a hopeless struggle. Even many northern editors expressed admiration when he died in 1870. For example, the *New York Herald* gushed that Lee "came nearer the ideal of a soldier and Christian general than any man we can think of," while the *New York Times* mentioned how Lee's "unobtrusive modesty and purity of life" after the war helped win "the respect even of those who most bitterly deplore and reprobate his course in the rebellion." In time, and quite remarkably, Lee transcended region to take his position among American heroes. Arlington, his home overlooking Washington, became a National Park Service site, and his visage adorned five U.S. postage stamps. What other rebel chieftain, anywhere at any time, has received comparable notice from the nation his military efforts almost dismembered?

III. RECONCILIATION—FOR SOME

A movement toward reconciliation gained power in the late nineteenth century. The Reconciliation Cause included major figures—military and political—from both sides who advocated a memory of the conflict that muted the divisive issue of slavery, seldom assigned relative value or virtue to the two causes, and cheered the bravery and steadfastness of white soldiers in Union and Confederate armies. It was because of *American* traits exhibited by men in blue and gray, the reconciliation-ist interpretation maintained, that the United States stood positioned by 1900 to emerge as an economic powerhouse on the world stage. Reconciliationists often summoned memories of Grant and Lee at Appomattox, where the two generals set a precedent for peaceful reunion and began a healing process that reminded all Americans of their shared history and traditions. Although sometimes combining with elements of the Union Cause and, much less often, the Emancipation Cause, the Reconciliation Cause most often reached out to the white South and its Lost Cause tradition.

Reconciliationists achieved considerable success but did not displace the memory traditions that took unabashedly partisan stances.

As already noted, most Union Cause advocates never ceased to assert the righteousness of their position, and most former Confederates nourished feelings of antipathy toward an enemy who had used military force to end their slavery-based social system. Reconstruction, with its Fourteenth and Fifteenth amendments conveying political and legal protections to freedpeople, deepened the white South's already substantial sense of outrage toward the North. In 1905, former Confederate general Clement A. Evans sputtered that the postwar era had been marked by "topsy-turvy conditions generally, domestic upheaval, negroes voting . . . disorder on plantations, Loyal Leagues and Freedmen's Bureaus, Ku Klux and Red Shirts"—all of which meant Evans, and huge numbers of other like-minded former Confederates, detested how the North forced unwelcome changes in the former slaveholding states' racial structures. The Jim Crow South stood as the defeated Confederates' most obvious, and enduring, reaction to the verdict of the battlefield.

Many Union veterans also clung to vitriolic sectional rhetoric. Almost sixty years after Appomattox, a publication of the Grand Army of the Republic eviscerated textbooks that included pro-Confederate material. Labeling the war a "Great Pro-Slavery Rebellion," the *Grand Army Record* referred to a "Lost Cause of Historical Truth." Union veterans sometimes took strident offense at public displays of the Confederate flag, as in 1891, when the Grand Army's national commander forbade members to participate in events that featured "the emblem of treason." Any veteran who ignored this instruction, he lectured, "violates his obligation 'to maintain true allegiance to the United States of America' . . . and brings disgrace upon the order of which he is a member." Republican politicians also kept animosities alive by heaping scorn on Democrats and ex-Confederates as purveyors of treason during the war. For their part, Democrats in the South excoriated scalawags and carpetbaggers, and candidates throughout the nation manipulated race and emancipation to suit their purposes.

What might be termed situational reconciliationists abounded in the North and the South. They said things in public that enhanced progress toward reunion but never achieved true forgiveness and acceptance vis-à-vis their old enemies. Robert E. Lee certainly fit into this category. He knew he was the most prominent ex-Confederate, and from Appomattox through his death he suppressed personal bitterness to set an example for the rest of the white South. On June 13, 1865, he formally requested a pardon from President Andrew Johnson (no pardon would be granted during his lifetime) and later that summer pronounced "it to be the duty of every one to unite in the restoration of the country, and the reestablishment of peace and harmony." Privately, Lee seethed about congressional legislation and constitutional amendments designed to place black people on a more equal footing with white Americans and worried that the federal government was assuming too much power and applying it inappropriately to the former Confederate states. If federal power outstripped that of the states by too wide a margin, predicted Lee darkly in 1866, the result could be calamitous: "The consolidation of the states into one vast republic, sure to be aggressive abroad and despotic at home, will be the certain precursor of that ruin which has overwhelmed all similar nations in the past."

Yet reconciliationists prevailed in many prominent forums. John Brown Gordon of Georgia, who had led a corps in Lee's army at Appomattox, typified the reconciliationist approach. A highly successful politician after the war, much sought-after speaker, and longtime commander in chief of the United Confederate Veterans, Gordon accepted the standard Lost Cause ideas relating to northern numbers, slavery, and Lee's brilliance. But he also sought to get beyond sectional animosity in his reconciliationist 1903 memoirs. "The unseemly things which occurred in the great conflict between the States should be forgotten, or at least forgiven," he advised readers, "and no longer permitted to disturb complete harmony between North and South." Looking to the future, Gordon closed with a paean to the modern nation: "So the Republic, rising from its baptism of blood with a national life more robust, a national union more complete, and a national influence ever widening, shall go forever forward in its benign mission to humanity." In 1895, William McKinley heard Gordon deliver a lecture titled "The Last Days of the Confederacy." "The lecture was intensely interesting," commented the Union veteran who would be elected president in 1896, "and was permeated by a highly patriotic spirit."

Two Democratic presidents used the fiftieth and seventy-fifth anniversaries of the battle of Gettysburg to pursue reconciliationist themes. Woodrow Wilson arrived at Gettysburg in 1913 as one who had been born in Virginia, lived as a boy in Georgia and South Carolina, and treasured a youthful memory of seeing Robert E. Lee, of whom he later wrote: "It is not an exaggeration to say that in all parts of this country the manhood and the self-forgetfulness and the achievements of General Lee are a conscious model to men who would be morally great." At Gettysburg, as "these gallant men in blue and gray sit all about us here," Wilson celebrated the masculine virtues and capacity for forgiveness those aged warriors had exhibited. "We have found one another again as brothers and comrades in arms," proclaimed Wilson, "enemies no longer, generous friends rather, our battles long past, the quarrel forgotten—except that we shall not forget the splendid valour, the manly devotion of the men then arrayed against one another, now grasping hands and smiling into each other's eyes."

Franklin D. Roosevelt chose similar rhetoric at Gettysburg on July 3, 1938. Speaking at the unveiling of the Eternal Peace Light Memorial on Oak Hill with approximately 1,800 aged veterans in attendance, Roosevelt remarked, "Men who wore the blue and men who wore the gray . . . . are brought here by the memories of old divided loyalties, but they meet here in united loyalty to a united cause which the unfolding years have made it easier to see." Of the veterans present, said Roosevelt to an audience that could read the words "Peace Eternal in a Nation

United" on the white stone of the monument, "All of them we honor, not asking under which flag they fought then—thankful that they stand together under one flag now." Photographs and motion picture footage from that same anniversary celebration showed old soldiers, decked out in uniforms adorned with reunion ribbons, shaking hands across the stone wall on Cemetery Hill that had sheltered Union troops firing into the ranks of North Carolinians and Virginians in Pickett's Charge. The president's words and former enemies fraternizing on a once bloody field epitomized the Reconciliation Cause.

IV. ACKNOWLEDGING THE WAR'S DARK SIDE

Participants who embraced all four memory traditions tended to highlight the most appealing elements of their preferred interpretation. In memoirs, accounts of famous battles and campaigns, regimental histories, and public speeches, they often created narratives of gallantry and sacrifice in pursuit of worthwhile causes. This is not to say they completely ignored less savory aspects of the war. Each side accused the other of atrocities in their handling of prisoners of war, generals and subordinate officers leveled charges of ineptitude against comrades, and former Confederates insisted that Union armies too often had targeted civilians and private property.

In assessing public understanding of the war in the 21st Century, some scholars insisted that the conflict's "dark side" remained unduly muted. They especially complained that the huge number of books about storied campaigns and commanders, typically written for popular rather than academic audiences, often cloaked the war in romantic trappings. The overlooked war, these historians argued, featured brutality, atrocities, cowardice, vicious guerrilla activity, and physical and psychological wounds that left veterans profoundly damaged. A striking example of how succeeding generations fashion their own interpretations of seismic historical events, the scholarly turn toward the dark side reflected, among other influences, the impact of the American military experiences in Vietnam and later in the Middle East, as well as the often-volatile political currents of the era.

The writings of a handful of Civil War veterans had anticipated some of this new scholarship, none more graphically than Frank Wilkeson's Recollections of a Private Soldier in the Army of the Potomac (1886). Wilkeson enlisted as a teenager and saw action with a New York artillery unit during the Overland campaign and at Petersburg. His Recollections opened with an unsparing portrait of men who accepted bounties to enlist. "If there was a man in all that shameless crew who had enlisted from patriotic motives," he wrote dismissively, "I did not see him." Wilkeson devoted an entire chapter to severe wounds. During action on May 5 in the Wilderness, a young soldier's "head jerked, he staggered, then fell, then regained his feet. A tiny fountain of blood and teeth and bone and bits of tongue burst out of his mouth." At the North Anna River later that month, an infantryman passed through Wilkeson's battery: "A solid shot, intended for us, struck him on the side. His entire bowels were torn out and slung in ribbons and shreds on the ground. He fell dead, but his arms and legs jerked convulsively a few times. It was a sickening spectacle."

Wilkeson also chronicled how the war crushed civilians. Deployed to the Tennessee/Alabama border late in the war, he encountered white refugees who had suffered from guerrilla activity. Gaunt, unwashed, and infested with vermin, these "Defenceless women and children . . . starved out of their homes" had been given shelter in camps set up by the Union army. Overall, guerrillas on both sides had wreaked havoc "through the southern highlands, killing men, burning houses, stealing cattle and horses." Such uncontrolled mahem, thought Wilkeson, virtually guaranteed postwar years "of bloodshed, of assassination, of family feuds, that would spring from the recollections of the war, handed from widowed mothers to savage-tempered sons . . . ."

V. BEYOND THE WARTIME GENERATION

By the time Franklin D. Roosevelt spoke at Gettysburg in 1938, the individuals who had done most to create the four interpretive traditions were long dead. Had they been alive to witness the shifting landscape of Civil War memory through the decades of the twentieth century and into the twenty-first, some would have been encouraged and others left frustrated. Novelists, artists, academic historians, and filmmakers, among others, had a hand in shaping perceptions of the conflict. The popularity of each of the four traditions ebbed and flowed, at once reflecting and influencing popular culture.

Reconciliation has maintained a steady presence in popular culture. It softens the hard edges of the war, props up the comforting, if deeply misleading, notion that the war was really just a quarrel between members of one national family whose antipathies did not run very deep and fell away rather quickly after Appomattox. Prominent during the centennial commemoration of the war in 1961-65, reconciliation showed up in the film *How the West Was Won* (1962). After the first day's fighting at Shiloh, an Ohio soldier finds himself by a pond with a Confederate. The two talk, and soon they reveal little inclination to fight one another. "This fool war started in the East," remarks the Rebel. "What's us westerners doin' in it?" The Yankee mutters, "I don't rightly know anymore." Although circumstances lead the Ohioan to bayonet the Texan a bit later, their scene underscores the similarity of two antagonists disgusted by the war and unconcerned with national causes. The year before *How the West Was Won* debuted, *National Geographic* published an article by Ulysses S. Grant III, the Union hero's grandson, that struck a clear reconciliationist chord. "Our forefathers fought to the limit of endurance for four years," observed Grant. "When the echo of the last shot died away, they saw in the unity of their land something that overshadowed the bitterness of the struggle." Out of the unimaginable carnage of the Civil War, continued Grant in lan-

Plate 23. Union and Confederate veterans shake hands in Gettysburg on the 50th reunion of the battle. Such photographs promoted public reconciliation between former enemies though bitter memories remained common among the wartime generation.

guage recalling that of Wilson and Roosevelt at Gettysburg, "emerged a more firmly united country—a country that has become the leader of the Free World."

As the scene from *How the West Was Won* suggests, films reveal a good deal about how Americans have understood the Civil War. For much of the twentieth century, the Lost Cause thrived. Films wield enormous cultural influence, and *Birth of a Nation* (1915) and *Gone with the Wind* (1939), by far the two most influential movies that have dealt with Civil War themes, sent viewers out of theaters with images of Confederate gallantry and suffering, racist stereotypes of black people, graphic evidence of Sherman's destructive campaigns in Georgia and South Carolina, and heavy-handed critiques of Reconstruction as a time of profound unfairness to ex-Rebels. Many less important films followed similar interpretive paths, and Lost Cause echoes continue in the form of repeated showings of old films on television. But the post-civil rights era trend has been strongly anti-Lost Cause, with most cinematic treatments of the late-twentieth century and later featuring strong disapproval of the Confederacy.

The Emancipation Cause, long relegated to obscurity in white popular culture, reemerged in stirring fashion with *Glory* in 1989. That gripping drama of the 54th Massachusetts Infantry's black soldiers and white colonel, Robert Gould Shaw, proved a revelation for filmgoers who had no idea there had been African American units in the war. Subsequent films, including *Lincoln* in 2012, helped situate the Emancipation Cause as the primary interpretive framework for Americans approaching the war. Events and popular writings relating to the sesquicentennial of the conflict predominantly followed an Emancipation Cause story line as well. Typical was an article that appeared as an insert in innumerable newspapers in April 2011. "[W]e must remember our nation's history fully, not selectively," wrote the author, who had won a Pulitzer Prize two years earlier: "If we truly want to be faithful stewards of the past, Americans need to recall what the war was about: slavery and the definition of human liberty. . . . As we reflect on the war, let us never forget that it was fought to rid us of a monumental prejudice and that we must remain vigilant about confronting inequality in our time."

Moving toward the third decade of the twenty-first century, evidence of the continuing power of the Civil War to stir emotional reactions and political controversy abounds. The Confederate memorial landscape—which includes statues and monuments, portraits hanging in courthouses and other public buildings, and schools named after military and political leaders in the rebellious republic—inspired a wave of heated exchanges at the local and national levels. Two violent

incidents spurred debate. On June 17, 2015, a shooting at the Emanu-
el African Methodist Church in Charleston, South Carolina, left nine
black parishioners dead, three wounded, and the white shooter, who
had posed for an image holding a Confederate flag, facing execution.
Two summers later on August 12, 2017, a Unite the Right rally in
Charlottesville, Virginia, triggered clashes between supporters of the
event and counterprotesters that resulted in multiple injuries and one
death when a self-identified white supremacist drove his car into a
crowd. An equestrian statue of Robert E. Lee figured prominently in
the events at Charlottesville, becoming part of a much larger effort
to remove such sculptures from cities across the nation. Confederate
statues in many places, including New Orleans, Baltimore, St. Louis,
and Austin, came down, and others were repositioned in the Capitol
Building in Washington, D.C.

The question of how best to deal with the Confederate memorial landscape occasioned honest disagreement among well-intentioned
people. Some opposed statues and portraits as relics of the Jim Crow
era, holdovers from a white supremacist past that offend modern
Americans, black and white, and have no historical or cultural value.
Others thought the monuments represent parts of the nation's complex
narrative that should be left to stand as reminders that history has hard
and sometimes unpleasant edges. Those who opposed removal typically
called for adding new text at the sites to situate the memorials within
the full sweep of how Americans have remembered the war and for
erecting new monuments dedicated to previously slighted groups or
events.

Ironically, appreciation of the Union Cause has disappeared almost
entirely from the memory of the war. In fact, few modern Americans
have any sense of what Union meant in the mid-nineteenth century—though no other word at the time carried as much ideological
and political weight. This would come as a great surprise to anyone
who believed preservation of the Union held surpassing importance in

terms of the legacy of the Founders and the prospects for democratic self-government in the Western world. Any firm understanding of Civil War-era America must start with the importance of Union, of the slavery-related issues that menaced it, and of the reasons so many people, whether living in the North or South, accepted the awful option of seeking armed resolution of intractable political and social divisions.

FURTHER READING

THE LITERATURE ON the Civil War and Reconstruction is massive and continues to grow. Estimates of the number of titles relating to the war itself range between 50,000 and 70,000, with works devoted to Abraham Lincoln forming a separate and immense part of the whole. Anyone seeking a comprehensive introduction to the scope and richness of the field should consult Aaron Sheehan-Dean, ed., *A Companion to the U.S. Civil War*, 2 vols. (2014), and Lacy K. Ford, ed., *A Companion to the Civil War and Reconstruction* (2005). For an annotated list of 1,100 titles that emphasizes military topics and personalities, see David J. Eicher, *The Civil War in Books: An Analytical Bibliography* (1997). Thomas J. Pressly, *Americans Interpret Their Civil War*, revised edition (1962), remains very useful on how the literature developed between the nineteenth century and the mid-twentieth century.

Our brief guide to further reading is highly selective and favors titles that combine accessibility and sound scholarship rather than rigorously academic ones that speak to a more specialized audience. The selections should be considered representative examples of reliable, informative works, and they include a number of older titles as well as more recent ones.

Among general one-volume treatments, James M. McPherson and James K. Hogue, *The Civil War and Reconstruction*, 4th edition (2009), is balanced and comprehensive, while McPherson's *Battle Cry of Freedom: The Civil War Era* (1988) covers the antebellum and war years.

David Herbert Donald, Jean Harvey Baker, and Michael F. Holt, *The Civil War and Reconstruction* (2001), offers a particularly fine treatment of the postwar years. Scott Nelson and Carol Sheriff, *A People at War: Civilians and Soldiers in America's Civil War* (2007), takes a thematic, socially focused approach. Three other noteworthy surveys are Michael Fellman, Lesley J. Gordon, and Daniel E. Sutherland, *This Terrible War: The Civil War and Its Aftermath*, 3rd edition (2015); Allen C. Guelzo, *Fateful Lightning: A New History of the Civil War and Reconstruction* (2012); and Elizabeth R. Varon, *Armies of Deliverance: A New History of the Civil War* (2019). Allan Nevins's *The Ordeal of the Union*, 8 vols. (1947-71), with four volumes devoted to the prewar years and four to the war, contains a wealth of information and excellent analysis. E. B. Long and Barbara Long, *The Civil War Day by Day: An Almanac, 1861-1865* (1971) is a handy reference work.

The photographic and artistic record of the war instructs and entertains in equal measure. Bob Zeller's *The Blue and the Gray in Black and White: A History of Civil War Photography* (2005) provides an excellent introduction to the subject. Two foundational titles are Francis Trevelyan Miller, ed., *The Photographic History of the Civil War*, 10 vols. (1911), and William C. Davis, ed., *The Image of War: 1861-1865*, 6 vols. (1981-84), which between them contain nearly 8,000 images. For representative work from a leading photographer, see Alexander Gardner, *Gardner's Photographic Sketchbook of the War* (1866; reprinted many times under the title *Gardner's Photographic Sketchbook of the Civil War*). William A. Frassanito compared wartime photographs with modern images of the same sites from the same angles in *Gettysburg: A Journey in Time* (1975), *Antietam: The Photographic Legacy of America's Bloodiest Day* (1978), and *Grant and Lee: The Virginia Campaigns of 1864-1865* (1983). Frassanito discovered that many of the original captions for photographs were highly misleading. *Lens of War: Exploring Iconic Photographs of the Civil War* (2015) and *Civil War Places: Seeing the Conflict through the Eyes of Its Leading Historians* (2019), both co-edited by Gary W. Gallagher and J. Matthew Gallman, feature essays about wartime and modern images. Mid-19th-century cameras could not capture action, but depictions of battles and other aspects of soldier life can be found in the work of artists who accompanied various armies. Harry L. Katz and Vincent Virga, eds., collected notable examples in *Civil War Sketch Book: Drawings from the Battlefront* (2012). *The American Heritage Picture History of the Civil War* (1960), with a splendid text by Bruce Catton, combines period and modern photographs, artworks, and sketches in what remains the best pictorial history of the war, and *Mine Eyes Have Seen the Glory: The Civil War in Art* (1993), edited by Harold Holzer and Mark E. Neely, Jr., offers a fine overview of paintings and prints. For the war's most celebrated artist, see Julian Grossman, *Echo of a Distant Drum: Winslow Homer and the Civil War* (1974).

A good starting place for the background of the conflict is Elizabeth R. Varon, *Disunion! The Coming of the American Civil War, 1789-1859* (2008). David M. Potter's *The Impending Crisis, 1848-1861* (1976) traces the arc of sectional politics; Bruce Levine's *Half Slave and Half Free: The Roots of Civil War*, revised edition (2005) takes an expansive approach to the antebellum years; and James L. Huston's *Calculating the Value of the Union: Slavery, Property Rights, and the Economic Origins of the Civil War* (2003) illuminates the centrality of property in slaves. James Brewer Stewart's *Holy Warriors: The Abolitionists and American Slavery* (1976) introduces an important group of actors, and Eric Foner's *Free Soil, Free Labor, Free Men: The Ideology of the Republican Party before the Civil War* (1995 edition with new introduction) is essential on the formation of the GOP. William W. Freehling's *The Road to Disunion: Secessionists at Bay, 1776-1854* and *The Road to Disunion: Secessionists Triumphant* (New York, 1990, 2007) examine the southern impulse toward separation that ended in establishment of the Confederacy. Robert E. Bonner, *Mastering America: Southern Slaveholders and the Crisis of American Nationhood* (2009), examines proslavery nationalists during the antebellum period and into the Confederate years; Peter S. Carmichael similarly illuminates the importance of generational differences in *The Last Generation: Young Virginians in Peace, War, and Reunion* (2005). The testimony in Charles B. Dew, *Apostles of Disunion: Southern Secession Commissioners and the Causes of the Civil War* (2001), underscores the importance of slavery and race in the secession crisis. On the North's reaction to secession, see David M. Potter, *Lincoln and His Party in the Secession Crisis* (1995 edition with introduction by Daniel W. Crofts); Russell McClintock, *Lincoln and the Decision for War: The Northern Response to Secession* (2008); Bridget Ford, *Bonds of Union: Religion, Race, and Politics in a Civil War Borderland* (2016); and Daniel W. Crofts, *Lincoln and the Politics of Slavery: The Other Thirteenth Amendment and the Struggle to Save the Union* (2016).

On the U.S. home front, Philip Shaw Paludan's *"A People's Contest": The Union and the Civil War* (1988) is the best detailed overview and J. Matthew Gallman's *The North Fights the Civil War: The Home Front* (1994) the best brief one. Joel H. Silbey, *A Respectable Minority: The Democratic Party in the Civil War Era, 1860-1868* (1977), Mark E. Neely, Jr., *The Union Divided: Party Conflict in the Civil War North* (2002), Adam I. P. Smith, *No Party Now: Politics in the Civil War North* (2006) and *The Stormy Present: Conservatism and the Problem of Slavery in Northern Politics, 1846-1865* (2017), and Jennifer L. Weber, *Copperheads: The Rise and Fall of Lincoln's Opponents in the North* (2006), explore, from various angles, the political dimension of the war. On questions relating to loyalty, the limits of opposition to the government, and ideas about patriotic behavior, see William A. Blair, *With Malice toward Some: Treason and Loyalty in the Civil War Era* (2014), and J. Matthew Gallman, *Defining Duty in the Civil War: Personal Choice, Popular Culture, and the Union Home Front* (2015). Specialized studies of value include James W. Geary, *We Need Men: The Union Draft in the Civil War* (1991); Melinda Lawson, *Patriot Fires: Forging a New American Nationalism in the Civil War North* (2002); Gary W. Gallagher,

The Union War (2011), which seeks to recover the importance of the concept of Union to the U.S. war effort; and Christopher Phillips, *The Rivers Ran Backward: The Civil War and the Remaking of the American Middle Border* (2016).

No satisfactory recent history of the Confederacy exists, but Emory M. Thomas's *The Confederate Nation: 1861-1865* (1979) provides a perceptive introduction. Historians have debated the presence or absence of Confederate national sentiment and whether internal fractures or Union military power contributed more to the Confederacy's demise. Key titles on these themes include Drew Gilpin Faust, *The Creation of Confederate Nationalism: Ideology and Identity in the Civil War South* (1988); Gary W. Gallagher, *The Confederate War* (1997); Anne Sarah Rubin, *A Shattered Nation: The Rise and Fall of the Confederacy, 1861-1868* (2005); Paul D. Escott, *The Confederacy: The Slaveholders' Failed Venture* (2010); Stephanie McCurry, *Confederate Reckoning: Power and Politics in the Civil War South* (2010); and Paul Quigley, *Shifting Grounds: Nationalism and the American South, 1848-1865* (2012). George C. Rable's *The Confederate Republic: A Revolution against Politics* (1994), Stephen V. Ash's *When the Yankees Came: Conflict and Chaos in the Occupied South, 1861-1865* (1995), Richard D. Goff's *Confederate Supply* (1969), Harold S. Wilson's *Confederate Industry: Manufacturers and Quartermasters in the Civil War* (2002), and Adrian Brettle's *Colossal Ambitions: Confederate Planning for a Post-Civil War World* (2020) are important titles.

Many books deal with both the U.S. and Confederate sides of important topics. Richard Franklin Bensel, *Yankee Leviathan: The Origins of Central State Authority in America, 1859-1877* (1990), shows that national power expanded as rapidly in the Confederacy as in the United States. For excellent treatments of various topics, see also George C. Rable, *God's Almost Chosen Peoples: A Religious History of the American Civil War* (2010); Howard Jones, *Blue and Gray Diplomacy: A History of Union and Confederate Foreign Relations* (2010); Andrew F. Lang, *A

Contest of Civilizations: Exposing the Crisis of American Exceptionalism in the Civil War Era (2021), Stephen C. Neff, *Justice in Blue and Gray: A Legal History of the Civil War* (2010); Don H. Doyle, *The Cause of All Nations: An International History of the American Civil War* (2015); Joan E. Cashin, *War Stuff: The Struggle for Human and Environmental Resources in the American Civil War* (2018); and Aaron Sheehan-Dean, *The Calculus of Violence: How Americans Fought the Civil War* (2018). For an in-depth look at two communities at war, see Edward L. Ayers, *In the Presence of Mine Enemies: The Civil War in the Heart of America, 1859-1863* (2003) and *The Thin Light of Freedom: The Civil War and Emancipation in the Heart of America* (2017).

The military literature relating to the Civil War is staggering. Campaign and battle studies and biographies of generals and lesser leaders appear at an especially brisk pace. The best overviews are Herman Hattaway and Archer Jones, *How the North Won: A Military History of the Civil War* (1983), which packs an impressive amount of descriptive and analytical detail into more than 700 pages, and Williamson Murray and Wayne Wei-Siang Hsieh, *A Savage War: A Military History of the Civil War* (2016). Also important are Mark Grimsley, *The Hard Hand of War: Union Military Policy toward Southern Civilians, 1861-1865* (1995); Daniel E. Sutherland, *A Savage Conflict: The Decisive Role of Guerrillas in the American Civil War* (2009); Paddy Griffith, *Battle in the Civil War: Generalship and Tactics in America, 1861-65* (1986), a well-illustrated primer on military nuts and bolts; Earl J. Hess, *Civil War Infantry Tactics: Training, Combat, and Small-Unit Effectiveness* (2017); *Civil War Field Artillery: Promise and Performance on the Battlefield* (2022); and Andrew F. Lang, *In the Wake of War: Military Occupation, Emancipation, and Civil War America* (2017). Two multivolume narratives have rewarded readers across several generations: Bruce Catton's *Mr. Lincoln's Army, Glory Road*, and *A Stillness at Appomattox*, which compose his "Army of the Potomac Trilogy" (1951-53); and Douglas Southall Freeman's *Lee's Lieutenants: A Study in Command*, 3 vols.

(1942-44). Exemplary titles on single campaigns, all of which demonstrate the potential of such studies, are Stephen W. Sears, *Landscape Turned Red: The Battle of Antietam* (1983); Albert Castel, *Decision in the West: The Atlanta Campaign of 1864* (1992), John J. Hennessy, *Return to Bull Run: The Campaign and Battle of Second Manassas* (1993); Kenneth W. Noe, *Perryville: This Grand Havoc of Battle* (2001); Allen C. Guelzo, *Gettysburg: The Last Invasion* (2013); and A. Wilson Greene, *A Campaign of Giants: The Battle for Petersburg, Virginia* (2018). Superior studies of individual armies are Joseph T. Glatthaar's *The March to the Sea and Beyond: Sherman's Troops in the Savannah and Carolinas Campaigns* (1985) and *General Lee's Army: From Victory to Collapse* (2008). Caroline E. Janney's *Ends of War: The Unfinished Fight of Lee's Army after Appomattox* (2021) assesses the final phase of the war for the Confederacy's premier army. For collections of essays that place military operations within a wider political and social framework, see Gary W. Gallagher, ed., "Military Campaigns of the Civil War," 10 vols. to date (1994-2015), of which *Cold Harbor to the Crater* (2015; co-edited with Caroline E. Janney) is a typical example.

Bell I. Wiley virtually invented the subfield devoted to common soldiers with his *The Life of Johnny Reb: The Common Soldier of the Confederacy* (1943) and *The Life of Billy Yank: The Common Soldier of the Union* (1952). Beginning in the late 1980s, men in the ranks (often together with their officers) came in for significant attention. Reid Mitchell's *Civil War Soldiers* (1988) and *The Vacant Chair: The Northern Soldier Leaves Home* (1993) stand with James M. McPherson's *For Cause and Comrades: Why Men Fought in the Civil War* (1997) as influential titles. Earl J. Hess examines the experience of combat in *The Union Soldier in Battle: Enduring the Ordeal of Combat* (1997); Peter S. Carmichael examines some of the more brutal aspects of soldiering in *The War for the Common Soldier: How Men Thought, Fought, and Survived in Civil War Armies* (2018); Chandra Manning highlights attitudes toward slavery, emancipation, and race in *What This Cruel War Is*

Over: Soldiers, Slavery, and the Civil War (2007); Kathryn Shively Meier addresses the impact of the environment on men's mental and physical health in *Nature's Civil War: Common Soldiers and the Environment in 1862 Virginia* (2013); and Clayton J. Butler explores white men in the Confederacy who fought for the United States in *True Blue: White Unionists in the Deep South during the Civil War and Reconstruction* (2022). A small number of women served in both armies, a phenomenon DeAnne Blanton and Lauren M. Cook cover in *They Fought Like Demons: Women Soldiers in the American Civil War* (2002). Joseph T. Glatthaar, *Forged in Battle: The Civil War Alliance of Black Soldiers and White Officers* (1990), Noah Andre Trudeau, *Like Men of War: Black Troops in the Civil War, 1862-1865* (1998), and John David Smith, ed., *Black Soldiers in Blue: African American Troops in the Civil War Era* (2002), treat the African American experience in the U.S. Army. On sailors, see Michael J. Bennett, *Union Jacks: Yankee Sailors in the Civil War* (2004).

A convenient collection of testimony about slavery, emancipation, and African Americans is Ira Berlin and others, eds., *Free at Last: A Documentary History of Slavery, Freedom, and the Civil War* (1992). On the process of emancipation, see Joseph P. Reidy, *Illusions of Emancipation: The Pursuit of Freedom and Equality in the Twilight of Slavery* (2019); James Oakes, *Freedom National: The Destruction of Slavery in the United States, 1861-1865* (2013); Eric Foner, *The Fiery Trial: Abraham Lincoln and American Slavery* (2010); Michael Vorenberg, *Final Freedom: The Civil War, the Abolition of Slavery, and the Thirteenth Amendment* (2001); and Louis Gerteis, *From Contraband to Freedom: Federal Policy toward Southern Blacks, 1861-1865* (1973). Thavolia Glymph, *Out of the House of Bondage: The Transformation of the Plantation Household* (2008), gives a persuasive, and thoroughly revisionist, assessment of black and white women during the transition from slavery to freedom. On slavery and slavery-related issues in the Confederacy, important studies include Clarence Mohr, *On the Threshold of Freedom: Masters and Slaves in Civil War Georgia* (1986); Bruce Levine, *Confederate Emancipation: Southern Plans to Free and Arm Slaves during the Civil War* (2006); Jaime Amanda Martinez, *Confederate Slave Impressment in the Upper South* (2013); and Colin Edward Woodward, *Marching Masters: Slavery, Race, and the Confederate Army during the Civil War* (2014).

Historians working on women and gender have created a rich component of the overall literature on the Civil War era. The best brief treatment is Nina Silber, *Gender and the Sectional Conflict* (2008). *Divided Houses: Gender and the Civil War* (1992), ed. by Catherine Clinton and Nina Silber, anticipated major trends in the field, while LeeAnn Whites's *The Civil War as a Crisis in Gender: Augusta, Georgia, 1860-1890* (1995) opened the way for similar studies. Elizabeth D. Leonard's *Yankee Women: Gender Battles in the Civil War* (1994), Nina Silber's *Daughters of the Union: Northern Women Fight the Civil War* (2005), and Judith Ann Giesberg's *Army at Home: Women and the Civil War on the Northern Home Front* (2009) deal with the United States; George C. Rable's *Civil Wars: Women and the Crisis of Southern Nationalism* (1989), Drew Gilpin Faust's *Mothers of Invention: Women of the Slaveholding South in the American Civil War* (1996), and Laura F. Edwards's *Scarlett Doesn't Live Here Anymore: Southern Women in the Civil War Era* (2000) do the same for the Confederacy. Thavolia Glymph's *The Women's Fight: The Civil War's Battles for Home, Freedom, and Nation* (2020) offers a range of useful insights. More narrow titles include Judith Ann Giesberg, *Civil War Sisterhood: The U.S. Sanitary Commission and Women's Politics in Transition* (2000); Lyde Cullen Sizer, *The Political Work of Northern Women Writers and the Civil War, 1850-1872* (2000); Jacqueline Glass Campbell, *When Sherman Marched North from the Sea: Resistance on the Confederate Home Front* (2003); Jane E. Schultz, *Women at the Front: Hospital Workers in Civil War America* (2004); and Amy Murrell Taylor, *The Divided Family in Civil War America* (2005). On manhood and military service, see Stephen W. Berry II, *All that Makes a Man: Love and Ambition in the Civil War South* (2003), and Lorien Foote, *The Gentlemen and the Roughs: Violence, Honor, and Manhood in the Union Army* (2010).

Biographies afford readers one of the best ways to engage with the mid-nineteenth century, and they number in the thousands. A few titles will suggest the potential of biographical studies. On the respective presidents and two most important generals, see Richard Carwardine, *Lincoln: A Life of Purpose and Power* (2006); Ronald C. White, Jr., *A. Lincoln: A Biography* (2009); William J. Cooper, Jr., *Jefferson Davis, American* (2000); Brooks D. Simpson, *Ulysses S. Grant: Triumph over Adversity, 1822-1865* (2000); Ron Chernow, *Grant* (2018); Emory M. Thomas, *Robert E. Lee: A Biography* (1995); Allen C. Guelzo, *Robert E. Lee: A Life* (2021); and William C. Davis, *Crucible of Command: Ulysses S. Grant and Robert E. Lee—The War They Fought, the Peace They Forged* (2015). Ethan S. Rafuse's *McClellan's War: The Failure of Moderation in the Struggle for the Union* (2005), John F. Marszalek's *Sherman: A Soldier's Passion for Order* (1993), and James I. Robertson, Jr.'s, *Stonewall Jackson: The Man, the Soldier, the Legend* (1997), assess three complicated, and often controversial, figures, while Kent Masterson Brown's *Meade at Gettysburg: A Study in Command* (2021) covers a leading general in the war's most famous battle. David Herbert Donald's *Charles Sumner and the Coming of the Civil War* and *Charles Sumner and the Rights of Man* (1960, 1970) meet the highest standard of the biographical craft. The best examination of the most prominent black leader is David W. Blight, *Frederick Douglass: Prophet of Freedom* (2018). Jean H. Baker, *Mary Todd Lincoln: A Biography* (1987), and Joan E. Cashin, *First Lady of the Confederacy: Varina Davis's Civil War* (2006), are excellent on the first ladies. For other notable biographies of women, see Elizabeth Brown Pryor's *Clara Barton: Professional Angel* (1987), Elizabeth R. Varon's *Southern Lady, Yankee Spy: The True Story of Elizabeth Van Lew, a Union Agent in the Heart of the Confederacy* (2003), Catherine Clinton's *Harriett Tubman: The Road to Freedom* (2004), and

J. Matthew Gallman's *America's Joan of Arc: The Life of Anna Elizabeth Dickinson* (2006).

The number of published memoirs, diaries, and sets of letters can be daunting. For selections of presidential materials, consult William E. Gienapp, ed., *This Fiery Trial: The Speeches and Writings of Abraham Lincoln* (2002), and William J. Cooper, ed., *Jefferson Davis: The Essential Writings* (2003). The two best accounts by generals are *Personal Memoirs of U. S. Grant*, 2 vols. (1885; reprint in one vol. edited by John F. Marszalek, David S. Nolen, and Louis P. Gallo, 2017), and *Fighting for the Confederacy: The Personal Recollections of General Edward Porter Alexander*, ed. Gary W. Gallagher (1989). Other essential titles include *The Civil War Diary of Gideon Welles, Lincoln's Secretary of the Navy*, ed. William E. Gienapp and Erica L. Gienapp (2014); *The Diary of George Templeton Strong*, ed. Allan Nevins and Milton Halsey Thomas, 4 vols. (1952); *"Journal of a Secesh Lady": The Diary of Catherine Ann Devereux Edmondston, 1860-1866*, ed. Beth Crabtree Gilbert and James W, Patton (1979); *Mary Chesnut's Civil War*, ed. C. Vann Woodward (1981); and John B. Jones, *A Rebel War Clerk's Diary*, 2 vols. (1866). Three superb sets of letters from the battle front are *Three Years in the Army of the Cumberland: The Letters and Diary of Major James A. Connelly*, ed. Paul M. Angle (1959); *Hard Marching Every Day: The Civil War Letters of Private Wilbur Fisk, 1861-1865*, ed. Emil and Ruth Rosenblatt (1992); and Edwin S. Redkey, ed., *A Grand Army of Black Men: Letters from African-American Soldiers in the Union Army, 1861-1865* (1992). For a superb set of letters between a general and his wife, see William C. Davis and Sue Heth Bell, eds., *The Wharton's War: The Civil War Correspondence of General Gabriel C. Wharton and Anne Radford Wharton, 1863-1865* (2022). Two classic common soldiers' memoirs are Frank Wilkeson, *Turned Inside Out: Recollections of a Private Soldier in the Army of the Potomac* (retitled 1997 reprint of 1886 original), and Sam R. Watkins, *"Co. Aytch," Maury Grays, First Tennessee Regiment; or, a Side Show of the Big Show* (1882; reprinted many times).

Good places to confront the literature on Reconstruction are Eric Foner's *Reconstruction: America's Unfinished Revolution, 1863-1877* (1988), since its publication the most influential title on the topic; Mark Wahlgren Summers's *The Ordeal of the Reunion: A New History of Reconstruction* (2014), which challenges parts of Foner's work; and a pair of short treatments—Michael W. Fitzgerald's *Splendid Failure: Postwar Reconstruction in the American South* (2007) and Allen C. Guelzo's *Reconstruction: A Concise History* (2018). W. E. B. DuBois's *Black Reconstruction* (1935) anticipated many of the directions the field would take after 1960. Leon F. Litwack's *Been in the Storm So Long: The Aftermath of Slavery* (1979) chronicles the transition to a post-emancipation world in the South. Willie Lee Rose's *Rehearsal for Reconstruction: The Port Royal Experiment* (1964) and Janet Sharp Hermann's *The Pursuit of a Dream* (1981), both engagingly written, examine specific localities in South Carolina and Mississippi. On the waning of Reconstruction, see William Gillette, *Retreat from Reconstruction, 1869-1879* (1979); Heather Cox Richardson, *The Death of Reconstruction: Race, Labor, and Politics in the Post-Civil War North, 1865-1901* (2001); and Michael F. Holt, *By One Vote: The Disputed Presidential Election of 1876* (2008). On postwar violence and Union military forces in the former Confederacy, see Alan W. Trelease, *White Terror: The Ku Klux Klan Conspiracy and Southern Reconstruction* (1971); Stephen V. Ash, *A Massacre in Memphis: The Race Riot that Shook the Nation One Year after the Civil War* (2013); Gregory P. Downs, *After Appomattox: Military Occupation and the Ends of War* (2015); and William A. Blair, *The Record of Murders and Outrages: Racial Violence and the Fight over Truth at the Dawn of Reconstruction* (2021).

Discussion of memory and commemoration of the Civil War should start with David W. Blight, *Race and Reunion: The Civil War in American Memory* (2001); Alice Fahs and Joan Waugh, eds., *The Memory of the Civil War in American Culture* (2004); and Caroline E. Janney, *Remembering the Civil War: Reunion and the Limits of Reconcil-*

iation (2013). Two influential earlier titles are Gaines M. Foster, *Ghosts of the Confederacy: Defeat, the Lost Cause, and the Emergence of the New South, 1865 to 1913* (1987), and Nina Silber, *The Romance of Reunion: Northerners and the South, 1865-1900* (1993). On Ulysses S. Grant's centrality, see Joan Waugh, *U.S. Grant: American Hero, American Myth* (2009). Other noteworthy titles are William A. Blair, *Cities of the Dead: Contesting the Memory of the Civil War in the South, 1865-1914* (2004); John R. Neff, *Honoring the Civil War Dead: Commemoration and the Problem of Reconciliation* (2005); Drew Gilpin Faust, *This Republic of Suffering: Death and the American Civil War* (2008); Barbara A. Gannon, *The Won Cause: Black and White Comradeship in the Grand Army of the Republic* (2011); and Thomas J. Brown, *Civil War Monuments and the Militarization of America* (2019). On the Civil War in recent American culture, see Tony Horwitz's *Confederates in the Attic: Dispatches from the Unfinished Civil War* (1998) and Gary W. Gallagher's *Causes Won, Lost, and Forgotten: How Hollywood and Popular Art Shape What We Know about the Civil War* (2008).

ILLUSTRATION CREDITS

Plate 11   Library of Congress, Prints and Photographs Division, reproduction number LC USZ62-33407

Plate 12   *Harper's Weekly*, September 6, 1862, pages 568-69

Plate 13   *Illustrated London News*, August 29, 1863, page 216

Plate 14   *Frank Leslie's Illustrated Newspaper*, May 23, 1863, page 141

Plate 15   Robert Underwood Johnson and Clarence Clough Buel, eds., *Battles and Leaders of the Civil War*, 4 vols. (New York: Century, 1887-88), 4:736

Plate 16   Library of Congress, Prints and Photographs Division, reproduction number LC DIG-cwpb-02807

Plate 17   Library of Congress, Prints and Photographs Division, reproduction number LC-DIG-ppmsca-33070

Plate 18   Library of Congress, Prints and Photographs Division, reproduction number LC DIG-pga-00291

Plate 19   *Harper's Weekly*, April 11, 1868, pages 232-33

Plate 20   *Harper's Weekly*, October 24, 1874, page 878

Plate 21   Library of Congress, Prints and Photographs Division, reproduction number LC DIG-ppmsca-17564

Plate 22   Paul F. Mottelay and T. Campbell-Copeland, eds., *The Soldier in Our Civil War: Columbian Memorial Edition. A Pictorial History of the Conflict, 1861-1865*, 2 vols. (New York: Stanley Bradley Publishing Company, 1893), 2:392

Plate 23   Library of Congress, Prints and Photographs Division, reproduction number LC DIG-ppmsca-32660

INDEX

A

Abolitionism and abolitionists
  Emancipation Proclamation, 92, 95,
    99–100
  Land ownership, 110
  Newspaper, 13
  In South, 10
  USCT, 103, 104
  Women's support, 159
Adams, Charles Francis, 151, 152
Adams, Charles Francis Jr., 129
African American Civil War Memorial,
  Washington, D.C., 254
African Americans
  Benefits of freedom, 247
  Citizenship dispute, 214
  Colonization, 98
  As contraband of war, 90, 92
  Education, 111
  Equal pay for soldiers, 104
  Franchise dispute, 217–214
  Free labor ideology, 108–109
  Land ownership/redistribution,
    109–111, 207, 213, 233
  Legislators, 232, 233, 234, 242
  Presidential employment, 85
  Refugee settlements, 92–94,
    96–97
  As sharecroppers, 214, 233–234
  Suffrage for, 210, 216–217, 214
  Three-fifths compromise, 14–15
  Two-parent household, 213
  Voting rights, 207, 216–217, 230
  - *See also* Slaves and slavery
Akerman, Amos T., 240
Alabama, during Reconstruction, 234
Alcohol consumption, 75–76
Alcorn, James L., 235
Alcott, Louisa May, 164
Alexander, Edward Porter, 28
Amendments to Constitution
  Thirteenth, 21–22, 92, 112–113,
    208, 214
  - *See also* Corwin Amendment
  Fourteenth, 219–221
  Fifteenth, 226, 230
  South's reaction to, 259
American Freedmen's Inquiry
  Commission, 97
American Missionary Association,

C

G

H

M

N

T

Made in the USA
Columbia, SC
04 February 2025

53289313R00185